Black Feminist Mothering in 21st Century Literature

Black feminist mothering can birth new worlds. As today's world becomes increasingly hostile—with the rising costs of food coupled with global warming's devastating impact—we are in need of a feminism bold enough to imagine new pathways for survival. Black feminist mothering may well be the remedy. This volume positions Black feminist mothering as much more than a biological or caregiving role. Building on key Black feminist tenets, Carr examines Black women's maternal labors as a practice and proclamation for mothering ourselves, tending to each other, and nourishing our communities. Far too often, Black women's maternal, intellectual, and political labors are recognized only in service to white supremacist capitalism. Mammy. Breeder. Welfare queen. This text counters these dehumanizing iconographies to focus instead on the Black maternal's imaginative possibilities. Not only does Carr address Black women's resistance to white supremacist power plays, but she also attends to Black heteropatriarchy and the burdens racial solidarity imposes on Black women. The Black maternal, Carr argues, is a cradle for Black revolution. As Assata Shakur famously declared, "We are pregnant with freedom."

Nicole Carr is Assistant Professor of African American Literature.

Routledge Studies in African American Literature

Pathologizing Black Bodies
The Legacy of Plantation Slavery
Constante González Groba, Ewa Barbara Luczak and Urszula Niewiadomska-Flis

Street, Text, and Representation in African American Literature
Urban Writing/Dwelling
Mattius Rischard

Black Feminist Mothering in 21st Century Literature
I Am Not Your Mammy
Nicole Carr

For more information about this series, please visit: https://www.routledge.com/Routledge-Studies-in-African-American-Literature/book-series/RSAAL

Black Feminist Mothering in 21st Century Literature
I Am Not Your Mammy

Nicole Carr

First published 2025
by Routledge
605 Third Avenue, New York, NY 10158

and by Routledge
4 Park Square, Milton Park, Abingdon, Oxon, OX14 4RN

Routledge is an imprint of the Taylor & Francis Group, an informa business

© 2025 Nicole Carr

The right of Nicole Carr to be identified as author of this work has been asserted in accordance with sections 77 and 78 of the Copyright, Designs and Patents Act 1988.

The Open Access version of this book, available at www.taylorfrancis.com, has been made available under a Creative Commons Attribution-Non Commercial-No Derivatives (CC-BY-NC-ND) 4.0 International license.

Any third party material in this book is not included in the OA Creative Commons license, unless indicated otherwise in a credit line to the material. Please direct any permissions enquiries to the original rightsholder.

Trademark notice: Product or corporate names may be trademarks or registered trademarks, and are used only for identification and explanation without intent to infringe.

ISBN: 9781032719986 (hbk)
ISBN: 9781032720005 (pbk)
ISBN: 9781032719993 (ebk)

DOI: 10.4324/9781032719993

Typeset in Sabon
by Deanta Global Publishing Services, Chennai, India

An electronic version of this book is freely available, thanks to the support of libraries working with Knowledge Unlatched (KU). KU is a collaborative initiative designed to make high quality books Open Access for the public good. The Open Access ISBN for this book is 9781032719993. More information about the initiative and links to the Open Access version can be found at www.knowledgeunlatched.org.

For my daughter, my son, and my mother.

Contents

List of Figures		*viii*
Acknowledgments		*ix*
	Introduction	1
1	Riding with Death: Assata Shakur, Fannie Lou Hamer, and Revolutionary Black Matrilineal Consciousness	7
2	The Motherwork Continues: Merciful Mothering in the Black Lives Matter Era	32
3	Sisters in Bloom: Tending to the Garden of Sisterhood	56
4	We Can Learn to Mother Ourselves: Sisterwork in the Time of Betty, Coretta, and Myrlie	80
5	I Am Not My Brother's Keeper: Black Women M(o)thering Themselves	100
6	I Am Not Your Mammy: Kamala Harris and the Politics of Refusal	126
	Index	*163*

List of Figures

3.1 Child's Drawing of Phillis Wheatley-Peters Sitting in Her Room Surrounded by Books 75
4.1 Coretta Scott King Holding Her Daughter Bernice at Martin Luther King's Funeral 83
5.1 1978 Flyer Listing Various Statistics Concerning African American Men 104
5.2 Huey P. Newton Seated in a Rattan Chair, Holding a Gun and Spear 106
6.1 Bring U.S. together. Vote Chisholm 1972 133

Acknowledgments

Writing a book for the first time has been a daunting task. I am grateful for all the love and support that I have received along the way.

To my students, Naimah, LoRen, Simone, Maya, and Anita, I hope you are all navigating life with all the grace and tenderness deserving of you. Thank you for always asking me questions that I pondered long after class was over—they helped shape the fifth chapter.

My mentor, David Ikard, who read the very first, very bad chapter of this manuscript and did not laugh but only encouraged me to keep writing. Your support over the years has really made me believe I am everything you say I am. For Cheryl, who prayed for me *and* over me right on campus when I needed it most. And everything did work out just as you said it did. Somehow I finished the book despite it all.

At my university, Katherine Gillen's support in the form of course reassignments helped me carve out a bit more time to focus. Best chair ever. James Finley's reading of an early draft helped me gain a better idea of where I wanted the book to go. Librarians are superheroes. I learned this whenever Sarah Timm renewed books for me when I needed a bit more time with the books that seemed to overflow in my home, bed, and car. My writing partners, Stephanie Rambo and Jana Knibb, for holding me accountable by always finding time for us to write. Our chitchat afterwards also felt spirit-renewing because who else can talk about Kendrick Lamar and then segue into the family tree of Hagar and Milkman? Let's do it again sometime soon, ladies.

To my sisters, the Doublemint twins. Thanks for doing my hair and letting me fall asleep in your chair. Thanks for making me laugh even when I was tired. To my partner, thank you for putting up with me long enough for me to finish this book so that I could return back to the living. And for the plaintains, my goodness, the plaintains.

For my mama. For the home-cooked meals and store-bought ones. For never once getting sick of me. For looking after my child like she was your own (and I suppose she is). For adorning my home with flowers just because. Thank you.

For my beautiful baby girl. You never once complained when I told you Mommy would be very busy for the next few months and we wouldn't have time to do all things we usually do. Instead you let me borrow your bubble gum when I needed something to snack on late at night. You have been with me since the dissertation and now you are with me for the book. Strange now to have created something that I can hold in my hands but is not one of my babies. I hope you find wisdom in this book one day.

To Harlem. You changed the entire direction of this book. It's as much your book as it is mine.

Introduction

Her neighbors knew her simply as "Thelma." Hollywood knew her as Butterfly McQueen. By 1989, McQueen was no longer the 27-year-old woman famous for her role as Prissy, the high-pitched enslaved Black nitwit in *Gone with the Wind*. Unable to support herself as an actress, she left New York and settled in Georgia. She purchased a one-bedroom cottage for herself and two other rental cottages near Augusta. For the next five years, McQueen either offered generous discounts on her cottages to low-income families or let them live there for free. To a mother of five who had been in an abuse shelter looking for a home but could not afford rent, McQueen smiled and simply said, "You're welcome, and don't worry about the rent."[1] Her pragmatic vision motivated McQueen to clean the streets and around her neighbors' homes, "They say the streets are going to be beautiful in Heaven. Well, I'm trying to make the streets beautiful here … When it's clean and beautiful, I think America is heaven."[2] McQueen, though she never defined her labors as such, embodied the spirit of Black feminist mothering.

Black feminist foundations, as Joan Morgan writes in *When Chickenheads Come Home to Roost*, are "often laid by women" who have "little use" for the terms and theories brandished by academics. For my Black feminist project, Black feminist mothering is the work required for "birthing new" worlds.[3] The complex life of McQueen reflects her engagement with Black feminist mothering as a sustained practice of communal care. After completing a course in nursing at the Georgia Medical School, she managed Belles Noires Enfante, a community service club for Black children. She supported the project by selling butter sandwiches and cold drinks in a local shop.[4] Her labors model for us a version of Black feminist mothering at work.

As a set of sustained practices, Black feminist mothering extends caregiving beyond that of one's children to include the nurturing of one's self and community. Structured along a continuum of care, Black feminist mothering has roots in the development of free breakfast and healthcare programs generated by Black women in the Black Panther Party. Therefore, this book highlights the critical care work necessary for nourishing ourselves and our relationships with other Black folks.

The framework for Black feminist mothering is grounded in scholarship by Black feminists Patricia Hill Collins, Kaila Adia Story, Jennifer C. Nash, and Alexis Pauline Gumbs. In her 2018 article, "Mama's Gon' Buy You a Mockingbird: Why #BlackMothersStillMatter," Story sources Black women's maternal labors as sites of resistance. Her theorizing of maternal care as political activism punctuates my own articulations of Black feminist mothering as crucial to the Black freedom struggle. As such, the first chapter, "Riding with Death: Assata Shakur, Fannie Lou Hamer, and Revolutionary Black Matrilineal Consciousness," provides a blueprint for utilizing mothering as a political strategy against reproductive injustice.

In my second chapter, Collins' definition of motherwork as labor "whether it is on behalf of one's own biological children, or for the children of one's own racial ethnic community, or to preserve the earth for those children who are yet unborn" guides my examination of the weight white supremacist violence bears on Black caregivers. In "The Motherwork Continues: Merciful Mothering in the Black Lives Matter Era,"[5] I begin with an analysis of Toya Graham beating her son following the police officers' killing of Freddie Gray. I further explore the ramifications of the viral moment via a literary analysis of key scenes in three works of African American literature: Toni Morrison's *A Mercy*, N.K. Jemisin's *The Fifth Season*, and Edward P. Jones' *The Known World*. The chapter's final pages address Diamond Reynolds' livestreaming of Philando Castile's fatal encounter with Minnesota police as an instance of reproductive violence since Reynolds' daughter witnessed Castile's execution unfold from the car's backseat. The first half of this book is concerned with motherwork as the vehicle by which Black women mobilize and labor for a better world. For Alexis Pauline Gumbs, China Martens, and Mai'a Williams, this labor is the "revolutionary mothering" offering us a "generous space for life in the face of life-threatening limits."[6] Birth-givers, birth-workers, and caregivers alike unite toward building collective solutions for our communities.

As such, *Black Feminist Mothering in 21st Century Literature* does not focus exclusively on the parent–child dynamic. And while I use mothering as a term for quantifying labor, I frequently use the terms caregivers, parents, birth-givers, and Black mothers almost interchangeably. This is done so that I may outline more clearly the wide-ranging dimensions of our beloved communities. As the legacies of chattel slavery and Jim Crow violence continue wreaking havoc, I explore Black resistance through the lens of what Joy James calls the "captive maternal." Describing those individuals "most vulnerable to violence, war, poverty, police, and captivity" as "Captive Maternals," James explains that "Captive Maternals" can "be either biological females or those feminized into caretaking and consumption."⁷ As such, a significant portion of my project is concerned with the expectations placed on Black women's maternal, intellectual, emotional, and political labors. As the subtitle of my book suggests, I also explore how Black women wrestle with the burdens of the mammy image. Although the work of deconstructing "mammy" has been undertaken by Black scholars, the persistence of the mammy myth necessitates my sustained focus on how Black women unburden themselves from the image.

As one of the most significant ideological tools for justifying Black women's economic exploitation, "mammy" remains central to unlocking constructions of Black women's labor as a boundless resource readily accessible to all except Black women. Mammy, "by loving, nurturing, and caring for her white children better than her own, symbolizes the dominant group's perception of the ideal Black female relationship to elite white male power."⁸ Since enslaved Black mothers within the United States were relegated to the position of "breeders" tasked with producing "property" to generate wealth for white patriarchal capitalism, the concept of motherhood is often conceptualized as the exclusive property of white women. This is what Saidiya Hartman calls the "afterlife of slavery" in which Black mothers are stereotyped as "welfare queens," "hypersexual breeders," or "bitter baby mamas." Significantly, Black women's position to labor has been that of sustaining the lifeblood of the community against onslaughts of structural violence. Therefore, I examine how Black women "feminized into caretaking and consumption" resist the expectation that they labor tirelessly on behalf of everyone else but themselves.

One of the ways to combat this expectation is to stage Black feminist mothering as an ethics of care between Black women. In "Sisters in Bloom, Tending to the Garden of Sisterhood," I reframe the relationship between Phillis Wheatley-Peters and Obour Tanner-Collins as a cultural vehicle for creativity, sisterwork, and survival. Juxtaposing their correspondence with letters between Pat Parker and Audre Lorde makes clear Black women's cultivation of a "mother tongue." It is a sisterhood aligning with what Johnnie M. Stover defines as a set of African American language forms consisting of "words, rhythms, sounds, and silences that [Black women encode] with veiled meaning."⁹ Framing Black women's use of letter writing as a literary call-and-response builds creative pathways for publication *and* self-actualization. The correspondence between Wheatley-Peters and Tanner-Collins is also examined in relation to Celie's letters to God in *The Color Purple*.

In my fourth chapter, "We Can Learn to Mother Ourselves: Sisterwork in the Time of Betty, Coretta, and Myrlie," I consider what the Civil Rights icons may teach us about nurturing and tending to other Black women. The trio, forced to navigate the dual pressures of being both the grieving widow and potentially bitter Black woman, forged a lasting friendship. Their sisterhood, formed amid a white American public eager to see them divided, encourages us to consider the barriers blocking us from clearing room in our hearts to love other Black women.

This book then is also concerned with America's investment in the enduring power of myths. Black women, as Hortense Spillers avers, are marked but not everyone knows our name. As a result, rarely are Black women's maternal labors rendered visible beyond a handful of dehumanizing iconographies. Mammy. Breeder. Welfare queen. Throughout her lifetime, McQueen was spectacularly misunderstood, disrespected, and defamed. Fellow actress Lena Horne called McQueen a dog. Malcolm X said that he "felt like crawling under the rug" when she appeared on screen—a sentiment still widely held by most Black Americans. Shame kept McQueen from embracing her role in a film as she hated performing as Prissy. Myths shaped and altered McQueen's life. In 1979, two security guards accused her of being a vagrant and thief, throwing her to the ground and holding her until police officers arrived. Though the police officers eventually recognized her and let her go, McQueen sued for $300,000 in damages, securing an out-of-court settlement for $60,000.

The complexities of McQueen's life invite us to rethink what we think we know about Black legacies of resistance. For instance, though she endured relentless racism on the set of the 1939 film, *Gone with the Wind*, McQueen's version of Prissy outraged Margaret Mitchell, the author of the novel. Perhaps Mitchell sensed the subversive elements of McQueen's depiction lurking just beneath the surface. McQueen, in a pivotal scene where Scarlett O'Hara's world is crumbling around her, situates enslaved Black women's resistance as blissful apathy. When an exhausted Scarlett, reeling from enslaved Black people fleeing the plantation at the news of the Confederacy's loss in the Civil War, travels and seeks aid to help deliver Melanie's baby, she peeks out the window and sees Prissy. Here, the enslaved Black woman is not rushing to Scarlett's side but blithely strolling up the walkway, even singing an upbeat tune. McQueen's Prissy is completely oblivious to the utter ruin Scarlett's life has become. Although Scarlett slaps her for lying about her ability to deliver babies, it is difficult to dismiss Prissy as the incompetent fool Mitchell imagined for her. Instead, Prissy, in McQueen's version, reserves her energy for herself. Why should I care, McQueen's Prissy seems to say, that white folks' world is falling apart? McQueen's Prissy would much rather ponder the beauty around her.

The myriad forms of Black women's resistance unfold in the final two chapters. *Black Feminist Mothering in 21st Century American Literature* ponders how Black women preserve and reclaim their energies for themselves. Drawing heavily from Audre Lorde's rejection of white supremacist patriarchal capitalism in that marginalized Black women caring for themselves "is not self-indulgence but self-preservation," I investigate Black women mothering themselves and their aspirations, becoming, as June Jordan wrote, "the ones we have been waiting for." In the fifth chapter, "I Am Not My Brother's Keeper: Black Women M(o)thering Themselves," I explore Black patriarchal stealth's shielding of Black men and boys from accountability. In turning to contemporary discussions about Korryn Gaines' defense of her home and Megan Thee Stallion's domestic assault at the hands of Tory Lanez, I address the longstanding intraracial tensions among Black men and women. Via an examination of Black women's political writings like Toni Cade Bambara's *The Black Woman Anthology* and Michele Wallace's *Black Macho and the Myth of the Superwoman*, I contextualize the contemporary moment as producing a mother wound in which Black women and girls seek, but do not receive, nurturing from within our communities.

The final chapter, "I Am Not Your Mammy: Kamala Harris and the Politics of Refusal," examines the phenomenon by which Black women emerged as saviors of 21st-century American democracy even as they were denied high-ranking leadership roles. However, the chapter goes beyond examining the co-opting of Black women's political labors to also address the seductive quality of power. Using *Sula* as a theoretical lens, I consider the ways in which political Black women weaponize their oppressed and gendered identities, contributing to the harm of those within their communities. Exploring Black women's resistance to *and* adoption of pathological tools of white supremacist power, I focus on the political careers of Shirley Chisholm, Condoleezza Rice, and Kamala Harris. Importantly, the chapter does not pathologize them. Rather, I argue that their desire for power confirms Black women's humanity as flawed individuals swayed by ambition, whim, and desire.

Black Feminist Mothering in the 21st Century comes at a time when Black birth-givers and birth-workers are urging mainstream media to showcase Black resistance, resilience, and joy. As such, I center Black women as actors rather than passive participants in their own demise. Exploring the nexus between gender, race, and politics requires a broad approach. My method of examination incorporates literary, cultural, and auto-ethnography into each chapter. My chief goal, in incorporating such a wide range, is to extend and expand the discussion on the various means Black women and birth-givers mobilize in the ongoing fight for reproductive justice. The Black maternal is a radically imaginative space. And in the pages that follow, we will bear witness to its manifestations, possibilities, and contradictions.

Notes

1 Bourne, 104.
2 Bourne, 104.

3 Gumbs, Martens, and Williams.
4 Bourne, 78.
5 Collins.
6 Gumbs, Martens, and Williams.
7 James, 255.
8 Collins, 266
9 Stover, 140.

Bibliography

Bourne, Stephen. *Butterfly McQueen Remembered*. Lanhan: Scarecrow Press, 2007.

Collins, Patricia. "Shifting the Center: Race, Class and Feminist Theorizing about Motherhood." *American Families: A Multicultural Reader*, edited by Stephanie Coontz, Maya Parson, and Gabrielle Raley, New York: Routledge, 1999, p. 9.

Gumbs, Alexis Pauline, China Martens, and Mai'a Williams. *Revolutionary Mothering: Love on the Front Lines*. New York: PM Press, 2016.

James, Joy. "The Womb of Western Theory: Trauma, Time Theft and the Captive Maternal." *Carceral Notebooks*, vol. 12, 2016, pp. 253–296.

Lorde, Audre. *A Burst of Light: And Other Essays*. New York: Ixia Press, 2017.

Stover, Johnnie M. "Nineteenth-Century African American Women's Autobiography as Social Discourse: The Example of Harriet Ann Jacobs." *College English*, vol. 66, no. 2, 2003, pp. 133–154.

1 Riding with Death
Assata Shakur, Fannie Lou Hamer, and Revolutionary Black Matrilineal Consciousness

In 1966, Fannie Lou Hamer was riding with death. The Black political activist's 22-year-old daughter had begun hemorrhaging following her second child's birth.[1] Mississippi doctors refused to treat Dorothy, so Hamer drove her to Memphis. But this white supremacist discrimination soon proved lethal. Unfortunately, Dorothy did not survive the drive and died on the way to the hospital. Of Dorothy's death, Hamer lamented: "We couldn't get a doctor to attend my daughter and she died as we were driving her 127 miles to Memphis."[2] In implicating Mississippi doctors for claiming Dorothy's life, Hamer names the "death-bound conditions" articulated by Treva B. Lindsey as the slow "wearing down of marginalized and vulnerable communities." In *America, Goddamn: Violence, Black Women, and the Struggle for Justice*, Lindsay outlines the intersecting harms of capitalism, poverty, and economic deprivation as a form of state-sanctioned violence. These "death-bound conditions" were at play even before Hamer raced to get Dorothy to a hospital. Indeed, the ill-fated drive was ultimately another link in the chain of Mississippi forces constricting the lives of Dorothy and her mother.

Because local white officials regarded Hamer as an enemy of the state due to her political activism, they blacklisted Dorothy. Following a series of repeated rejections and firings, Dorothy secured a job only because, as Hamer said, "they don't know she's my child."[3] Being Hamer's child carried with it the threat of constant job instability and exposure to violence. Hamer had experienced this firsthand. In 1962, she joined the Student Nonviolent Coordinating Committee and worked tirelessly to register Black voters in Mississippi. For her efforts, both she and her husband, Perry Hamer, were fired by B.D. Marlowe, the white plantation owner of the farm where they had worked for years as sharecroppers. Thus, Dorothy's untimely death exposes the Mississippi doctors colluding with state officials to deny her potentially life-saving treatment as a premeditated, targeted attack on Black women resisting Jim Crow rule.

Her battle for reproductive justice is eerily similar to contemporary Black women's fight against an American healthcare system in which

Black women are three to four times more likely to die in childbirth or as a result of pregnancy-related complications. Today, medical staff administer similar lethal forms of discrimination that healthcare officials reserved for Dorothy. Doctors and nurses often redirect resources away from Black women, withhold treatment, and deny and dismiss our legitimate concerns. Anthropologist and reproductive scholar Dána-Ain Davis defines this neglectful behavior as obstetric racism. As a threat to positive maternal and neonatal outcomes, obstetric racism is medical abuse producing a higher exposure of Black women to pain, illness, misdiagnoses, and death. It is no exaggeration to say that the US healthcare system functions as one of the most efficient killing machines in the world. In what Saidiya Hartman calls the "afterlife of slavery," Black mothers and birth-givers experience "skewed life chances, limited access to health and education, premature death, incarceration, and impoverishment." Slavery's lingering impact on conceptualizations of motherhood scripts it as a title belonging exclusively to white women in 21st century America. As Black feminist scholar Alexis Pauline Gumbs explains, motherhood is largely "a status granted by patriarchy to white middle-class women, those women whose legal rights to their children are never questioned, regardless of who does the labor of keeping them alive."[4] Motherhood, thanks in part to white mainstream media, exists as an extension of citizenship rights, privilege, power, and American exceptionalism for white children. This hierarchical ordering of motherhood requires a permanent underclass of non-mothers serving to make white motherhood more visible. In fact, as Ross reminds us, "the nobility of white, middle-class maternity depends on the definition of others as unfit, degraded, and illegitimate" (Reproductive Justice 3–4). Because images of white women as ideal mothers saturate advertisements, television shows, and magazines, motherhood is inextricably bound to a handful of white maternal archetypes first introduced on shows like *Leave It to Beaver* and *Little House on the Prairie*. Images of June Cleaver, Carol Brady, and other married heterosexual white women cement white women's status as the inheritors of faultless motherhood. As Rickie Solinger and Loretta Ross explain, the media's impact on shaping motherhood has been instrumental in championing a certain kind of mother:

> For decades, TV shows, movies, and other cultural expressions typically portrayed white, middle-class, heterosexual, married women as the mothers we all want to be and have: "legitimate" mothers. So what are Americans to think about persons who do not have all of these assets and resources to bring to motherhood? Our political culture conditions us to regard these mothers as inappropriate, illegitimate" mothers in comparison.
>
> (Reproductive Justice 3–4)

Although Dianne Carroll's eventual role as a widowed single mother in the 1968 television series, *Julia*, paved the way for more Black mother images to emerge in the portrayal of Florida Evans and Claire Huxtable, notions of the "illegitimate" Black mother persist. However, the historical turning point at which Black women could reserve our labors exclusively for our own children, our labors are still either rebuked or go unnoticed. Today, single Black mothers raising their children are derided as "bitter baby mamas." This rhetorical violence is part of the devaluing of Black mothers and children. It is little wonder then that healthcare officials outright refuse to administer care and support to Black mothers and birthgivers. In hospitals across the country, Black mothers are "riding with death."

As this chapter and title draw heavily from one of Jean-Michel Basquiat's final artworks, it bears a brief analysis. In the 1988 painting, a brown-hued rider sits atop a white skeletal figure crouching on all fours. Brown flesh dangling from the white creature's mouth hints at a bloody battle between the parasitical pair. The duo are locked in a battle that neither can seem to escape. Other telltale signs include the brown rider's arms, which appear faintly as if severed. But it is the white creature that appears almost decomposed, hauntingly skinless. What is most remarkable about the painting, at least to me, is that the brown figure appears to be transforming into something wholly different despite suffering clear injuries.[5] Because of the painting's clear allusions to Black people's hard-fought battles for freedom in America, "Riding with Death" informs my examination into how Black women give birth to a Black matrilineal consciousness.[6] Borne from prolonged exposure to centuries of reproductive violence in the holds of slave ships, plantations, and rice fields, Black matrilineal consciousness operates as "a second sight" in the DuBoisian sense. We may locate Black matrilineal consciousness in Black women's oral histories, testimonies, and indigenous ways of knowing. Writer Toni Morrison recalled this phenomenon when her mother defied the doctor's orders, refusing to enter her children into the hospital after tuberculosis exposure:

> But for my mother to decide that myself and my sister, when we were infants, would not go into a tuberculosis hospital as this doctor said we should because we had been exposed to tuberculosis was not based on scientific evidence. She simply saw that no one ever came out of those sanatoriums in the '30s and also she had visitations.[7]

Here, Morrison blends her mother's power of observation with a spiritual connection to her past ancestors. In Black American households, "visitations" from ancestors are not wholly dreams nor moments rooted in actual occurrences. Rather, these visions contain meaningful tips for surviving an anti-Black world. Throughout her career, Morrison insisted that visitations from ancestors and dreams carried the same weight as other scientific, but perhaps more widely accepted, forms of knowledge:

> I grew up in a house in which people talked about their dreams with the same authority that they talked about what really happened. They had visitations and did not find that fact shocking and they had some sweet, intimate connections with things that were not empirically verifiable.[8]

Morrison's placing of the spiritual world on equal footing with the physical world establishes a flow of life-sustaining information passing between ancestors and descendants. That her mother's maternal decision-making also drew on visitations from her ancestors speaks to the development of a Black matrilineal foundation, one standing in stark opposition to Western scientific medicine as the apex of knowledge. Amid the Black maternal healthcare crisis, Morrison's embrace of alternative forms of knowledge opens up a path for considering Black matrilineal consciousness as a resistance tool against America's long silencing of Black maternal knowledge.

My own ride with death emphasizes an American healthcare system hell-bent on discrediting Black women's maternal wisdom. In 2016, I was pregnant with my second child. At the time, I was living in South Florida completing my PhD and going through a difficult divorce. I shared with my doctor, a middle-aged Black woman, that all of the stress was having a profound effect on me, so much so that I believed it would affect my son. However, she consistently reassured me that everything was fine. But I could not shake the fear that my son was not safe inside of me. The source of my fears stemmed from my first pregnancy. Though I delivered my daughter in our apartment with my mother, midwife, and then-husband present, when her head began crowning I struggled to push her 8-pound, 12-ounce, 22-inch body out. She was trapped inside of me. When I finally pushed her out, piece by piece, she was not breathing on her own. At the hospital, doctors diagnosed her with shoulder dystocia. In Greek, *dys* means difficult and *Tokos* means birth. Dystocia: *difficult birth*. The kind that occurs when one or both of the baby's shoulders become lodged against the pelvic bone. My difficult birth weighed heavily on my mind during my second pregnancy. At my first prenatal appointment for my son, I requested additional monitoring. All the research that I had done on shoulder dystocia suggested that the complications of my first labor warranted close monitoring.

But whenever I broached the subject with my OB-GYN, she dismissed my concerns. My first delivery was difficult because I had chosen a midwife, she insinuated. Regrettably, I accepted her sentiments. She was not the first to tell me this. My doctor's dismissal of my legitimate concerns echoed the paramedics who, upon arriving at our apartment, quipped through mocking laughter, "People have these babies at home and then are shocked when it doesn't work out." The attending doctor at the hospital told his staff, "Of course she was delivered by a midwife. That's the problem right there." A shared disdain for midwives and home births by both the doctor and paramedics aligns with the overall suspicion aimed at midwifery and its African origins.

When Europeans stole African women from their homelands, some of these African women brought with them a unique set of maternal knowledge practices to the Americas. Once enslaved, they cultivated plants, herbs, spices, and teas capable of opening the cervix and shortening labor. Their maternal practices were a combination of motherwit, observation, and medicinal wisdom, encouraging women to "remain active during labor, being awake and aware for birthing, using alternative upright birthing positions, and creating a welcoming environment that encourages women and others to gather to provide comfort throughout the birthing process."[9] All of these processes are what women's health activist Linda Janet Holmes calls the "hallmarks of traditional midwife practices." Following slavery's decline, Black midwives served as a crucial resource in segregated Jim Crow America. In rural Black communities far away from hospitals, midwives not only served the community but were so firmly ensconced within it that they were sometimes affectionately called "granny midwives." However, federal, local, and state authorities only tolerated these midwives as they continued refusing Black women seeking care at white hospitals.

Still, by the Progressive Era of the 1900s, American healthcare officials launched a smear campaign depicting home birth-workers as dirty and incompetent. One of the first national healthcare bills, the Sheppard-Towner Act of 1921, enforced strict certification and licensure rules for midwives, making it difficult for them to retain their practices in the communities that they served. Black midwifery's eventual decline cleared the way for white, mostly male physicians to occupy obstetric positions previously reserved for Black women. This erasure had dire consequences, particularly for Black women and women of color. As midwife specialist Shafia M. Monroe explains, "One of the darkest moments in US history was the systematic eradication of the African American midwife from her community, resulting in a legacy of birth injustices." I had not been thinking of this tortured past when I was pregnant with my son, but I had been thinking of my maternal grandmother, who had been a midwife. She had helped deliver nearly everyone on my mother's side of the family. Yet, despite this, I believed that trusting a midwife to deliver my first child had been a foolish decision. Worse, I felt stigmatized as a poor, uneducated mother in the presence of doctors. Although I knew a midwife would be the best option, I felt compelled to choose a doctor for my second child.

This time my child would be safe, I told myself. Delivered in a hospital. By a doctor. A *Black woman doctor*. This time my child would be safe.

And for a while, he was. After completing my PhD and moving to Upstate New York for my first tenure-track appointment, my mother and I arranged a 45-minute taxi drive to the doctor's office. But by the time the doctor performed the routine prenatal check-up, using the stethoscope to scan my belly for a heartbeat, she could find none. At 33 weeks, my son, Harlem Mackenzie Rose, died nearly a month short of his due date. Not until I lay in the hospital bed, recovering from the C-section, waiting to at least hold Harlem, did the doctor confirm my suspicions as valid. "You should have been considered high risk and put on bed rest," he said, after learning of my first pregnancy's complications and the tremendous stress of my impending divorce while pursuing my PhD. His anger and disbelief were palpable. He was a middle-aged white man, but his medical opinion was more than palliative; his own wife had delivered a stillborn baby during her second pregnancy. In recounting my birthing stories, I mention the race of each healthcare professional to make clear the healthcare system's pervasive practice of dismissing Black maternal knowledge in order to prioritize Western scientific practices.

Because testing results for abnormalities did not reveal any problems, doctors in Florida failed to take my personal challenges into account when addressing a healthcare plan. In midwifery, patients are not simply treated for physical health, but for emotional and mental health as well. But because midwifery is rooted in enslaved Black women's labor, these Black maternal practices are often regarded with suspicion, if not outright disdain. From the moment healthcare staff arrived to assist my infant daughter at our apartment, my decision-making was questioned, challenged, and dismissed as inferior—a pattern of obstetric racism that would continue even with my second pregnancy. To be clear, it certainly matters that the race of EMT staff, nurses, and doctors was mostly white at the time of my first pregnancy. Statistics have shown that Black patients fare better while under the care of Black doctors and nurses. However, my inability to convince a Black woman doctor to take my concerns seriously during my second pregnancy registers the healthcare system as a state apparatus at odds with Black indigenous ways of knowing.

In telling my personal birthing story, I am guided by the Black feminist anthropologist Irma McLaurin's insistence that "we all carry an archive inside us." Black feminist archive-making is a central tool for avowing Black maternal knowledge in the fight against reproductive injustice. The archive we carry inside us is what McLaurin defines as a repository of "memories, music, creativity, family lines, ancestry, experiences of grief, joy, trauma, and walking embodiments of our historical presence as Black people in the United States and on this planet." Autoethnography—the practice of connecting personal experiences to larger cultural events and history—is essential for the survival of Black communities as testifying connects past generations to the next generation. In this chapter, I position my own birthing experiences alongside two Black revolutionary figures, Assata Shakur and Fannie Lou Hamer. Although a 30-year age difference between the women distinguishes them, their lives and political organizing often intersect in meaningful ways. Specifically, both Hamer and Shakur strike out against state-sanctioned reproductive violence.

As with Shakur, Hamer's personal and political battles for reproductive rights are often overshadowed by an overemphasis on her voting rights activism. Whenever I present speeches on Hamer and ask the audience if they are aware that she was forcibly sterilized, a few hands raise. Far fewer hands raise when I ask if they are also aware of her labor as a mother and her national fight for reproductive justice in the Deep South. In many ways then, this chapter is an attempt to spotlight the centrality of reproductive politics to the Black freedom struggle. As both their political labors demonstrate, neither Hamer nor Shakur believed the fight for reproductive justice to be ancillary to the Black Revolution. They understood that the "racial calculus" marking Black women's pregnant bodies and children as expendable not only shortens lifespans but also threatens the sustainability of communities. Engaging Shakur and Hamer as reproductive justice advocates expands the scope of the Black Revolution. Thus, rather than singularizing Hamer and Shakur, this chapter tethers Hamer's fight against Mississippi healthcare officials in the 1960s to Shakur's prolonged battle for reproductive justice beginning with her 1973 solitary confinement at the Rikers Island Correctional Facility for Women for 21 months and her subsequent 1977 imprisonment and escape from the Clinton Correctional Facility for Women in New Jersey.[10] The Black maternal, when spotlighted through the pragmatic maternal visions of Shakur and Hamer, emerges as a cradle for revolutionary potential.

Black Matrilineal Legacies

> It is our duty to fight for our freedom.
> It is our duty to win.
> We must love each other and support each other.
> We have nothing to lose but our chains.[11]

In the 21st century, "Assata's Chant" rose as a soundtrack for the Black Power and Black Lives Matter era. Often recited at protests, Democratic speeches, and rallies, her steely command gifts us with what Audre Lorde called "a litany for survival." Indeed, the origins of Assata's Chant began first as a poem penned during her 1974 incarceration.

The poem was first published in *Assata: An Autobiography*, the 1988 autobiography written by Shakur in Cuba during her political exile to the island country. In *Assata: An Autobiography*, the poem appears as a love letter of sorts titled, "To My People." The letter opens with a declaration: "Black brothers, Black sisters, I want you to know that I love you and I hope that somewhere in your hearts you have love for me."[12] Her conciliatory tone emphasizes Shakur's precarious position while penning the letter. Severely wounded during a traffic stop, she survived only to be promptly charged with murder. Both Zayd Malik Shakur and Werner Foerster were killed during the traffic stop, which left Shakur and Acoli wounded. But the death of the white New Jersey highway patrol officer sparked the most outrage, sealing Shakur's subsequent conviction. Of this incident, Shakur writes: "I want to apologize to you, my Black brothers and sisters, for being on the New Jersey Turnpike. I should have known better. The turnpike is a checkpoint where Black people are stopped, searched, harassed, and assaulted."[13] Throughout the letter, Shakur rejects the mantelpiece of exceptionality, drawing attention to the Black freedom struggle as a praxis of communal care. In praising "jobless Black veterans and welfare mothers" for forging better worlds together, she urges a reproductive politics grounded in ensuring daily living needs are met. This is the kind of communal labor Shakur spearheaded as a member of the Black Panther Party for Self-Defense, the Marxist Black Power organization started in Oakland, California, by Bobby Seale and Huey P. Newton. From her headquarters in the Harlem branch of the Black Panther Party, Shakur established free healthcare clinics and the Free Breakfast for Children program, which was later adopted by the federal government and instituted in public schools throughout America.

The accessibility of Shakur's poem and her ability to capture the spirit of revolution in such a concise manner lends its repackaging simply as "Assata's Chant." It is perhaps the brevity and accessibility of the poem that has concealed its origins as a reservoir of Black matrilineal resistance. The popularity of "Assata's Chant" within the Black Power movement converges around 5-year-old Malkia Cyril attending a rally with their mother, Black Panther Janet Cyril. Once there, the mother–daughter duo denounced the United States' inhumane treatment of Haitians fleeing President Jean "Baby Doc" Duvalier's murderous regime and reframed Black mothering as transformational politic.[14] As a Black Panther Cub, Cyril's early exposure to "Assata's Chant" left an indelible mark. While working as an Oakland activist, they incorporated lines from "A Letter to My People" into every protest. Artist and Black Lives Matter cofounder Patrisse Cullors, upon hearing Cyril recite "Assata's Chant," carried the tradition with her to Ferguson, Missouri, to protest Darren Wilson's murder of Michael Brown.[15] The poem's Black matrilineal history registers Shakur's investment in laboring for a better world amid the United States' government reign of terror via a set of Black maternal practices.

And yet, Shakur's reliance on the Black maternal as a revolutionary tool is rarely addressed. As Black feminist activist Charlene Carruthers notes, Shakur "is a full human being, who, like other freedom fighters, greets many of us in pithy quotes."[16] Indeed, rappers evoke her name in songs; protestors recite her poetry at rallies; and activists sport T-shirts with her resolute image. Lionizing Shakur is no doubt borne from pride and respect. Her successful evasion of the US government, a behemoth of a nation eager to crush her, is a testament to Black resiliency. Shakur's ride with death culminated in a victory. But, as with any Black Civil Rights leader, it is difficult to pinpoint where Shakur's cause célèbre ends and humanity begins. As a member of the Black Liberation Army, Shakur would be indicted more than eight times between 1971 and 1973. Because the Black Liberation Army championed armed struggle as a means of liberation, Shakur engaged in activism designed to shift property and resources into the hands of Black people. Her charges—attempted robbery, felonious assault, reckless endangerment, and possession of a deadly weapon—present a snapshot of a Black revolutionary figure determined to reallocate resources to Black people by any means necessary. For her efforts, Shakur would be shot in the stomach during one of her attempts. But she was never convicted until the fateful traffic stop. However, extolling her risks flattening Shakur into a one-dimensional figure. Even Shakur herself cautioned against relying on one sole means of activism, insisting "the armed struggle, by itself, can never bring about a revolution." Her words encourage us to consider the myriad strategies for resistance available to activists in the long struggle for freedom.

Because Shakur's visions for freedom cohere around pregnancy, birth, and reproductive justice, *Assata: An Autobiography* emerges as a Black maternal manifesto. Although *Assata* mirrors other prison narratives by incorporating memoirs, poetry, and polemical writings, the text scripts Black matrilineality as revolutionary from its beginning pages. Shakur envisions Black foremothers as oracles, knowingly and perhaps unknowingly, passing vital information onto their descendants. While incarcerated in New Jersey, Shakur turns to this rich maternal legacy to empower herself when contemplating if she should bring a child into the world.

> My head was swimming. What had my mother and grandmother and great-grandmother thought when they brought their babies into this world? What had my ancestors thought when they brought their babies into this world, only to see them flogged and raped, bought and sold? I thought and thought.[17]

In theorizing her ancestors as bearers of knowledge, albeit forged from oppressive conditions, Shakur repositions Black women as inheritors of ancestral wisdom necessary for survival. In many Black communities, dreams are portals through which we commune with ancestors holding the keys crucial for ensuring safe passage through a virulent anti-Black world. One of the single most terrifying aspects of my second pregnancy was my dreaming in complete darkness. These pitch-black dreams had the finality of a film's closing credits. This spiraling black abyss, coupled with the fact that I dreamed of Harlem only once, convinced me that he was not safe inside my womb. It disturbed me that there were no "visitations" from my maternal ancestors carrying vital information. In the hospital, after recovering from the C-section, I held my son's tiny body and thought of my grandmother. I wondered how she had endured giving birth to a boy who did not survive outside of her womb. I thought of her and my great-aunt. Both delivered stillborn babies. Both survived. Had they not visited me because they could not find the words for waking up from leathery, cold blackness to being thrust into a hospital holding a silent baby? *Dreams hold secrets, child*, my grandmother would often say.

Shakur too privileges her dreams as signposts for life-sustaining information. Following her 1977 murder conviction, Shakur eagerly awaits her grandmother's arrival at the Clinton Correctional Facility for Women. It is quite a journey; her grandmother travels all the way from North Carolina to New Jersey. But it is no ordinary visit. Shakur writes, "My grandmother's dreams have always come when they were needed and have always meant what we needed them to mean."[18] Perhaps because of this, Shakur, in spite of her incarceration, describes the air as "confident and victorious" upon her grandmother's arrival. As her grandmother "catches her eyes and stares down at her," she predicts Shakur's swift escape from prison:

> You're coming home soon. I don't know when it will be, but you're coming home. You're getting out of here. It won't be too long, though. It will be much less time than you've already been here.[19]

Indeed, Shakur's grandmother delivers crucial information to her by recounting a dream. The exchange between Shakur and her grandmother is "loaded with information."[20] When her grandmother shares the vision she had of dressing Shakur in their old house in Jamaica, Shakur initially fears that this is perhaps a sign of her impending death. But her grandmother reassures her:

> You're alive. It's just as plain as the nose on your face. You're coming home. I know what I'm talking about. Don't ask me to explain it anymore, because I can't. I just know you're going to come home and that you're going to be all right.[21]

Not only does her grandmother accurately predict Shakur's asylum to a Caribbean nation—Cuba to be exact—but the message acts as a survival tactic for Shakur, instantly buoying her hopes despite her dismal conditions in prison. Shakur returns to her cell convinced that "no amount of scientific rational thinking could diminish the high that I felt."[22] Tellingly, her grandmother's "Don't ask me to explain it anymore, because I can't" speaks to the ways in which alternative maternal wisdom, the kind at odds with Western scientific logic, gets passed down through generations of Black women.

This maternal storehouse of wisdom among Black women surfaces again and again in the works of Toni Morrison. The women of Toni Morrison's 2012 novel, *Home*, tap this knowledge base when nursing Ycidara "Cee" Money back to health. In Morrison's tenth novel, she casts the United States as a haunted space for Korean War veteran Frank Money. However, Frank's sister, Cee, despite never leaving the United States, is so brutalized *within it* that she may as well be at war. After she is unknowingly sterilized by her white employer and doctor, her brother Frank Money rushes a nearly lifeless Cee to Miss Ethel's front porch. There, in Miss Ethel's Georgia home, the neighborhood women take turns nursing Cee back to health. In their attempts to save her, the women enact a series of traditional healing cures and imbue Cee with a solid dose of skepticism for the medical industry:

> And nothing Cee remembered—how pleasant she felt upon awakening after Dr. Beau had stuck her with a needle to put her to sleep; how passionate he was about the value of the examinations; how she believed the blood and pain that followed was a menstrual problem—nothing made them change their minds about the medical industry.[23]

Like Black midwives before them, Miss Ethel and the women reject the US healthcare system as the sole gynecological authority. Indeed, the unconventional cures Miss Ethel and the women instruct Cee to perform—opening her legs to the sun—allude to the practices Black midwives enacted as a means of addressing their clients' physical as well as emotional well-being. Because it was not uncommon for midwives to treat women for any number of reproductive health issues, their skill set ranged from contraception to abortion.[24] Traditionally, women were rubbed, massaged, and talcum-powdered by midwives during labor. Rituals like these were deemed essential for welcoming new life into the world. Speaking of her mother's midwifery practice, Alabama midwife Onnie Logan articulated a clearly defined set of treatment practices among midwives: "In those days the doctors didn't tell 'em what to do. They used the old home remedies, mostly come from Indian remedies."[25] Though fictional, *Home* elucidates Black women's oracular vision via relentless state-sanctioned reproductive terror. The women of *Home* command Cee to adopt a more defensive stance, insisting that "Misery don't call ahead. That's why you have to stay awake—otherwise it just walks on in your door"[26] echo midwife and doula Erykah Badu's crooning refrain for Black people to "stay woke" in the face of soul-crushing oppression.

High-Risk Rage and Its Uses

From inside her white frame house with a sprawling pecan tree in the front yard, Fannie Lou Hamer declared to an interviewer there to visit her that the white man was "the scaredest person on earth."[27] Her assertion, published by *The Nation* in 1964, was risky even for her. It had only been a year since Byron de la Beckwith murdered NAACP field activist Medgar Evers outside his Mississippi home. After the murder, Beckwith had not fled. Generous financial donations pouring in from the KKK allowed him to freely roam Mississippi. Like Evers and most Black Mississippians, Hamer loved a state that could not love her back. Three years before racing Dorothy to Memphis, she had been arrested and beaten in Winona, Mississippi. Hamer's crime: conducting a voter education workshop in South Carolina. Officers beat her so severely that she walked with a permanent limp. Kidney damage and the blood clot in her eye plagued Hamer until her death in 1977. Of this savage beating, Hamer said: "After I got out of jail, half dead, I found out that Medgar Evers had been shot down in his own yard."[28] Yet despite the very real possibility of her own assassination, Hamer resolved to never leave. Working Mississippi into a Black homespace, tending to its people and its land, Hamer *rose* in the face of white supremacy: "But I'm goin' to stay in Mississippi and if they shoot me down, I'll be buried here."[29] Evers too refused to flee Jackson, Mississippi, loving the land "as a farmer loves the soil."[30] In continuing to rebuke cowardly white supremacists, Hamer put Black rage on full display. She did not hesitate to call out murderous white men despite their clear retaliation against her, "Out in the daylight he don't do nothin'. But at night he'll toss a bomb or pay someone to kill."[31] A native daughter of Mississippi, Hamer's audacious nerve informs my definition of high-risk rage as a tool for strategizing against reproductive violence.

High-risk rage embodies the politics of refusal articulated by Kellie Carter Jackson as a "forceful no" to "white violence that seeks to steal, kill, and destroy Black lives." As Carter Jackson explains, this refusal is "packed full of energy and meaning." My naming of Black women's rage as high risk is also "packed full of energy and meaning" as it alludes to the medical term reserved for mothers and birthing people requiring additional maternal monitoring due to pre-existing factors. In defining rage in this way, I intend to emphasize the vulnerable, too often deadly, condition

Black mothers experience as a result of hostile, racist-based healthcare. Importantly, high-risk rage originates in Audre Lorde's 1981 essay, "The Uses of Anger: Women Responding to Racism." Like Carter Jackson, Lorde argues: "Anger is loaded with information and energy."[32]

And, as Lorde argued in her essay, this kind of informative anger rejects blind fury that swings wildly but hits no target. My own definition of high-risk rage does not champion aimless rage. Neither does high-risk rage hinge on biologically defined mothers or even women. Although deploying high-risk rage often serves as a barrier for protecting our children from the terror that the white supremacist state enacts, it may be best explained as a creative force for envisioning a more equitable world. High-risk rage is Nina Simone, after learning of the 1963 Birmingham bombing which killed Denise McNair, Addie Mae Collins, Carole Robertson, and Cynthia Wesley, contemplating shooting the white supremacists responsible before ultimately writing "Mississippi Goddam" in one sitting.[33] Rage motivated her during the conception of the song, as she would tell interviewers that the crushing violence of the 1960s was taking its toll on her,

> And I was beginning to get angry then. First you get depressed and then you get mad. And when these kids got bombed, I sat down and wrote this song. And it's a very moving, violent song cause that's how I feel about the whole thing.

Performing the song at Carnegie Hall before a mostly white audience, Simone's opening stanza captured the trauma, fear, and violence haunting Black people throughout the United States: "Hound dog on my tail/ School children sitting in jail/Black cat across my path/I think every day's gonna be my last." When Simone calls out America for "being full of lies," she unleashed a rage so fierce that the song was banned in most states. Years later, Simone recalled the radio stations returning the physical tracks back to the recording company broken in half. As Treva B. Lindsay writes, "Those who viewed the song as a threat to a white supremacist status quo railed against the profanity of the song's title and lyrics and the possibility that it could further galvanize and intensify support for Black freedom struggles." Simone then embodies the kind of high risk rage that mobilizes us toward not only challenging the status quo but also harvesting our creative labors for change.

Like Simone, I learned to marshal high-risk rage's creative potential. Lying in the hospital bed, crying but not too hard because I was afraid of rupturing my stitches, I listened to the doctor. This time, she was an older Indian woman whose pained expression told me that this was not her first time delivering a stillborn baby. "The umbilical cord was wrapped very tightly around his neck, but he was a perfect baby," she said. He likely died 24–48 hours before the check-up appointment. His 4-pound, 22-inch body was in pristine condition. No flaky skin. Cheeks slightly rosy. All I heard as she relayed this information was that he could have survived had I received additional monitoring during my pregnancy. In the years following his death, my rage swelled, not only for him but for many Black infants delivered stillborn or fatally injured during childbirth. *Treveon Taylor, Jr. Lula Mika.*[34] For Black women dying after childbirth. *Felicia West.*[35] *Dr. Shalon Irving.* While working on this book, I began collecting names of mothers and infants who had not survived the healthcare industry. I committed their names to memory while wondering if rage could function as an emancipatory tool, a proclamation declaring our worth beyond white supremacist savagery.

I found my answers in Hamer's relationship with her closest maternal figure: her mother. Praising Mrs Lou Ella Townsend as a "great woman," Hamer roots her path toward activism first in the lessons taught by her mother. "She went through a lot of suffering to bring the twenty of us up, but she still taught us to be decent and to respect ourselves, and that is one of the things that has kept me going."[36] Recollecting an early memory, Hamer tells the story of a white man on a horse riding into the field to inform Mrs Townsend that he would be taking her niece home with him, but not before giving "her a good whipping first." However, Mrs Townsend refutes the white man's demands with the promise of *his* bloodshed: "My mother just stood there, popped her cork and said, 'You don't have no Black children and you not goin' to beat no Black children. If you step down off that horse, I'll go to Hell and back with you before Hell can scorch a feather.'"[37] The scene, exemplifying the terrorist regimes Black women endured following slavery's decline, reframes Black women as tacticians skilled in the art of war. Going toe-to-toe with him in the Jim Crow fields of Mississippi, Mrs Townsend advances a Black maternal praxis under threat of lethal backlash. She thwarts the white man's intended physical and sexual exploitation of her niece, refusing to pay him a mammy-like deference.

Mrs Townsend's commitment to fighting b(l)ack and speaking b(l)ack was not coincidental. In another childhood memory, Hamer witnessed her mother tussling with the "bossman" after he struck her youngest child in the face. The rueful laugh and warning Mrs Townsend issued to her boss guaranteed that none of her children were ever assaulted again. But Mrs Townsend's reputation for defending her children in the face of white violence meant some Black people feared her. Some even called her crazy "since she didn't have the sense enough to be afraid of white folks."[38] As Britney Cooper explains, this brand of rage places those practicing it at risk since it "can't be reasoned with, can't be forced to accept the daily indignities of racism, and more than likely will fight back, rather than fleeing or submitting."³⁹ Similarly, high-risk rage is dangerous precisely because too often Black people wielding it pay for it in blood. Those fortunate enough to escape with their lives often become pariahs.

Still, the revolutionary aims of Hamer's political labors lie in bearing witness to her mother creating life-sustaining spaces for Black children. Celebrated and feared for her fiery speeches, Hamer is less well known for her mobilizing against reproductive injustice. In 1964, she struck out at state sterilization programs targeting Black women and other welfare recipients. Joining forces with the Student Nonviolent Coordinating Committee (SNCC), Hamer denounced the "Genocide Bill" for proposing to make the birth of a second illegitimate child punishable by sterilization or imprisonment. Hamer's work with SNCC to repudiate the bill—she helped develop a pamphlet rebuking it as a thinly veiled attempt to "cut down the rise of illegitimate children on the welfare rolls and force many Negroes to leave the state"—no doubt contributed to the bill's failure to pass. Although the "Genocide Bill" was struck down, Black women in Mississippi were routinely sterilized without their consent. So common were these procedures that Hamer called them "Mississippi appendectomies." In 1961, Hamer herself had been forcibly sterilized. It is not surprising then that she consistently advanced reproductive politics arising out of her personal pursuit of reproductive agency. Hamer, despite being in her early 40s and suffering two stillborn pregnancies, never missed an opportunity to admonish the doctor responsible for sterilizing her:

> If he was going to give that sort of operation, then he should have told me. I would have loved to have children. I went to the doctor who did that to me and I asked him, Why? Why had he done that to me? He didn't have to say anything—and he didn't.

In 1964, when Hamer traveled to New Jersey to speak at the Democratic National Convention, she once again drew attention to the reproductive attacks impacting Black women in her hometown.

> One of the other things that happened in Sunflower County, the North Sunflower County Hospital, I would say six out of ten Negro women that go to the hospital are sterilized with their tubes tied. They are getting up a law that said if a woman has an illegitimate baby and then a second one, they could draw time for six months or a five hundred dollar fine. What they didn't tell you is that they are already doing these things, not only to single women but to married women.⁴⁰

Hamer continued pinpointing the role of racism in threatening and shortening Black lives. "Is this America," she asked with tears in her eyes, "the land of the free and the home of the brave, where ... our lives are threatened daily because we want to live as decent human beings?" The power, fury, and rage of Hamer's testimony were so compelling that President Lyndon B. Johnson called for an impromptu televised press conference from the White House. Although Martin Luther King joined Hamer on the panel, President Lyndon B. Johnson feared her testimony would stoke the ire of Southern Democrats. However, his silencing tactic to detract attention away from her speech backfired. Television networks simply aired the speech in its entirety during their primetime viewership slots, widening her reach within all American homes. Hamer's testimony galvanized a nation, imprinting her resolute image as the face of Black female resistance. That Hamer linked the retaliatory tactics enacted on her by police officials to her sterilization speaks to her activism's rootedness within a reproductive justice framework.[41]

Thus, Hamer's strategic praxis of communal care is representative of a deeply personal reproductive politics of care. Although she never had biological children, Hamer and her husband, Perry, raised two girls. One of the girls was so badly burned in a hot water accident that Hamer and Perry adopted her after the impoverished family struggled to provide the necessary care. The couple's other daughter was a young unmarried woman. Hamer, in caring for children not her own in the biological sense, epitomizes Patricia Hill Collins' definition of an "othermother."[42] According to Hill Collins, "othermothers" are "those sharing or even taking on all primary responsibilities of raising children regardless of a biological connection." Black families, having never confined themselves to the whitewashed two-parent American ideal, are often populated by grandmothers, aunts, uncles, and "othermothers," not always related by blood but responsible for performing the labor of keeping children alive, fed, and physically and emotionally safe. The prominence of othermothers within African American communities today evidences the foundation for a Black matrilineal legacy, springing forth from forced familial separations during slavery. bell hooks, in naming the nurturing and care extended to her via her grandmother's laboring, cites "homeplace" as a "site of resistance."[43] These homecomings teach hooks "dignity, and integrity of being."[44] Black women's caregiving labors underscore the genesis of a Black matrilineal resistance.

Hamer, unflinching in her pursuit of justice and in remaking Mississippi into a less hostile world for her children, engaged in what Patricia Hill Collins calls "motherwork." This maternal labor, or motherwork, is done "on behalf of one's own biological children, or for the children of one's own racial ethnic community, or to preserve the earth for those children who are yet unborn." Motherwork attests to the boundless creative possibility produced by Black matrilineal consciousness. Of paramount importance to this kind of mothering is the tending to and caring for the community. Much like the Black Panther Party's offering of free healthcare clinics, Hamer launched the Freedom Farm Collective, securing a $10,000 charitable donation and purchasing 40 acres of land for over 1500 families.[45] A former sharecropper herself, Hamer knew most families could not afford the monthly $1 membership, so she provided them with land to plant cash crops like soybeans and cotton to cover the taxes and administrative costs. The farmworkers used the rest of the land for planting peas, squash, and collard greens. The following year, using funds from the National Council of Negro Women, Hamer's co-op purchased 40 pigs. For years, the families survived off the "pig bank." Often overlooked, this kind of labor is crucial for sustaining liberation. Poet June Jordan, shortly after Hamer's death, paid tribute to the woman she felt was like a mother to her by memorializing her maternal care work. In "1977: Poem for Mrs. Fannie Lou Hamer," it is not only Hamer's "lion spine" that Jordan remembers, but also her "singin' face" and the handpicked okra and turnip greens she called for everyone to gather around to eat, saying, "BULLETS OR NO BULLETS! THE FOOD IS COOKED AN' GETTIN COLD!" Of Hamer's labors, Jordan ascribes them with the motivation needed to continue the work, "We ate/A family tremulous but fortified." Forging pathways for others while facing down white supremacists who wanted Hamer dead evinces her maternal vision as integral to the Black freedom struggle.

High-Risk Rage and Subterfuge

Ten years after Hamer traveled to New Jersey to testify at the Democratic National Convention, word of Assata Shakur's pregnancy began trickling out of Rikers Island Correctional Institution for Women. *The Atlanta Journal-Constitution* announced the news without mentioning her name: "Jailed Black Militant Is Reported Pregnant."[46] *The Washington Post* followed suit, declaring, "Militant Pregnant."[47] Both headlines, in shifting attention toward the circumstances of her imprisonment, trouble Shakur's ties to motherhood. Subtly calling her reproductive right to have children when, where, and how into question, the newspapers subtly condemn her pregnancy as a potentially dangerous event to the nation state. This rhetorical assault is not unique to Shakur. Black mothers, as Christen Smith avers,

> bear a unique burden under the weight of anti-Black state violence not because they are the idyllic symbols of maternal purity, loss, or innocence, but because they are enemies of the state—subjects that challenge the ideology of anti-Blackness, which undergirds the state's structure.[48]

In *Assata*, Shakur contextualizes the constant surveilling and restricting of her reproductive rights as representative of Black women's protracted battle against white supremacist incursions on Black caregiving. "Black life expectancy is much lower than white and they do their best to kill us before we are born," she warns.[49] For weeks, Shakur faces off against the healthcare machine, with the prison doctor denying her access to prenatal treatment. Despite the intense pain traveling down her lower body, the doctor repeatedly denies and dismisses Shakur's concerns. When he finally confirms that she is indeed pregnant, he regurgitates eugenicist rhetoric coding pregnant Black women as a drain on the nation's resources:

> "There's a chance that you're going to abort."
> "I don't want no abortion," I cried out.
> "It's probably the best course you could take now, and I'd recommend it. But that's not what I was talking about. I said that there was a chance you could spontaneously abort, have a miscarriage."
> "Oh no!" I moaned. "What are you going to do?"
> "Relax. It's probably nothing serious. It's nothing much to worry about."
> "What do you mean, nothing much to worry about. I want this baby."
> "Well, I can't force you to do anything, but my advice is to have an abortion. It will be better for you and for everyone else."[50]

This torrent of verbal abuse parallels the state sterilization programs, such as the ones Hamer mobilized against in Mississippi, accusing Black mothers of exploiting their pregnancies for increased state financial assistance. Worse still, the doctor's "it will be better for you and for everybody else" tacitly chastises Black mothers for birthing too many "fatherless" children. Years before Ronald Reagan vilified "the welfare queen" using coded racist language to suggest that she was a Black mother scamming the government by collecting funds in her Cadillac, social scientist and politician Daniel Moynihan described Black households headed by single Black women as a "dangerous tangle of pathology." In his report, Moynihan overlooked the institutional racism crippling Black families, instead reducing poverty and health issues to overbearing Black women. In the years since, this kind of language has been mobilized even within Black communities. When Democratic nominee Senator Barack Obama began his 2008 presidential campaign run, he tacitly implicated Black mothers for failing to provide solid domestic foundations while assailing absent Black fathers. Speaking to a predominantly Black crowd about the rising numbers of gang-related deaths in Chicago, Obama insisted that Black families were "weaker because too many fathers are M.I.A, too many fathers are AWOL, missing from too many lives and too many homes." In light of his own white mother's status as a single parent, Obama's allusions to Moynihan's matriarchal thesis expose the different set of standards for Black mothers. Similarly, the prison doctor, believing Shakur's maternal labors as insignificant precisely because they cannot be redeemed for white capitalist exploitation, justifies denying her adequate treatment:

> My advice to you is that you should go to your cell and lie down. Just lie down and rest your mind. Just lie down and stay off your feet. And if you go the bathroom and see a lump in the toilet, don't flush it. It's your baby.[51]

Racing back to her cell, a weeping Shakur thinks: "As far as I could see, they were out to kill my baby."[52] Black, poor, and incarcerated, she exists beyond the bounds of care. Shakur's medical neglect while imprisoned underscores the oppressive conditions foisted upon pregnant incarcerated women and birthing people. As Michele Goodwin notes,

> a poor woman determined to carry a pregnancy to term often unwittingly exposes herself to nefarious interagency collaborations between police and physicians, quite possibly leading to criminal prosecution, incarceration, and giving birth while in highly unsanitary prison conditions, sometimes without the appropriate aid of hospital physicians and staff.[53]

Indeed, the prison hospital staff withholds Shakur's treatment for so long that she develops monilia—a vaginal discharge that impacts her physical health so severely that her thighs become "chapped raw." At one point, she can "barely walk."[54] Although her personal doctor insists she not be shackled to the bed during her labor, Shakur is handcuffed to "round-the-clock guards" sitting outside her hospital room. They train shotguns at her head.[55] As heartbreaking as Shakur's experience is, her resistance tactics reveal the degree to which Black women rely on subterfuge during their pregnancies. While laboring, Shakur becomes keenly aware of the fact that she bleeds each time the doctor performs an examination. In response, Shakur circumvents healthcare professionals' attempts to harm her unborn child:

> Then a nurse told me to walk around to ease the pain and encourage labor. I got up, then pretended to fall out (knowing how afraid they were of lawsuits), and the doctors rushed over to pick me off the floor. I knew they were worried. I stated again, "I am delivering the baby

myself." I checked the baby's heart with the stethoscope. It was beating normally.⁵⁶

Though incarcerated, Shakur's strategizing here compels us to consider how Black women, across class and gender lines, develop dissembling tactics as a means of ensuring one's survival and that of their offspring. Feigning falls, sporting wedding rings, and announcing educational degrees and certifications are all machinations Black women employ in the face of a hostile medical apparatus.⁵⁷ My own mother suggested that I go to the hospital and "fall out" since the medical doctors and specialists refused to take my concerns seriously. In devising a strategy for refusal, Shakur repels the probable *and intended lethal* health outcomes for her and her child. Vowing to never let "any of them touch me again," she springs into action, demanding the medical staff bring her a stethoscope so that she can monitor her *own* child's heartbeat. Surrounded by a room full of white doctors and nurses, Shakur repeatedly declares, "I am delivering this baby myself."⁵⁸ Her declaration is an avowal, an assertion of high-risk rage as the sustained process of constructing routes and pathways for our children's safety amid potentially lethal anti-Black antagonisms.

Birthing New Worlds

The extraordinary details of Shakur's escape from prison—a small group of Black Liberation Army members held two prison officers at gunpoint before seizing a prison vehicle—are well-documented. But less attention has been paid to the simultaneously tender and violent mother–daughter moment that Shakur deems pivotal in her escape from prison. In *Assata*, Shakur identifies a prison visit from her 4-year-old daughter as the deciding factor motivating her to first imagine for herself a life beyond the prison's bars:

> I go over and try to hug her. In a hot second she is all over me. All I can feel are these little four-year-old fists banging away at me. Every bit of her force is in those punches, they really hurt. I let her hit me until she is tired. "It's all right," I tell her. "Let it all out." She is standing in front of me, her face contorted with anger, looking spent. She backs away and leans against the wall. "It's okay," I tell her. "Mommy understands." "You're not my mother," she screams, the tears rolling down her face. "You're not my mother and I hate you." I feel like crying too. I know she is confused about who I am. She calls me Mommy Assata and she calls my mother Mommy. I try to pick her up. She knocks my hand away. "You can get out of here, if you want to," she screams. "You just don't want to." "No, I can't," I say weakly.⁵⁹

Though she delivers the message with an intensity characteristic of a 4-year-old—screaming, hitting, and contorting herself with anger—Kakuya's articulation of freedom is anything but facile. Structuring resistance along a generational expanse, she positions freedom as a collaborative task, to be worked on by caregivers and children alike, whether childfree or child-full. Direct as a missile, Kakuya's rage transforms the physical conditions under which her mother is imprisoned, provoking a visceral reaction from Shakur:

> "Yes you can." She accuses. "You just don't want to." "I can't open the door," "I tell my daughter. I can't get through the bars. You try and open the bars." My daughter goes over to the barred door that leads to the visiting room. She pulls and she pushes. She yanks and she hits and she kicks the bars until she falls on the floor, a heap of exhaustion. I go over and pick her up. I hold and rock and kiss her. There is a look of resignation on her face that I can't stand. We spend the rest of the visit talking and playing quietly on the floor. When the guard says the visit is over, I cling to her for dear life. She holds her head high, and her back straight as she walks out of the prison. She waves good-bye to me, her face clouded and worried, looking like a little adult. I go back to my cage and cry until I vomit. I decide that it is time to leave.[60]

Kakuya's attempt at breaking down the prison bars provides Shakur a model for what she *must* do, echoing her mother's command in "For My People": "It is our duty to win." And her "You can get out of here, if you want to," reminds Shakur of her parental duty to Kakuya. As activist and educator Alexis Pauline Gumbs asks,

> How often do we think about the fact that one of the rare success stories of the Black Liberation Army or of the effective escape of a political prisoner is at its heart a story of [B]lack mother/daughter rage and love?[61]

Perhaps the beginnings of a response to Gumbs' question lie in hinging Shakur's survival on a triptych of Black matrilineal resistance starting with grandmother, mother, and child. Kakuya taps into this generative source much like Shakur's grandmother when she visits the prison. In so doing, she draws on the legacy of Black matrilineal consciousness and the Black women carving out spaces for their children's survival against anti-Black regimes of reproductive terror.

These are the "headragged generals" lauded by Alice Walker for not only leading armies across "booby-trapped ditches," but also for "discovering books, desks, and making a place for us."⁶² Walker's wise words affirm the presence of an innovative Black maternal inheritance from which we draw strength for survival. This Black maternal genius is frequently praised by the chorus of Black writers marveling at their mothers for making a dollar out of 15 cents. It is instrumental in shielding our children from lethal harm while planting the seeds for creativity. As this chapter was inspired by Basquiat's "Riding with Death," I close it with a childhood story from the artist as a means of making clear the oracular power of Black maternal visions of freedom. At just 7 years old, Jean-Michel Basquiat was seriously injured after being hit by a car while playing in the street. A broken arm and ruptured spleen were just two of his injuries, causing him to stay in the hospital for weeks. For Basquiat's mother, Matilde, to know that gifting him *Gray's Anatomy Descriptive and Surgical* during his hospitalization would provide the emotional sustenance necessary for his development speaks to Black maternal consciousness as a life-affirming resource.⁶³ While some parents may have thought the dissection manual, complete with drawings of bodily organs, was too mature, Matilde awakened her son's capacity for new ways of seeing. Indeed, Basquiat's paintings, distinguished by anatomical renderings of stark white thyroids, tracheas, and scapulas thrown against black canvases, often center the body as a site of critical inquiry, a wounded space lodged with racism's corporeal toll. Of his artistic vision, Basquiat credited his mother: "I'd say my mother gave me all the primary things. The art came from her."⁶⁴ Our children, inheritors of so much more than the wretched afterlife of slavery, birth new worlds.

Notes

1 Mills, 191.
2 Mills, 191.
3 Demuth.
4 Gumbs, Martens, and Williams.
5 Basquiat.
6 Hartman, 6.
7 Davis, 144.
8 Davis.
9 Holmes, 35.
10 McLaurin, 21.
11 Shakur, 52.
12 Shakur.
13 Shakur.
14 Cyril.
15 "Patrisse Cullors Shares the History of the Protest Chant Inspired by Assata Shakur."
16 Carruthers, 222.
17 Shakur, *Assata: An Autobiography*, 93.
18 Shakur, 260.
19 Shakur, 260.

20 Lorde, 278.
21 *Assata: An Autobiography*, 261.
22 *Assata: An Autobiography*.
23 Morrison, 123.
24 Logan, 146.
25 Logan, 126.
26 Morrison, *Home*, 123.
27 Demuth, "Fannie Lou Hamer: Sick and Tired of Being Sick and Tired."
28 Demuth.
29 Demuth.
30 Evers-Williams, 3.
31 Demuth.
32 Lorde, 278.
33 Fields.
34 "Black Mothers Respond to Our Cover Story on Maternal Mortality."
35 Kelly.
36 Mills, 17.
37 Lee, 12.
38 Lee, 12.
39 Cooper, 118.
40 Houck and Brooks, 41.
41 Lee, 22.
42 Collins, 178.
43 hooks, 42.
44 hooks, 42.
45 Mills, 255.
46 "Jailed Black Militant Is Reported Pregnant."
47 "Militant Pregnant."
48 Smith, 32.
49 *Assata: An Autobiography*, 51.
50 *Assata: An Autobiography*, 126.
51 *Assata: An Autobiography*, 125.
52 *Assata: An Autobiography*, 127.
53 Goodwin, x.
54 Shakur, 142.
55 Shakur, 141.
56 Shakur, 143.
57 Sacks, 4.
58 Shakur, 143.
59 Shakur, 257.
60 Shakur, 258.
61 Gumbs.
62 Walker, 242.
63 Gipson.
64 Hagar, 56.

Bibliography

"Black Mothers Respond to Our Cover Story on Maternal Mortality." 19 April 2018. https://www.pbs.org/wnet/americanmasters/the-story-behind-nina-simones-protest-song-mississippi-goddam/16651/.

"Jailed Black Militant Is Reported Pregnant." *The Atlanta Journal Constitution* 27 January 1974.

"Militant Pregnant." *The Washington Post* 27 January 1974.

"Patrisse Cullors Shares the History of the Protest Chant Inspired by Assata Shakur." 5 March 2019. 2 May 2024. <https://www.youtube.com/watch?v=zmuaWInh8BQ>.

Basquiat, Jean Michel. *Riding with Death*. Estate of Jean-Michel Basquiat. New York: Artestar, 1988.

Carruthers, Charlene. "Hearing Assata Shakur's Call: A Black Feminist Reflection on 'To My People.'" *Women's Studies Quarterly*, vol. 46, no. 3, 2018, pp. 222–225.

Collins, Patricia Hill. *Black Feminist Thought: Knowledge, Consciousness, and the Politics of Empowerment*. New York: Routledge, 2000.

Cooper, Brittney. *Eloquent Rage: A Black Feminist Discovers Her Superpower*. New York: St. Martin's P, 2018.

Cyril, Malkia. "Magazine: Black Panther Cub on New Era of Civil Action." 8 August 2015. 1 May 2023. https://www.aljazeera.com/features/2015/8/8/magazine-black-panther-cub-on-new-era-of-civil-action.

Davis, Christina. "Interview with Toni Morrison." *Présence Africaine*, vol. 145, 1988, pp. 141–150.

Demuth, Jerry. "Fannie Lou Hamer: Sick and Tired of Being Sick and Tired." 1 June 1964. 1 June 2020. https://www.thenation.com/article/archive/fannie-lou-hamer-tired-being-sick-and-tired/.

Evers-Williams, Myrlie. *For Us, the Living*. Mississippi: U P of Mississippi, 1996.

Fields, Liz. "The True Story behind Nina Simone's Protest Song, 'Mississippi Goddam.'" 14 January 2021. 2 June 2023. https://www.pbs.org/wnet/americanmasters/the-story-behind-nina-simones-protest-song-mississippi-goddam/16651/.

Gipson, Ferren. "Jean-Michel Basquiat—The Artist's Sisters Guide Us Through Their Family Album." 2021. https://wepresent.wetransfer.com/artists/jean-michel-basquiat.

Goodwin, Michelle. *Policing the Womb: Invisible Women and the Criminalization of Motherhood*. London: U of Cambridge, 2020.

Gumbs, Alexis Pauline. "Kakuya Collective: A Visionary Daughtering Webinar." 16 November 2016. https://brokenbeautiful.wordpress.com/.

Gumbs, Alexis Pauline, China Martens, and Mai'a Williams. *Revolutionary Mothering: Love on the Front Lines*. New York: PM Press, 2016.

Hagar, Steven. *Art After Midnight: The East Village Scene*. New York: St. Martins Press, 1986.

Hartman, Saidiya. *Lose Your Mother: A Journey Along the Atlantic Slave Trade*. New York: Farrar, Straus and Giroux, 2008.

Holmes, Linda. *Safe in a Midwife's Hands Birthing Traditions from Africa to the American South*. Ohio: Ohio State U P, 2023.

hooks, bell. *Yearning: Race, gender, and cultural politics*. Boston: South End Press, 1990.

Houck, Davis W., and Maegan Parker Brooks. *The Speeches of Fannie Lou Hamer: To Tell It Like It Is*. Mississippi: U P of Mississippi, 2011.

Hoybert, Donna L. "Maternal Mortality Rates in the United States, 2021." 16 March 2023. 2 June 2020. https://www.cdc.gov/nchs/data/hestat/maternal-mortality/2021/maternal-mortality-rates-2021.htm.

Kelly, John. "Hospitals Blame Moms When Childbirth Goes Wrong. Secret Data Suggest It's Not That Simple." 23 April 2020. 1 June 2023. https://

www.usatoday.com/in-depth/news/investigations/deadly-deliveries/2019/03/07/maternal-death-rates-secret-hospital-safety-records-childbirth-deaths/2953224002/.

Lee, Chani Kai. *For Freedom's Sake: The Life of Fannie Lou Hamer*. Illinois: U of Illinois P, 2000.

Logan, Onnie Lee. *Motherwit: An Alabama Midwife's Story*. San Francisco: Untreed Reads Publishing, 1989.

Lorde, Audre. "The Uses of Anger." *Women's Studies Quarterly*, vol. 9, no. 3, Fall 1981, 8; vol. 25, no. 1/2, 1981, pp. 278–285.

McLaurin, Irma. *Black Feminist Anthropology: Theory, Politics, Praxis, and Poetics*. New Jersey: Rutgers U P, 2001.

Mills, Kay. *This Little Light of Mine: The Life of Fannie Lou Hamer*. Kentucky: U P of Kentucky, 2007.

Morrison, Toni. *Home*. New York: Vintage, 2012.

Sacks, Tina K. *Invisible Visits: Black Middle-Class Women in the American Healthcare System*. London: Oxford U P, 2019.

Shakur, Assata. *Assata: An Autobiography*. Chicago: Lawrence Hill Books, 1987.

Shakur, Assata. *Assata: An Autobiography*. Chicago: Lawrence Hill Books, 2001.

Smith, Christen. "Facing the Dragon: Black Mothering, Sequelae, and Gendered Necropolitics in the Americas." *Transforming Anthropology* 19 April 2016, pp. 37–63.

Walker, Alice. *In Search of Our Mothers' Gardens: Womanist Prose*. Orlando: Mariner Books, 2003.

2 The Motherwork Continues
Merciful Mothering in the Black Lives Matter Era

I had every intention of spanking my children. "Better tan them legs," the Southern Black American euphemism for lightly tapping a small child on their bottom, had been passed around at family gatherings for as long as I could remember. It was not only advice but a warning. *Better tan them legs before someone else does.* That someone could be the trigger-happy police, a quick-to-suspend school principal, or a random racist white person. My parents believed that whuppings would keep us in line and teach us the right way. After each whupping, which was always scheduled from eldest to youngest, my mother would sit on my bed, look at me, and say, "I'm doing this because I love you." For a while, I believed this too. I knew that I would administer whuppings as a preventive tool in much the same way. But two things happened. First, I had my daughter. When I went to tan her legs, I found that I simply could not. My raised hand remained suspended in the air. Fear settled in. Because if I wasn't going to whup her, then what was I supposed to do when she inevitably began challenging my authority? What would my family think?

Then the second thing happened. I read Stacy Patton's *Spare the Kids: Why Whupping Children Won't Save Black America*. In it, Patton makes a compelling argument linking spanking to the brutal disciplinary measures meted out on the bodies of enslaved Black people. But a single sentence fundamentally shifted my perspective: "Black Americans have been allowed to legally parent their children for only 150 years."[1] Importantly, Patton does not define this legal permission as a freedom granted to Black caregivers but as a provision that can be revoked at any time. In colonial America, the legal doctrine of *partus sequitur ventrem* relegated enslaved Black women's children to chattel property even when their fathers were white. This increased slaveholders' supply of exploitable labor while reducing Black parents to breeders. Today, Black caregivers parenting children in this newly acquired legal provision are imagining new ways to parent, though we are living under the old oppressive regimes of terror. Therefore, despite having obtained legal permissions to parent our children, Black parents navigate through what I call deathscapes. These deathscapes may be understood as "geographies of domination."[2] In *Demonic Grounds: Black Women and the Cartographies of Struggle*, Katherine McKittrick explores these "geographies of domination" as transatlantic slavery and the racial and sexual violence this practice imposed on Black women. Our constant exposure to reproductive violence highlights the hostility of American terrain devaluing Black lives. In these deathscapes, whether within the holds of slaving ships, forced work camps, or over-policed ghettos, Black parents operating under these oppressive forces are stirred by an anticipatory grief compelling them to harm their children. To be a Black parent raising children in "the mouth of the dragon" is to be an unwilling accomplice to the powerful state apparatus.[3]

The fight to raise our children in these deathscapes is the kind of maternal strategizing defined by sociologist Patricia Hill Collins as motherwork. As discussed in the previous chapter, motherwork is "work done on behalf of one's own biological children, or for the children of one's own racial ethnic community, or to preserve the earth for children who are yet unborn."[4] Motherwork is the radical labor necessary for imagining pathways for survival.[5] However, our fight to cultivate spaces for resistance in these deathscapes siphons our energies, labors, and resources. As Professor Ruha Benjamin reminds us, the "deep social fault lines and deadly inequalities ... impact not only our everyday lives but our ability to imagine something different."[6] Black caregivers, desperate to save our children, imagine "something different" and deploy a kind of mothering that calls forth a new definition of mercy.

For Black parents, mercy is the relentless pursuit of tenderness amid American white supremacist capitalism. Mercy is a love offering, albeit marred and warped under the threat of reproductive violence. No wonder then that Farrah Jasmine Griffin declares that "the question of mercy revolves around Black children who are the most vulnerable."[7] "Who," Griffin ponders, "can be more deserving of mercy than a child?" As mercy so often eludes Black children, Black parents must be the ones to extend it. In the pages that follow, I examine Black parents' merciful mothering against the state's prevention of these attempts. In considering the weight white supremacy bears on Black caregivers and children, this chapter conducts a literary analysis of key scenes in three works of African American Literature: Toni Morrison's *A Mercy*, Edward P. Jones' *The Known World*, and N.K. Jemisin's *The Broken Earth* trilogy. I have chosen to analyze the trio of texts because they each attend to the challenges facing Black parents across various time periods. Colonial 17th-century America is the setting for *A Mercy*; the antebellum plantation household takes center stage in *The Known World*; the dystopian nightmare in *The Broken Earth* trilogy mirrors the horrific conditions Black people navigate currently. The texts provide a compelling lens for understanding the negotiations Black parents are forced to make when confronting the threat of reproductive violence. Contemporary Black mothers Toya Graham and Diamond Reynolds, through their experiences navigating reproductive violence, highlight Black reproductive health scholar Dana-Ain Davis' assertion that the threat of losing one's child engenders a perpetual state of sorrow within Black caregivers.

Deathscapes: Past and Present

When a news camera crew recorded Toya Graham pummeling her teenage son upside the head in the middle of a Baltimore street, they tapped into white America's centuries-long obsession with Black mothers harming their children. The smashing success of Harriet Beecher Stowe's *Uncle Tom's Cabin*—the 1852 novel sold 10,000 copies in its first week, 300,000 in its first year in the United States, and 1.5 million in Great Britain—normalized Black child abuse. In one of its opening scenes, enslaved Black mother Aunt Chloe slaps her children, "pushing away their woolly heads."[8] Aunt Chloe's violent blows, despite landing "very formidably," only elicit laughter from her children who "fairly [scream] with merriment" as the slaps rain down on their heads. Therefore, we may think of *Uncle Tom's Cabin* as conditioning white audiences to accept Black children's abuse. We may also use the text's popularity in spite of its trite stereotypes to contextualize the media's fascination with Graham's 2020 public beating of her son.

Within 24 hours, Graham became a viral sensation, appearing on news stations and newspapers across the country. Days after the incident, social media hailed her as "Mom of the Year."[9] Even Baltimore Police Commissioner Anthony Batts praised Graham, expressing his hope that more parents would follow her example.[10] *The New York Post* agreed, publishing the headline, "Forget the National Guard: Send in the Moms."[11] Lost in the praise was a sincere engagement with the harrowing circumstances compelling 16-year-old Michael Singletary to leave school. He had planned to attend the protest rally for Freddie Gray, a 25-year-old man arrested by local police and subsequently killed in their custody. Gray's murder had badly shaken Michael. When he pulled a black skull cap over his head, he had been thinking of his friends who had been beaten by police. Yet in interview after interview, reporters conveniently sidestepped the issue of police violence, its role in Gray's death, and its potential threat to Michael's life. In an interview with CNN, Graham tethered her plight to other Black mothers navigating a specific kind of invisible trauma. "People looking in can't see what we go through," she explained, "No one sees us mothers, our pain."[12] Lensing her pain through a frame of mourning, Graham's violence may be understood as the kind of anticipatory grief every Black parent has likely spent considerable time contemplating.

As reproductive scholar Dana-Ain Davis asserts, "Black mothering can be sorrowful when we lose our children but also just the threat of losing our children can precipitate a constant state of sorrow."[13] Though media outlets marveled at Graham's tenacity in raising six children alone, they made less effort to interrogate her violent response as primarily spurred by the crushing fear that police officers would kill her son, as they had Gray, and get away with it. Reporters unwilling to engage Graham beyond the socially constructed image of her as a lone single mother figure evaded the more important question of how police violence compels Black parents' complicity in harming our own children. Therefore, the scene may be understood as what Christina Sharpe articulates as "the still unfolding aftermaths of Atlantic chattel slavery."[14] The police state's continued oppression in our lives situates Graham's beating of Michael as a gathering of ancestral suffering in her bones, a deep sorrow over the threat of losing her child. The scene unfolding on the Baltimore street between mother and son embeds the desperation and hope for mercy that enslaved Black parents like Sojourner Truth cried out for when "none but Jesus heard."

For Black caregivers, spending considerable time preparing children for navigating anti-Black state apparatuses is a necessity. These defensive strategies are nothing new. Family scientist Leslie A. Anderson identifies "The Talk" as the stern discussion Black parents have with their children about "racial profiling and diffusing negative perceptions and stereotypes to avoid being hurt or killed by police during routine activities, such as driving or walking down the street."[15] As a girl, I witnessed the urgency of "The Talk" while listening to my mother repeatedly brief my older teenage brothers. Perhaps sensing that three young Black boys needed more defense against the targeting they would experience in white suburbia, my mother drilled the already known information into their heads until the warnings bored them. When, not if, the police stop you, keep your hands on the steering wheel. Call the officer sir. Roll the window all the way down. Turn the music off before the officer gets to your door. My mother's fears were no doubt intensified by the very suburban white area we lived in at the time. Amplifying her anxiety was my eldest brother's refusal to perform any of these rituals whenever he was stopped, which was often. Now, as a parent, I understand her anxiety as grief, boundless and bottomless, gnawing at her during sleepless nights. Because our children are rendered disposable, we have developed a set of strategies for combating their potentially fatal demise within this system. However, these defensive strategies can have the unintended effect of conveying to our children that they must shrink themselves to survive, or even contort themselves into impossible versions of the perfect non-stereotypical Black person. Never angry. Never loud. Articulate even in the face of injustice. In this light, my brother's rebellion was not aimed at my mother, but at a system refusing him the right to be as free as any other teenager his age.

In the historical fiction of *The Known World*, Edward P. Jones treads similar ground by constructing an antebellum deathscape responsible for effectively severing the relationship between father and son. The novel begins first with Augustus Townsend, a formerly enslaved Black man and skilled carpenter, purchasing himself, his wife, and later, his son's freedom. His participation in Virginia's slave market economy, though for compassionate purposes, signals his entanglement within a brutal system of white supremacist capitalism. That is, Augustus' freedom does not preclude him from experiencing, participating, and engaging in the parasitical practices endemic to slaveholders. As if to underscore this, Jones places Augustus and Mildred in a tenuous position further illustrating their illusory position as parents. As Augustus must save more money to purchase his young son Henry, he and Mildred are forced to visit their son on William Robbins' plantation. One of the wealthiest slaveholders in the county, Robbins restricts the couple's movement around his property: "Robbins had told them not to take the boy beyond where his overseer could see them from the entrance to his property."[16] Essentially, he assumes the role of a parent over Mildred and Augustus, ordering them to keep his property within eye's view. Under his watchful gaze, Augustus and Mildred "build a fire on no-man's-land," eating "with few words."[17] Robbins goes a step further, refusing to let Augustus and Mildred step foot on his property unless dropping off a payment for their son's eventual freedom. Geographical edicts like the one Robbins enacted have a long history in American slaveholding. In fact, Robbins' strict enforcement over the movements of Mildred and Augustus on his property mirrors the customary slaveholding practices imposed on Frederick Douglass' mother. In his autobiography, Douglass writes:

> It is a common custom, in the part of Maryland from which I ran away, to part children from their mothers at a very early age, Frequently, before the child has reached its twelfth month, its mother is taken from it, and hired out on some farm a considerable distance off, and the child is placed under the care of an old woman, too old for field labor.[18]

In this anti-Black terrain, short-circuiting chances for familial harmony is by design. As Douglass explains, these practices indeed "hinder the development of the child's affection toward its mother, [blunt] and destroy the natural affection of the mother for the child."[19] The efficacy of these tactics surfaces in Douglass being mostly unfazed by his mother's laborious efforts. The 12-mile trek she embarks on to see him, risking a whipping penalty for not being in the field at sunrise, impresses little memory of her onto Douglass. "I never saw my mother, to know her as such, more than four or five times in my life; and each of these times was very short in duration, and at night."[20] Not even news of his mother's passing sways him. "I received the tidings of her death with much the same emotions I should have probably felt at the death of a stranger."[21] Similarly, like the young Douglass, Henry remains oblivious to his parents' sacrifices and the power Robbins retains over them. Unable to step foot on Robbins' property, Augustus and Mildred wait and

> hope some slave would venture out, going to or from the mansion, so they could holler to him or her to go get their boy Henry. But even when they managed to see someone and tell them about Henry, they would wait in vain for the boy to show up.[22]

As with the 7-year-old Douglass, Henry attaches little significance to these two-hour visits. When he misses these visits, he offers a mere "I just forgot."[23] Like Douglass, Henry cannot fully understand the enormity of the danger, labor, and love involved in each visit. Especially difficult in the winter, the visits require Mildred to bake rocks so that they stay warm. When the stones turn cold, their time is up. Yet his parents are aware of every minute that passes and Robbins' watchful eye. Parenting, under such high stakes, becomes a pressure-inducing situation. Inevitably, Augustus snaps under the weight of it all.

During one of their meetings, Augustus interprets Henry's tardiness and absences as insolence, gently reminding the boy to take these visits seriously. "Try harder to remember, son," he cautions, "To know the right way."[24] His reprimand is purposefully tender: he has not yet bought Henry and cannot rebuke him too sternly. "Augustus had often been chastised as a boy but though Henry was his son, he was not yet his property and so beyond his reach."[25] Therefore, his reprimand is also rooted in fear. As he cannot fully parent Henry, Augustus fears losing his son to the whims of a slaveholder. Though absent, Robbins' omniscient presence limits Augustus' ability to imagine creative, life-affirming modes of parenting. The violence deployed by Augustus in a moment of misplaced frustration is the byproduct of Robbins' relentless continual interference in Mildred's and Augustus' attempts to parent Henry:

> Then, in mid February, after they had waited two hours beyond when he was supposed to appear on the road, Augustus grabbed the boy when he shuffled up and shook him, then he pushed him to the ground. Henry covered his face and began to cry. "Augustus!" Mildred shouted and helped her son up. "Everything's good," she said to him as she cradled him in her arms. "Everything's good."[26]

Augustus' pushing of Henry draws the paradox facing Black parents into sharp focus. In attempting to show Henry "the right way," Augustus not only does the wrong thing, but he also engages in cruel behavior on par with that of a slaveholder. And, he succumbs to the pull of power as a disciplinary tactic. Even worse, Augustus' momentary lapse in judgment reveals a devastating reality: Black parents, fearful of losing their children, often deploy the master's tools as an easier, quicker, seemingly more effective choice.

Because *The Known World* explores the ever-present threat of losing a child to a slaveholder's clutches and the waves of sorrow that this potential loss imposes, the novel expands our understanding of Graham's predicament. Augustus' cautious, ever-present looking over his shoulder recalls Graham's persistent fear of police harming her son—a fear shared by many Black parents in the 21st century. White supremacist violence monopolizes Black parents' time and health, and mental labors for imagining "something different" are limited. Consider, for instance, the day of the Freddie Gray protests. Graham, at the urging of her daughter who suspected Michael may have joined the protests, left her doctor's appointment. Her abruptly canceled appointment emphasizes the energy, time, and labor Black parents spend on steering our children away from death and misfortune at the whims of the state. Parenting in this "constant state of sorrow" inhibits us from imagining radical, life-affirming futures for our children. As with the state's constant surveilling and killing of Black men and women in Baltimore, slaveholding codes in antebellum Virginia limit and severely curtail Augustus' time with his son as Robbins uses his status as a wealthy slaveholder to maintain God-like overseer power. Though absent, Robbins' omniscient presence prevents Augustus from constructing life-affirming modes of parenting. Violence, deployed by Augustus in a moment of misplaced frustration, is the byproduct of Robbins' relentless interference in Mildred's and Augustus' attempts to parent Henry.[27]

An otherwise exemplary figure of heroic Black masculinity and morality, Augustus anchors the novel. His turn toward violence is a stunning deviation. In fact, he likely never would have physically touched Henry if permitted the time, space, and freedom. But Robbins, by moving Augustus and Mildred around his plantation like chess pieces, corrupts Augustus' love into the type reminiscent of the parasitical dynamics between enslaved and slaveholder. By succumbing to the patriarchal pull of power, Augustus is implicated as a chief participant in Henry's trauma. And his actions will have disastrous effects on Henry and generations to come. But his violence must be analyzed as an act made under extreme coercion. This is the brilliance of *The Known World*—the text exposes the psychological torture slaveholders inflicted on Black men and women without even laying a finger on them.

In a scene registering white supremacists' appetite for Black suffering, Robbins punishes Augustus and Mildred for daring to believe that they could parent Henry without his permission:

The next Sunday Robbins was waiting. "I heard you did something to my boy, my property," he said before Augustus and Mildred were down from the wagon. "No, Mr. Robbins. I did nothin," Augustus said, having forgotten the push.

"We wouldn't," Mildred said. "We wouldn't hurt him for the world. He our son."[28]

Robbins looked at her as if she had told him the day was Wednesday. "I won't have you touching my boy, my property." His horse, Sir Guilderham, was idling two or so paces behind his master. And just as the horse began to wander away, Robbins turned and picked up the reins, mounted. "No more visits for a month," he said, picking one piece of lint from the horse's ear.[29]

In a bitter twist of irony, Robbins assumes the moral high ground on behalf of "his boy, his property." He becomes, essentially, a quasi-father to Henry. Perched atop his horse, he chides Augustus: "It'll take a month for him to heal from what you did, Augustus."[30] The absurdity of a slaveholding, physically abusive, rapist of a man condemning a man he once owned makes visible white American capitalism's demented outcomes. Robbins' condemnation is not moral; he is not angered by Augustus for hurting Henry. Rather, Robbins denounces Augustus' use of violence because it neither enriches his property nor expands it. Thus, Robbins lashes out at Augustus for threatening the order of slaveholding capitalism.

Remnants of this perverse racial calculus surfaced in the years following Graham's viral beating of her son. Politicians and business officials who promised housing, scholarships, and mentoring programs for Michael disappeared. When none of these opportunities materialized, Michael fell into a deep depression. A dejected Graham told a local news reporter, "I'm tired of struggle, I feel broken. You try to hold on, you try to do everything, you try to be strong for your children. But this is a lot."[31] The speed with which the mainstream divested from Michael and Graham underscores the role of the deathscape in demoralizing children and parents when they do not conform to scripts reinforcing Black pathological family dynamics as championed in early novels like *Uncle Tom's Cabin*. Put another way, when violence against Black children cannot be reimbursed for capitalistic gain, then the parents are punished and the children are subsequently discarded by larger white mainstream society.

In the antebellum deathscape that Augustus navigates, Robbins positions himself as a wedge between Augustus and Henry by repurposing Henry's labors for his direct gain. In the years that it takes for Augustus to buy Henry's freedom, Robbins primes the intelligent 9-year-old to become his groom, shoemaker, and future slaveholder. Whereas he restricts Mildred and Augustus' time with their child, Robbins keeps Henry in close proximity to him. So determined is he to keep Henry as his groom, Robbins demands that Augustus pay a higher price for Henry than originally agreed upon. Thus, while Augustus eventually frees Henry, Robbins' targeted interference corrupts the love between Augustus and his son indefinitely. Perhaps even more devastating, Henry becomes a slaveholder. As *The Known World* revolves around a Black slaveholder and his ownership of 33 enslaved Black people, early critics of the historical novel accused Jones of absolving slaveholding whites of their predominant role in slavery.[32] However, Robbins' early grooming of Henry renders his decision a warped one, a consequence of surviving the brutalizing Virginia deathscape turning father against son. As Black parents' ability to raise their children is neutralized by the state's ceaseless intrusions upon Black families, Henry cannot inherit his father's legacy but rather that of Robbins' slaveholding power. Predictably, when Henry becomes a slaveholder, he "wanted to be a better master than any white man he had ever known."[33] Yet when Henry dies, none of the enslaved Black people shed a tear. Indeed, Henry's first purchase of an enslaved Black person devastates Augustus so deeply that he brutally attacks his son with one of his wooden carved sticks, landing blows so hard that they break Henry's shoulder. As the novel's moral center, Augustus' brutal condemnation registers the totality of Henry's betrayal of both his parents and Black people. Calculated, deliberate, and purposeful, Augustus' violence strikes out at Robbins' structuring of the early visits as constant checks and reassertions of his white slaveholding power.

Forever impacted by Robbins' powerful reach, Henry and Augustus regard each other as enemies. In *The Known World*, freedom comes with a heavy price. That is, Henry and Augustus will never love each other as father and son. When he does occasionally visit Henry on the Virginia plantation, Augustus refuses to sleep in his son's home, choosing instead to sleep in the slave cabins although he is a free Black man. Their fractured relationship serves as a cautionary tale for Black parents attempting to love their children today. Imagining better futures for our children will require dreaming of better ways to bestow mercy, even if we are not yet living in the freedom necessary to grant it.

Deathscapes: Futuristic Dystopias

The world that science fiction writer N.K. Jemisin imagines in *The Broken Earth* trilogy is one that, despite its setting in the far future, addresses issues of reproductive violence, environmental racism, and discrimination. In this futuristic deathscape, modern-day Earth is replaced by the Stillness, a continent plagued by powerful tectonic plate shifts strong enough to destroy entire cities. Locals refer to these disasters as Seasons. They are massive upheavals striking with such force that "the people of the Stillness live in a perpetual state of disaster preparedness."[34] To survive, people in the Stillness build walls, dig wells, "and put away food, and they can easily last five, 10, even 25 years in a world without sun."[35] The environmental crises facing the people in the Stillness parallel the apocalyptic nightmare shortening the lives of oppressed Black people today.

In America, Black people are 75 percent more likely to live near oil and gas refineries. The Louisiana Saint James parish is an indication of the ways Black communities are targeted by chemical plants. The small parish community of 19,000 residents is nearly 50 percent Black, and the high rates of cancer among residents due to the influx of industrial petrochemical plants have transformed resident Sharon Lavigne into an environmental activist. Her fight against companies building dangerous plants near her neighborhood highlights the racialized effects of environmental aggression. "So many people are dying of cancer, upper respiratory diseases, asthmatic conditions," Lavigne explains, "We have huge medical bills. We have to plan our final resting place. They have plans for us to die. Some call where we live 'Cancer Alley.' It's more appropriate to call it 'death row.'"[36] Lavigne's battles against the petrochemical plants crystallize the far reaches of reproductive injustice. The intersection between human rights and environmental injustice emphasizes the slow deaths we face under these oppressive forces. These dystopic anti-Black conditions persist in *The Broken Earth* trilogy. Surviving these anti-Black conditions healthy and whole is virtually impossible. But for Jemisin, this seems to be precisely the point. Of *The Broken Earth* series, Jemisin says,

> This has been a hard year, hasn't it? A hard few years. A hard century. For some of us, things have always been hard. I wrote *The Broken Earth* trilogy to speak to that struggle, and what it takes to just live, let alone thrive in a world that seems determined to break you.[37]

We may think about *The Broken Earth* as Jemisin's rumination on the many ways Black people are broken down daily. While the characters in *The Broken Earth* trilogy are never defined as Black or white, nor do they exhibit a set of consistent racial signifiers, their unique experiences maneuvering through a world designed to exploit their magical abilities or kill them off connect their plight to that of oppressed Black people around the world. More specifically, Jemisin examines the costs of raising children in a broken world. Therefore, *The Broken Earth* may be categorized as an extended meditation on the negotiations, calculations, and miscalculations Black parents make under an exploitative system rivaling that of an American slaveholding society. Here, in the Stillness, parents cannot love their children. They can only offer something akin to mercy.

In *The Fifth Season*, the first book of *The Broken Earth* series, the story begins with a woman named Essun returning home to a devastating scene.

Her husband, Jija, has beaten their 2-year-old son to death. Stunned, Essun sits with "Uche's broken little body" for days.[38] However, it is her resignation to suffering that positions reproductive violence as a continuous, relentless force in her life: "She will pay no attention to the world that is ending outside. The world has already ended within her, and neither is ending for the first time. She's old hat at this by now."[39] In the world Essun inhabits, to be an orogene is to be at the mercy of a stranger's fear. Neighbors kill them in a brutal fashion. Parents fear giving birth to them. Orogenes, though best suited for surviving harsh seasons, are a small class of magically gifted people capable of drawing power from deep within the earth. Their magic is capable of quelling dangerous shakes rippling through cities. Yet, despite their abilities to save entire cities, society regards them as cursed individuals, and their powerful magic casts them as outsiders. Ordinary people, known as non-magical stills, hold such distaste for orogenes that they refer to them using a derogatory slur, "rogga." Clearly an allusion to the hard double g sound found in the slur "nigger," roggas are disenfranchised by the state as they "have no right to get angry, to want justice, to protect what they love."[40] Because Essun is an orogene herself, she lives a severely constricted life. For years, she has hidden out in the "little nothing town of Tirimo" to escape discrimination and possible murder at the hands of stills for being an orogene.[41] She blends in as a non-remarkable teacher. Essun even gets married to Jija, a local still. Only three people in the town know her secret—two of them are her daughter, Nassun, and her son, Uche. A fact they only know because they are orogenes too.

Sitting on the floor, gazing at her dead son's lifeless body, Essun begins putting the pieces of the puzzle together as she covers "Uche's broken little body with a blanket—except his face, because he is afraid of the dark."[42] Jija, her husband, killed his own son after discovering his orogenic status. But the anti-orogene sentiment engulfing the community complicates Jija's brutal beating of Uche. When Essun, in a fit of mourning and rage, mobilizes her fury to split open the town's valley floor, she indicts the community for producing "the kind of hate that can make a man hate his own son."[43] As everyone screams and takes cover, Essun rebukes the tiny city of Tirimo, saying, "These people killed Uche. Their hate, their fear, their unprovoked violence."[44] But if Jija's murder of Uche is tethered to the wave of anti-orogene sentiment, then it must be analyzed as an act borne from mercy. In some ways, Jija takes a path similar to Margaret Garner, the enslaved Black woman whose decision to kill her infant daughter rather than let her suffer in slavery sparked nationwide interest. In refusing to prosecute Garner for murder and destruction of property, Ohio state officials avoided the larger question of enslaved Black people's humanity and being deserving of legal protection, rights, and responsibilities for their children. Defining 2-year-old Mary as property before the law tacitly confirms Garner's choice, though horrific, as justifiable. Though there is no slaveholding nation in Tirimo, Jija's choice is inflected by the state's rendering of children as non-citizens undeserving of equal protections before the law. Of murdering Uche, Jija thinks: "He loved his family, after all, and the truth was simply ... unthinkable."[45] The impossible bind Jija finds himself in mirrors the realities Black parents navigate in an anti-Black America. Jija's ability to love his children is severely restricted by the limited options available to orogenic children. Although he murders 2-year-old Uche, he cannot bring himself to murder his daughter. When Nassun tells him that she is an orogene and starts crying, Jija cannot comfort her. He can only stare at her "as if he has never seen her before." Then he realizes: "He cannot kill her. Not even if she is ... no. She is his little girl."[46] Placed in such an impossible dilemma, Jija seizes another option. He takes Nassun on a journey to find the Fulcrum, a forced labor camp masquerading as a training school for orogenes.

In the Stillness, all citizens are duty-bound by law to deliver orogenic children to guardians, the leaders of the Fulcrum. In no way a safe haven, the Fulcrum exists as a site of terror. Guardians abuse, murder, and coerce orogenes into using their magic for the benefit of the Fulcrum and the rest of the surrounding communities. It is impossible to ignore how closely the terroristic regimes of the Stillness parallel the pro-slavery conditions fostering the passage of the Fugitive Slave Act of 1850. The law deputized citizens, investing them with the legal force of the law to hunt down and return Black people fleeing slavery. Similarly, guardians fulfill the role of enforcer, appearing whenever parents, neighbors, or citizens suspect a child of practicing orogeny. Essun learns this lesson early. As a little girl, she lives as Damaya in a town with her mother, father, and brother. But after flashing her orogeny at school in response to a boy bullying her, her mother forbids her from entering the family home. Instead, Damaya must sleep outside in the barn on a pile of straw, even during the winter. Through these dysfunctional familial dynamics, the costs of raising children in a world designed to brutalize the most helpless among us are made visible. In the tangled pathology that this futuristic deathscape weaves, parents turn against children. But it is precisely because Damaya's parents cannot compassionately raise her that they call on the guardian to take her away, thereby protecting them from enduring the murderous wrath of their neighbors. Damaya does not realize this fact until her guardian Schaffa, though she refers to him as a "child-buyer," comes to take her to the Fulcrum.

> It takes a moment for Damaya to understand, and then she realizes: People from Palela want to kill Damaya. But that's wrong, isn't it? They can't really, can they?[47]

Damaya's childlike innocence prevents her from realizing the full extent of her own danger. That is, Schaffa takes the longer, more difficult road to dodge the townspeople harboring "the fine idea to come seek us out along the road, and make their farewells to Damaya in a ruder fashion."[48] That the local townspeople will kill her is not the only fact motivating her parents to give her away. Her brother is a non-orogene, and so they sacrifice Damaya to ensure that he may live. This is a realization that comes to Damaya only in the last moments before seeing her family for the final time:

> Mother has not sold Damaya. She and Father have given Damaya away. And Mother does not hate her; actually, she fears Damaya. Is there a difference?[49]

The question nipping at young Damaya's consciousness expands our conception of mercy. What Damaya struggles to articulate here is the extent to which her mother's decision to give her away goes beyond an act of cruelty and toward something far more tender. Damaya's predicament situates *The Broken Earth* trilogy as a text primarily concerned with how oppressive forces pervert the parent–child dynamic. It is a question Toni Morrison contemplates more fully in her 2008 novel, *A Mercy*. Set in 17th-century colonial America, *A Mercy* opens with a young woman named Florens recounting her early childhood memories of her mother. In this capitalist slave regime, "the beginning begins with shoes."[50] Demarcating the lines between free, enslaved, and runaway, shoes were distributed by slaveholders in yearly allotments or not at all. An indication of how cost-effective these practices are is the fact that Thomas Jefferson, a wealthy enslaver of over 600 people on his sprawling Monticello estate, did not issue shoes to any children he owned until they were 10 years old.[51] Scarcely dressed enslaved Black children appearing in *Narrative of the Life of Frederick Douglass* confirm this system as "the children unable to work in the field had neither shoes, stockings, jackets, nor trousers, given to them; their clothing consisted of two coarse linen shirts per year."[52] On some plantations, Douglass recalls, yearly allotments were so meager that it was not uncommon to see naked barefoot children until "the next allowance day."[53] Even when enslaved children were given shoes, they were often wooden-soled so uncomfortable that they were cast off.

Curiously, Florens prefers wearing shoes. "When a child I am never able to abide being barefoot and always beg for shoes, anybody's shoes, even on the hottest days."[54] However, she disdains the hard wooden shoes typically worn by enslaved children, desiring instead the fancy, high-heeled shoes commonly worn by free white Portuguese women. At her daughter's preference, minha mae frowns and discourages Florens from wearing the shoes, insisting, "Only bad women wear high heels." Florens' desire for fancy shoes is more than a bad omen. It is a frightening indication that she is daring to imagine herself as free; in the eyes of minha mae, this risky endeavor immediately makes her "dangerous" and "wild."[55] In slaveholding colonies, enslaved Black women and men stole clothing and shoes to assist them with blending into the free population. In the *Virginia Gazette*, published between 1736 and 1780, slaveholders placed ads describing fugitive clothing in great detail. When a young man named Tom ran away, his slaveholder emphasized the elaborate "white Virginia cloth jeans coat" and "good shoes" he wore precisely because he appeared free.[56] Florens' desire for fancy shoes also reflects a childlike naivete—she does not yet comprehend her enslaved status and the restrictive expectations that come with it. Thus, minha mae's rebuke embeds the same kind of anticipatory grief spurring Augustus towards physically hitting Henry. That is, Black parents' sorrow often manifests as a fierce defensive posturing, threatening and severely rupturing any chance of parent–child bonding.

In *The Broken Earth* deathscape, Essun cannot offer love to her daughter. She can only engage with Nassun through a series of forced negotiations. A significant portion of her maternal labor is directed toward teaching Nassun to constrain her orogenic power. Twelve-year-old Nassun recalls these trainings bitterly. First, Essun lies to Jija and tells him that they are having "girl talk."[57] In reality, Essun takes Nassun out into the valley and peppers her with "endless quizzes" and "discussions of wave mechanics and math."[58] If Nassun does not answer properly or quickly enough, her mother's anger rises. One memory in particular stands out as Nassun recalls that her mother threw a "boulder" at her. The young Nassun recalls her fear not only of the boulder hurtling toward her, but also the fear of her mother's unrelenting "lessons": "Terrifying to have three tons of stone rumbling along the ground towards me, and to wonder, If I can't do it, will Mama stop?"[59] The disheartening scene—a mother throwing a boulder at her child as a means of teaching her to restrain her powers in the face of her own abuse—compels a consideration of Black parents' sustained exposure to reproductive injustice and its bearing on the next generation.

In 21st century America, one of the most visible scenes of Black parenting under threat of reproductive violence was captured by Diamond Reynolds. She began livestreaming Officer Jeronimo Yanez after he fired and killed Philando Castile following a routine traffic stop. Speaking both calmly and clearly, she asserted Castile's innocence while narrating the moments transpiring before she began filming with her phone, "You shot four bullets into him, sir. He was just getting his license and registration, sir."[60] Reynolds' decision to record the brutal scene unfolding before her represents a kind of "Black witnessing, or the use of counter-surveillance measures to resist state violence."[61] This strategic witnessing, as the research of Shannon Malone Gonzalez and Faith M. Deckard demonstrates, dates back to Ida B. Wells-Barnett, who, spurred by her friend's lynching at the hands of an angry white mob, meticulously documented the lynchings of men, women, and children. Her 1895 *The Red Record* survives as the first example of "Black witnessing," or the tactic by which we advocate for the dead, the dying, and the persecuted among us. Indeed, Reynolds' stoic demeanor registers her terror for not only her own safety but also that of her 4-year-old daughter Dae'Anna in the back seat. Curiously, in the days following the shooting, national and international headlines praising Reynolds' "incredible calm" virtually invisibilized Dae'Anna. *The Washington Post* made no mention of Dae'Anna, "Whether it was instinct or shock that had taken over inside the car, she was the one whom millions of viewers remembered as dignified, as unafraid, as somehow calm at the center of an American crisis."[62] Although television host George Stephanopoulos praised her for being strong and having the foresight to remain calm, saying, "You and your daughter have been so strong," he does not yet again mention her daughter or the officer training a gun on her and 4-year-old daughter.[63] In the days after, Reynolds forced audiences to see her not as a strong Black woman unfazed by the barrel of a gun but as a mother negotiating her child's safety under the threat of sustained reproductive terror. Reynolds insisted that her attempts to mollify the officer grew from a hyper-awareness of her daughter's presence in the backseat: "I knew that if anything were to alarm that officer, he could have taken me and maybe my daughter."[64] In effusively praising Reynolds, interviewers missed an opportunity to address her polite exchanges with the officer as a familiar strategy for Black people navigating hostile anti-Black state apparatuses.

In fact, her decision to punctuate each sentence with "sir" mirrors a key scene in Toni Morrison's *Sula*. Helene, Nel's mother, finds herself in a difficult position while attempting to make her way through a segregated train car with her young daughter in tow. When the conductor accosts her for traveling through the white section of the car, Helene immediately slips into calling him "sir" despite the fact that he rudely dismisses her as "gal."[65]

"What you think you doin, gal?"
"We made a mistake, sir. You see, there wasn't no sign. We just got in the wrong car, that's all. Sir."
"We don't 'low no mistakes on this train. Now git your butt on in there."[66]

Helene's obsequious tone with the emphatic "Sir" recalls Reynolds' forced tone of politeness she adopts when talking to Yanez. But it is the fact that this scene occurs in front of Nel, Helene's daughter, that highlights the conundrum Black mothers find themselves in when attempting to extricate their children from the "mouth of the suicidal dragon."[67] Nel witnesses her mother ingratiate herself before a white man, and it sickens her.

> He stood there staring at her until she realized he wanted her to move aside. Pulling Nel by the arm, she pressed herself and her daughter into the foot space in front of a wooden seat. Then, for no earthly reason, at least no reason that anybody could understand, certainly no reason that Nel understood then or later, she smiled. Like a street pup that wags its tail at the very doorjamb of the butcher shop he has been kicked away from only moments before, Helene smiled. Smiled dazzlingly and coquettishly at the salmon-colored face of the conductor.[68]

Her mother's smile horrifies Nel precisely because it seems to thank the man for his dastardly behavior. Told through Nel's eyes, her mother's reaction underscores the less visible trauma inscribed on our children when they are conditioned to smile and maintain composure in the face of their own brutalization. We may understand Nel's witnessing of her mother's obsequious nature to the train conductor as evidence of the state's corruptive power in forever altering parent–child relationships. Returning to the modern-day deathscape of Dae'Anna, witnessing her mother's stoicism in the face of unspeakable violence affords us an opportunity to register reproductive violence's toll on Black children even when they survive in the mouth of the dragon. As Reynolds began attempting to piece her life back together after Castile's murder, she began worrying about her daughter's silence:

> Dae'Anna had said nothing, and so Diamond began to wonder: How was that possible? How could anyone, much less a 4-year-old, keep quiet during those four minutes? The force of four bullets fired from point-blank range shook the car, and Dae'Anna was quiet. Castile rolled his head back between the seats and gasped, "I can't breathe," and Dae'Anna was quiet. The officer screamed, "Keep your hands where they are!" and she was quiet. The gun, still aimed inside the car, began to shake in the officer's hand, and she was quiet. Diamond said, "Please don't tell me he's dead," and she was quiet. Castile gripped his bleeding stomach, moaned, slid back between the seats and dropped his head right toward Dae'Anna's lap, and she was quiet.[69]

Dae'Anna's silence, no doubt rooted in fear, may be understood as a byproduct of the conditioning Reynolds drilled into her head since the age of 2. In what Reynolds called "survival skills," she taught Dae'Anna to "duck at the sound of gunfire. Make yourself small whenever you feel threatened. Never touch guns or needles. The more scared you are, the less noise you should make."[70] Although perhaps some of these directives may be told to other children, it is impossible to ignore their specific import to Black children. Therefore, these directives surface as defensive maternal strategies employed as a means of keeping our children safe.

In the Stillness, the futuristic deathscape as imagined by Jemisin, caregiving emerges along a similar trajectory. Although Damaya's parents give her away in the hopes of sparing her life, she experiences a level of cruelty at the hands of her guardian, Schaffa, that inevitably corrupts her relationship with her future daughter, Nassun. As she rides next to Schaffa on the horse, he suddenly takes her hand and bears down on it so hard that she feels her bones breaking. To which he calmly replies, "Be still, and be brave. I'm going to break your hand now."[71] Though she screams, Schaffa does not stop until he "lifts her broken hand, adjusting his grip so that she can see the damage." Sickened by "seeing her hand bent in a way it should not be, the skin tinting and purpled in three places like another set of knuckles the fingers already stiffening and spasm," Damaya screams out no.[72] Perhaps more horrific than Schaffa's breaking of her hand is the threat accompanying this violence,

> Never say no to me ... Orogenes have no right to say no. I am your Guardian. I will break every bone in your hand, every bone in your body, if I deem it necessary to make the world safe from you.[73]

In *The Broken Earth* trilogy, the dual meaning of the term guardian underscores its connections to twisted paternalistic pro-slavery rhetoric justifying Black people's enslavement. If Black people could be reduced to "child-like" inferior subjects, then "masters" and "mistresses" were not slaveholders but guardians ensuring enslaved men and women were taken care of in colonial America. In flipping the image of a guardian into a frighteningly abusive figure, Jemisin seems to take a page out of the narratives written by formerly enslaved Black people. Exposing the perverse hypocrisy at play, the guardians of the Stillness function exactly as slaveholders did during the antebellum period. The Fulcrum, largely a forced labor camp where guardians harness orogenic power and kill all orogenes who fail this test, exists as a literal breeding ground where female orogenes are forced to breed with male orogenes. In fact, Damaya's training at the Fulcrum consists of screening her skills to prepare her for breeding with the most successful male orogene. While at the Fulcrum, Damaya must forgo her past identity. The guardians rename her Syenite. This forced identity—evident in the naming of her as an igneous rock—symbolizes her newly oppressed status as property of the Fulcrum.

Most interestingly, this renaming process mirrors the treacherous journey enslaved Africans undertook to secure their freedom in colonial slaveholding America. It is only when she finally flees the Fulcrum and settles in Tirimo with Jija that she freely selects her own name: Essun. Damaya's journey from her small town as an innocent but oppressed child, to a conscript within the Fulcrum as Syenite, and her flight to Tirimo as Essun situates her oppression as one consistent with enslaved Black people's ascent from enslaved to free. Formerly enslaved Black people could never be certain of their freedom. Slavecatchers, operating under The Fugitive Slave Act, traveled great distances to find people living freely in the North and Canada to bring them back. Like these formerly enslaved Black people, Essun, even when settling down in Tirimo with Jija, must constantly fear being outed as an orogene. For Essun and all Black people living under oppressive regimes, freedom comes with a price. That is, Essun's freedom is marred by her inability to parent her children without adopting the cruel lessons she learned at the Fulcrum.

As Nassun shares memories of her mother, Schaffa, who has now, in a perverted twist of irony, become her guardian, she remembers that "there wasn't time to teach me the gentle way, and anyway I was too strong. She had to do what would work."[74] What works is her mother crushing Nassun's hand with a large rock, effectively breaking and shattering bone. In Nassun's heartbreaking retelling of the moment, she notes that despite her screams, her mother does not comfort her. Instead, her mother's steady voice cuts "through the pounding blood in her ears" as she says, "You're fire, Nassun. You're lightning, dangerous unless captured in wires. But if you can control yourself through pain, I'll know your'e safe."[75] Complicating Essun's actions are the circumstances in which orogenic children are rendered dangerous and therefore disposable. Like Reynolds, Graham, and Augustus from *The Known World*, Essun feels compelled to teach Nassun that her subordinate status in the world makes her vulnerable to the murderous whims of others. Nassun, in processing the trauma Essun inflicts on her, is unaware of how large a role the guardians have played in whittling her mother's love down to a set of survival skills. Indeed, she is also unaware of the fact that Schaffa, the guardian she has grown to love, is the one who first broke her mother's hand. Therefore, classifying Essun's actions as abuse is difficult as she breaks her daughter's hand as a means of teaching Nassun the necessary self-control for surviving an anti-orogene world. Paradoxically, Nassun's ability to control her orogeny saves her life when she travels with her father on their journey to the Fulcrum. Yet, Essun's violent lessons transform Nassun into a sullen, quiet child nursing a growing and unyielding hatred for her mother.

Therefore, we may consider how these deathscapes pervert the ethics of care between child and parent. In the final pages of *The Stone Sky*, the last book in *The Broken Earth* trilogy, Essun and her daughter reunite for the first time. It has taken Essun three books to finally locate her daughter, but their meeting is less of a reunion. Although Nassun greets her mother with a "Hi Mama," it is with the coldness of a stranger. Essun finally realizes "that it is hopeless. That there can be no relationship, no trust, between you and her, because the two of you are what the Stillness and the Season have made you."[76] An explicit address to the oppressive conditions of the Stillness, Essun's shift from mother to that of enforcer speaks to the complicated position Black parents find themselves in. As if to render more clearly the hopeless realities of caregiving in this deathscape, Jemisin depicts Essun as lying on the ground where she has begun gradually fading into "brown sandstone."[77] On the bottom steps of the pylon, Essun whispers faintly and tries to reach her daughter, but her arm has "completely solidified" and her "torso is going."[78] Amid this transformation into stone, Essun manages to smile at her Nassun's growth, her beauty. So overwhelmed by her daughter's power and beauty, Essun bursts "into tears at the sight of her." Her smiling laughter momentarily stuns Nassun, who cannot "believe what she is seeing: her mother, so fearsome, on the ground. Trying to crawl on stone limbs. Face wet with tears. *Smiling*. You have never, ever smiled at her before." But just as the moment opens up a possible reconciliation between the two, Essun is gone, disappearing into a brown lump of sandstone. The implications of a mother turning into cold, hard stone and struggling mightily to embrace her only living child, ultimately failing in the end, offer a profound, yet perverse, tableau of merciful mothering.

That is, even small acts of mercy come with devastating costs. In *A Mercy*, minha mae, like Essun, envisions for her daughter a different future and thus permits Florens to "wear the throwaway shoes from Senhora's house, pointy-toe, one raised heel broke, the other worn and a buckle on top."[79] More than a small act of tenderness, this love offering is made poignant by minha mae's refusal to harden her daughter for all the brutalities facing an enslaved Black girl in 17th-century America.

But when the man comes into town looking to purchase an enslaved Black person, minha mae is terrified that the slaveholder will be drawn to her daughter standing "there in those shoes."[80] Here, minha mae comes face-to-face with the potential dangers involved in attempting to parent a child free from the strictures of slavery. Trapped within a devastating prism of sexual abuse, racism, and violence, Florens is easy prey. Her budding girlhood threatens her safety; minha mae reasons that she will suffer violations in a way that her son will likely never know: "To be female in this place is to be an open wound that cannot heal." Her gendered analysis of oppression situates Black female identities along a precarious spectrum of violation. And echoes of minha mae's plight appear in *The Fifth Season* when Essun, before destroying the town with her orogeny, rebukes the townspeople for dehumanizing children: "*You cowards. You animals, who look at a child and see prey.*"[81] Both women share the same plight as marginalized parents struggling to raise children in brutalizing deathscapes across time and space. Having few tools at her disposal to protect her daughter, minha mae, holding her infant son in her arms, uses her own horrors of sexual abuse at the hands of Senhor as knowledge to prevent Florens' sexual abuse. The choice is both desperate and calculating: "One chance, I thought."[82] Quickly, minha mae measures her daughter's worth by adopting a slaveholder's cold, objectifying gaze. Like Essun of *The Broken Earth* trilogy, she becomes cold and hard-hearted as she focuses solely on her daughter's survival. First, assessing her son as insignificant to the slaveholder's sexual desires, minha mae notes her daughter's growing physical body:

> Neither one will want your brother. I know their tastes. Breasts provide the pleasure more than simpler things. Yours are rising too soon and are becoming irritated by the cloth covering your little girl chest. And they see and I see them.[83]

Because minha mae gifts her daughter a mercy, Florens escapes the sexual assault her mother could not. Kneeling, minha mae forces herself to submit her daughter to the will of a man: "I said you. Take you, my daughter. Because I saw the tall man see you as a human child, not pieces of eight. I knelt before him. Hoping for a miracle. He said yes."[84] The violence of the scene—a Black mother kneeling before a white slaveholder as her young daughter watches, her tightly cradling her brother—lies not only in the white men consulting about buying enslaved people, but in minha mae's proffering her daughter up for sale. Confoundingly, this act is the closest thing to freedom that minha mae can offer her daughter.

But her actions, a recreation of the routine familial separations enforced by slaveholders, effectively rupture Florens' love for minha mae. A young girl, Florens cannot understand the gendered dimensions of minha mae's decision and misinterprets the act as her mother casting her off in favor of her brother. For Florens, it is a profound betrayal from which she cannot recover. The fateful moment is the origin of her anxiety:

> But I have a worry. Not because our work is more, but because mothers nursing greedy babies scare me. I know how their eyes go when they choose. How they raise them to look at me hard, saying something I cannot hear. Saying something important to me, but holding the little boy's hand.[85]

Because Florens never learns of the complexities informing minha mae's decisions, the physical gulf between mother and daughter widens to an impossible gulf. Unlike Essun and Nassun, the two never even see each other again.

In this new millennium, we are still plagued by antebellum deathscapes of the past. The difficult challenge of learning how to love our children without fear sometimes occurs in the most mundane moments. Over the summer, when I swim alongside my daughter in the pool, she spots a dark round object at the bottom of the pool and begins swimming to pick it up. But I stop her, grabbing her arm without thinking. I am only remembering the time my father beat my brother and me for touching a needle on the way home from school. I tell her, when she looks at me in confusion, how my father beat me to understand.

"I know," she says, bored from hearing a story that I have told her many times. She is already moving to another part of the pool, away from the object, away from my memories. Her "I know" asserts her right to be loved without lashes. Her knowing declares her right to be loved by a mother who will not allow fear to corrupt our bond. A mercy forged from caregivers tending to children in such dim futures that they could not even claim their children as their own.

Notes

1 Patton, 13.
2 Paddison, Routledge, Sharp, and Philo, 1.
3 Lorde, 33.
4 Collins, 9.
5 hooks, 383.
6 Benjamin, 38.
7 Griffin, 29.
8 Stowe Beecher, 33.
9 "Baltimore's 'mom of the year' on why she smacked rioting son."
10 "Baltimore Mom Toya Graham's Son-Smacking During Riot a 'Teachable Moment.'"
11 Engel.
12 Caviness.
13 Davis, 8.
14 Sharpe, 2.
15 Anderson, 475.
16 Jones, 18.
17 Jones, 18.
18 Douglass, 2.
19 Douglass, 2.
20 Douglass, 2.
21 Douglass, 3.
22 Jones, 18.
23 Jones, 18.
24 Jones, 18.
25 Jones, 18.
26 Jones, 19.

27 Jones, 19.
28 Jones, 19.
29 Jones, 19.
30 Jones, 19.
31 "Mom Seen Disciplining Son During Freddie Gray Riots Gives 5-Year Update."
32 Graham, 1089.
33 Jones, 40.
34 Jemisin, 8.
35 Jemisin, 8.
36 Surrusco.
37 Romano.
38 Jemisin, 1.
39 Jemisin, 1.
40 Jemisin, 418.
41 Jemisin, 4.
42 Jemisin, 1.
43 Jemisin, 58.
44 Jemisin, 58.
45 Jemisin, 58.
46 Jemisin, 10.
47 Jemisin, 40.
48 Jemisin, 38.
49 Jemisin, 33.
50 Morrison, 1.
51 Gruber.
52 Douglass, 10.
53 Douglass, 10.
54 Morrison, 2.
55 Morrison, 2.
56 Gruber.
57 Jemisin, 98.
58 Jemisin, 152.
59 Jemisin, 153.
60 Saslow.
61 Gonzalez and Deckard, 1.
62 Saslow.
63 Philando Castile | Diamond Reynolds on Livestreaming Police Shooting.
64 Philando Castile | Diamond Reynolds on Livestreaming Police Shooting.
65 Morrison, *Sula*, 21.
66 Morrison, *Sula*, 21.
67 Lorde, 33.
68 Lorde, 68.
69 Saslow.
70 Saslow.
71 Jemisin, 98.
72 Jemisin, 98.
73 Jemisin, 99.
74 Jemisin, 152.
75 Jemisin, 154.
76 Jemisin, *The Stone Sky*, 373.
77 Jemisin, *The Stone Sky*, 386.
78 Jemisin, *The Stone Sky*, 386.

79 Morrison, *A Mercy*, 2.
80 Morrison, *A Mercy*, 3.
81 Jemisin, 57.
82 Morrison, *A Mercy*, 190.
83 Morrison, *A Mercy*, 191.
84 Morrison, *A Mercy*, 191.
85 Morrison, *A Mercy*, 9.

Bibliography

Anderson, L. A., M. O'Brien Caughy, and M. T. Owen. "'The Talk' and Parenting While Black in America: Centering Race, Resistance, and Refuge." *Journal of Black Psychology*, vol. 48, no. 3–4, 2022, pp. 475–506.

Baltimore Mom Toya Graham's Son-Smacking During Riot a "Teachable Moment." 29 April 2015. 9 April 2020. https://abcnews.go.com/Lifestyle/baltimore-mom-toya-grahams-son-smacking-riot-teachable/story?id=30674966.

Baltimore's "Mom of the Year" on Why She Smacked Rioting Son. 2015. https://www.youtube.com/watch?v=qBpm-85GI5Y.

Benjamin, Ruha. *Imagination: A Manifesto*. New York: W. W. Norton & Company, 2024.

Caviness, Ylonda Gault. *Why Baltimore Mom Toya Graham Is My Shero—And, No, It's Not the Same Reason the Media is Using*. 27 October 2020. 1 September 2021. https://www.essence.com/news/why-baltimore-mom-toya-graham-my-shero-and-no-its-not-same-reason-media-using/.

Collins, Patricia. "Shifting the Center: Race, Class and Feminist Theorizing about Motherhood." *American Families: A Multicultural Reader*, edited by Stephanie Coontz, Maya Parson, and Gabrielle Raley, New York: Routledge, 1999, p. 9.

Davis, Dana-Ain. "'The Bone Collectors' Comments for Sorrow as Artifact: Black Radical Mothering in Times of Terror." *Transforming Anthropology*, vol. 24, no. 1, 2016, pp. 8–16.

Douglass, Frederick. *Narrative of the Life of Frederick Douglass*. Scotts Valley: CreateSpace Independent Publishing Platform, 2018.

Engel, Pamela. "Forget the National Guard, Send in the Moms." 29 April 2015. 29 March 2020. https://www.businessinsider.com/new-york-post-forget-the-national-guard-send-in-the-moms-2015-4.

Gonzalez, Shannon Malone, and Faith M Deckard. "'We Got Witnesses' Black Women's Counter-Surveillance for Navigating Police Violence and Legal Estrangement." *Social Problems*, vol. 71, no. 3, 2024, pp. 894–911.

Griffin, Farah Jasmine. *Read Until You Understand: The Profound Wisdom of Black Life and Literature*. New York: W. W. Norton & Company, 2021.

Gruber, Katherine. "Clothing and Adornment of Enslaved People in Virginia." July 2020. 1 March 2024. https://encyclopediavirginia.org/entries/slave-clothing-and-adornment-in-virginia/.

hooks, bell. *Yearning: Race, Gender, and Cultural Politics*. Boston: South End P, 1990.

Jemisin, N. K. *The Fifth Season*. London: Orbit, 2014.

Jemisin, N. K. *The Stone Sky*. London: Orbit, 2014.

Jones, Edward P. *The Known World*. New York: Amistad, 2004.

Jones, Edward P., and Maryemma Graham. "An Interview with Edward P. Jones." *African American Review*, vol. 50, no. 4, 2017, 1081–1098

Lorde, Audre. *Sister Outsider: Essays and Speeches*. Ontario: Crossing P, 1984.

Mom Seen Disciplining Son During Freddie Gray Riots Gives 5-Year Update. WBAL-TV 11 Baltimore. April 27 2020.

Morrison, Toni. *A Mercy*. New York: Vintage, 2009.

Morrison, Toni. *Sula*. New York: Vintage, 2004.

Paddison, Ronan, Paul Routledge, Joanne P. Sharp, and Chris Philo. *Entanglements of Power: Geographies of Domination/Resistance* London: Routledge, 2000.

Patton, Stacy. *Spare the Kids: Why Whupping Children Won't Save Black America*. New York: Beacon P, 2017.

Philando Castile | Diamond Reynolds on Livestreaming Police Shooting. 2016. 1 March 2023. https://www.youtube.com/watch?v=8CILL-cDxRU.

Romano, Aja. *The Hugo Awards Just Made History, and Defied Alt-Right Extremists in the Process*. 21 August 2018. 1 February 2020. https://www.vox.com/2018/8/21/17763260/n-k-jemisin-hugo-awards-broken-earth-sad-puppies.

Saslow, Eli. *For Diamond Reynolds, Trying to Move Past 10 Tragic Minutes of Video*. 10 September 2016. 10 September 2020. https://www.washingtonpost.com/national/stay-calm-be-patient/2016/09/10/ec4ec3f2-7452-11e6-8149-b8d05321db62_story.html.

Sharpe, Christina. *In the Wake: On Blackness and Being*. North Carolina: Duke U P, 2016.

Stowe Beecher, Harriet. *Uncle Tom's Cabin*. New York: Open Road Integrated Media, Inc., 2014.

Surrusco, Emilie. *Cancer Alley Rises Up*. 23 January 2024. 8 March 2024. https://earthjustice.org/feature/cancer-alley-rises-up.

3 Sisters in Bloom
Tending to the Garden of Sisterhood

In 1835, a seemingly simple gesture shifted Phillis Wheatley-Peters' historical legacy from that of a mimetic child prodigy to a complicated Black woman poet. That is, Obour Tanner-Collins hand-delivered six of Wheatley-Peters' letters to Katherine Edes Beecher. Yet so few traces of her exist in the archives. What little we do know about Tanner-Collins points toward a devotion to reading and writing. She served as president for the African Female Benevolent Society, a relief program dedicated to promoting literacy education.[1] Her X mark on an 1835 deed of sale transferring property serves as a testament to her long life, as she had grown too feeble to write her name.[2] Her hyphenated name indicates that she too had married and merged her husband's last name with her maiden name, as Wheatley-Peters did upon marriage. That the historical record stops here for the formerly enslaved Black woman and friend to Wheatley-Peters epitomizes the resounding silence of the archives and the truncated legacies that this silence produces for Black women.

Friendship between Tanner-Collins and Wheatley-Peters may well serve as the antidote to the flattened, one-dimensional portrayals of Black women during the colonial era. Sisterwork, what I define as Black women devoting their labors toward each other, is the critical care work necessary for maintaining Black women's creative genius. In some ways, this chapter is a response to the series of questions posed by Alice Walker in her classic text, *In Search of Our Mothers' Gardens*. "Did you," Walker asks, "have a genius of a great-great-great grandmother who died under some ignorant and depraved white overseer's lash?"[3] Casting the kitchen as the site of Black women's oppression, Walker continues, "Or was she required to bake biscuits for a lazy backwater tramp, when she cried out in her soul to paint watercolors of sunsets, or the rain falling on the green and peaceful pasturelands?"[4] These questions, made harrowing by Black women's historical realities, illuminate Black women's creative persistence in the face of targeted oppression, how, Walker ponders,

DOI: 10.4324/9781032719993-4

This chapter has been made available under a CC-BY-NC-ND license.

was the creativity of the Black woman kept alive, year after year and century after century, when for most of the years Black people have been in America, it was a punishable crime for a Black person to read and write?[5]

Her questions provide the critical backdrop for examining sisterwork's role as the maternal labor responsible for nourishing each other's creative possibilities. We may think of sisterwork as the development of an "interstellar mother tongue" cultivated among Black women and for Black women. This mother tongue, unburdened by time and space, surfaces in Black women's collective need to be mothered by other Black women. Echoes of a mother tongue surface again and again in the letters written by Black women. An aspect of this interstellar mother tongue is located in Johnnie M. Stover's definition of "mother tongue" as "a combination of words, rhythms, sounds, and silences that woman has encoded with veiled meaning. And it is more. It is also a look, a set of the lips, a positioning of the hand, hips, head."[6] While Stover situates this "mother tongue" as verbal and physical expressions of resistance, I am more interested in how Black women writers cultivate an alternative, coded language in their letters to each other.

In this chapter, I consider how Wheatley-Peters' letters to her "dear friend" Obour Tanner-Collins evidenced an interstellar mother tongue developed by Black women writers treading difficult paths. In placing Wheatley-Peters' letters alongside the tender exchanges between Pat Parker and Audre Lorde, and Zora Neale Hurston and her dispatches to the writing cousin duo, Dorothy West and Helene Johnson, I position this interstellar mother tongue as an ancestral garden, blooming with our maternal need to claim each other, to nourish each other's creative labors. This Black mother tongue speaks back, calls, and responds to our maternal ancestors. In conceptualizing Tanner-Collins as a Black literary foremother, I situate Black feminist writing as not only the literature we produce but also the circuitous publication pathways Black women construct as a means of preserving Black literature for generations to come.

Erotic Blooms of Sisterwork

Sisterwork's affirmative power surfaces in letters written by Black women. Scholar Desireé R. Melonas offers an overview of the medium as representative of "radical self-care through epistolary work." Letter writing, Melonas argues, opens "up a space of counter-resistance, healing, recognition, care, and creativity."[7] Melonas' viewpoint is helpful when considering Wheatley-Peters and Tanner-Collins creating for themselves an intimate space in 18th-century colonial America. Their letters, written between 1772 and 1779, reflect the carefully mediated society Black women maneuvered through as hyper-visible subjects.[8] As Tara Bynum reminds us, the letters first passed through the hands of white men, one of whom was anti-slavery advocate Reverend Samuel Hopkins and his son, and therefore "participate in a series of hand-to-hand transactions." Although Hopkins officiated Tanner-Collins' wedding and served as an ally to both women, the circuitous route that the letters took renders more clearly the closely surveilled circumstances under which formerly enslaved Black women maintained friendship.

In her letters, Wheatley-Peters repeatedly invoked Christian themes of holiness. Most striking, however, is that the subject of this blessed acknowledgment is none other than Tanner-Collins, a formerly enslaved Black woman. In a letter to Reverend Samuel Hopkins of Newport, Wheatley-Peters praises her friend for being one of the "living witnesses" of Ethiopia's inclination toward God.[9] As M'Baye argues, "Wheatley's description attests to her admiration and love for Obour Tanner's religiosity and humanity."[10] Identifying another Black woman as sacred, Wheatley-Peters challenged prevailing notions of Black women as impure, unworthy of God's grace. This kind of recuperative maternal labor is an element of Black feminist mothering as it presents an avenue for Black women's resistance to dehumanizing narratives. A constant in Black women's fiction, the recuperative maternal labor required for casting off societal markers of inferiority and ugliness is the first step in journeying toward constructing a liberated Black female identity. An example of this plays out in *The Color Purple* through the character of Celie. The novel's chief protagonist and Black teenage girl coming of age in rural Georgia, Celie, writes letters to God as a vehicle not only for documenting her traumas but also for recording her eventual triumphs over them.

Much like Wheatley-Peters addressing Tanner-Collins, 14-year-old Celie develops a spiritual pathway for herself via letter writing. In her first letter to God, she writes:

> Dear God, ~~I am~~ fourteen years old. I have always been a good girl. Maybe you can give me a sign letting me know what is happening to me.[11]

Celie's youthful oblivion registers the nature of her gendered oppression— "Maybe you can give me a sign letting me know what is happening to me." At only 14, she cannot process her now pregnant body and its ensuing changes. Nor can she process her father's rape of her and his taking of her children. Neither does she understand Mister's abuse. Thus, lodged within Celie's crossed-out "~~I am~~" to the more uncertain "I have always been a good girl" is the internalized self-blame of a sexual assault survivor.[12] If we assess Celie's shame through the long lens of history, the strikeout of "~~I am~~" visually negates Celie's victimhood status. Her doubt over whether she can still qualify as a "good girl" recalls pro-slavery scriptings of white men's sexual abuse of enslaved Black women and girls into a "discourse of seduction."[13] In this white supremacist rendering, Black women were cast as sexually immoral in order to conveniently shift blame away from white men. The erasure of Black women's sexual abuse, fueled by legal codes, blocked them from embodying an idealized feminine ideal. When given the chance to strike out against prevailing white supremacist rhetoric, formerly enslaved Black women penned narratives addressing the conundrum of being both sexually and racially oppressed. Indeed, in *Incidents in the Life of a Slave Girl*, Harriet Jacobs internalizes her subjugated status when defending herself against her enslaver, Dr. James Norcom. Jacobs, writing of her decision to initiate a relationship with a white attorney as an attempt to thwart Norcom's sexual abuse, all but pleads for forgiveness from her white female readers, reminding them that chastity is a luxury an enslaved Black girl cannot afford:

> But, O, ye happy women, whose purity has been sheltered from childhood, who have been free to choose the objects of your affection, whose homes are protected by law, do not judge the poor desolate slave girl too severely! If slavery had been abolished, I, also, could have married the man of my choice; I could have had a home shielded by the laws; and I should have been spared the painful task of confessing what I am now about to relate; but all my prospects had been blighted by slavery. I wanted to keep myself pure; and, under the most adverse circumstances, I tried hard to preserve my self-respect; but I was struggling alone in the powerful grasp of the demon Slavery.[14]

The teenaged Jacobs verbalizes the same guilt burdening Celie in her letters to God. Although they occupy vastly different worlds, Jacobs, Celie, and Wheatley-Peters situate Black women's resistance along an erotic continuum. As the bedrock of Black feminist mothering, the erotic serves as a guide for Black women surviving the crippling impact of structural racism, sexism, and poverty. The erotic, within a Black feminist context, encompasses far more than sexual desire. Redefined by Audre Lorde, the erotic is a field of dormant power suppressed by oppressive structures that diminish, overlook, and undervalue feminine energies. During her speech, the mother of two described the erotic as "a resource within each of us that lies in a deeply female and spiritual plane, firmly rooted in the power of our unexpressed and unrecognized feeling."[15] In shifting power away from material accumulations of wealth and property, Lorde encourages us to root power within an internalized feeling occurring along a "deeply female and spiritual plane." Scholar of early African American literature Tara Bynum locates the emancipatory power of the erotic in the correspondence between Wheatley-Peters and Tanner-Collins who "write in a language that not only speaks a spiritual liberation that prepares them for a heavenly afterlife but also a reclamation of the erotic and spiritual agency that encourages a self-realization and affirmation in this World."[16]. In the 1773 letter written by Wheatley-Peters, she activates the erotic rescripting of Black womanhood, beginning first with "My dear friend." Next, Wheatley-Peters praises her "dear friend" for contributing to a spiritual renewal, writing, "Your observations on our dependence on the Deity, & your hopes that my wants will be supply'd from his fulness which is in Christ Jesus, is truely [sp] worthy of your self."[17] The high compliment Wheatley-Peters pays Tanner-Collins counters anti-slavery rhetoric denigrating Black women as dirty, licentious, and unruly. In bestowing another Black woman with the blessed qualities of Jesus Christ, Wheatley-Peters attributes a godliness to Tanner-Collins that "is truly worthy of your self." Holiness, she seems to suggest, resides within Black women. It is an erotic concept, blooming from that "deeply spiritual plane" of knowledge articulated by Lorde.[18] The positive affirmations Wheatley-Peters doles out to her "dear friend" are not simply compliments, but wholesale refusals of societal conventions denigrating Black women. The presence of an interstellar mother tongue situates this exchange as an example of the maternal carework employed by Black women. Walker treads this familiar ground in *The Color Purple* when Celie begins doubting her intrinsic value in the face of unrelenting injustice. Of Celie's circumscribed position, Walker explains that her intentions were to

> explore the difficult path of someone who starts out in life already a spiritual captive, but who, through her own courage and the help of others, breaks free into the realization that she, like Nature itself, is a radiant expression of the heretofore perceived as quite distant divine.[19]

Therefore, because Celie can, as the old folks used to say, call up God on the main line, her letters to God resituate her as a divine being, worthy of God's direct mercy and grace. However, the "distant divine" lives within Celie and the other Black women in *The Color Purple*. This is the deep, abiding spiritual nourishment Celie longs for while isolated in Mister's home. She comes full circle with this "distant divine" when she finally meets Shug. One of the first things Celie notices is that Shug is "so stylish it like the trees all round the house draw themselves up for a better look."[20] From the moment Celie learns of Shug Avery's impending arrival, she awaits her presence as one would anticipate the arrival of a dignitary or goddess: "Lord, I wants to go so bad. Not to dance. Not to drink. Not to play cards. Not even to hear Shug Avery sing. I just be thankful to lay eyes on her."[21] That she understands its transformational power even before laying eyes on Shug speaks to her burgeoning development of an erotic consciousness. One representative of sisterwork's revitalizing capacities even if she does not yet name it as such.

Evidence of sisterwork's erotic power surfaces in the tenderness with which Wheatley-Peters extends to Tanner-Collins. Writing of how their relationship invigorated her, Wheatley-Peters routinely expresses her gratitude for their ability to sustain a friendship, "I rec'd your most kind Epistles of Augt. 27, & Oct. 13th by a young man of your Acquaintance, for which I am obliged to you."[22] In another letter, Wheatley-Peters writes, "I am exceedingly glad to hear from you."[23] Though she is in a rush and can only manage to scratch out a "hasty scrawl," she signs off with, "I am most affectionately, my dear Obour, your sincere friend."[24] Wheatley-Peters' compassionate dispatches to her "dear friend" parallel the high regard Celie extends to Shug as she gives her a bath, thinking, "I wash her body, it feel like I'm praying. My hands tremble and my breath short."[25] Once again, the reverence with which Celie regards Shug confers holiness onto another Black woman. She converts the image of God away from that of a white "patriarchal male supremacist" into a singing blues woman with dark skin. Shug is depicted as such a divine figure that becomes almost a Christ-like figure. As the unnamed woman in the Bible touches the hem of Jesus' garment in an effort to heal the bleeding condition afflicting her for the past 12 years, Celie's healing begins with Shug's arrival. In a particularly poignant scene, Celie combs Shug's hair, which she believes is "the nottiest, shortest, kinkiest hair I ever saw." However, Celie does not debase Shug's Afrocentric features, saying, "I loves every strand of it." So moved by Shug's hair, Celie decides to preserve a few strands, "The hair that come out of my comb I kept."[26] Here, Celie's rewriting of nappy, kinky hair as divine restructures our understanding of sisterwork among Black women as a revitalizing life-force. A bulwark against racist pronouncements deriding Black women as ugly and unrefined.

Sisterwork in Publishing

For Black women writers to thrive, we have had to make a home out of each other. Because Wheatley-Peters created amid persistent racist and sexist discrimination, her letters trace the alternative publication pathways Black women forged via sisterwork. Hints that Wheatley-Peters saw Tanner-Collins not only as a friend but also as an invaluable asset for furthering her literary career emerge in their correspondence. In a letter dated October 30, 1773, she writes to Tanner-Collins: "I enclose Proposals for my Book, and beg youd help use your interest to get Subscriptions as it is for my Benefit."[27] Tanner-Collins, heeding the call of her "dear friend," frequently acted as a literary agent of sorts, using her membership in the First Congregational Church and connections with Reverend Hopkins to solicit subscriptions for Wheatley-Peters' first book, *Poems on Various*

Subjects, Religious and Moral.[28] It would be Wheatley-Peters' first and only published book. Tanner-Collins' nurturing of Wheatley-Peters' poetic talents in a virulently hostile colonial society intent on siphoning Black women's energies and labors spotlights the critical care work necessary for nurturing and preserving Black female creativity. The trajectory of Black women's creative output has been shaped by our exclusion from mainstream publication pathways. On this alternative track, Black women need much more than a "room of one's own" and financial capital to sustain a writing career. As Black feminist scholar Barbara Christian noted, women marginalized via their race "cannot rely on inheritances or other benefits of class privilege to do the work we need to do." Therefore, sisterwork, the recuperative maternal labor necessary for maintaining our physical, mental, and spiritual well-being, is essential for Black women creating at the intersections of economic insecurity combined with racist and sexist discrimination. To better understand the creative fostering between Tanner-Collins and Wheatley-Peters, I turn to the constellations of Black women writers supporting each other during the 1920s, 1960s, and 1970s. As these time periods coincide with a blossoming Black feminist ethos, I analyze their letters to each other as examples of sisterwork.

Sisterwork's radical potential survives in Zora Neale Hurston's letters to Dorothy West and Helene Johnson. In the heady days of the Harlem Renaissance, Johnson and West were among the youngest members of the growing circle shaping the literary scene. They were also cousins. In 1926, a chance encounter with Hurston occurred after the pair gathered at an awards dinner to celebrate West's short story, "The Typewriter." A promising writer, West's short story earned her the second-place award from *Opportunity*, the National Urban League's journal. West shared the second-place prize with none other than Hurston. A mere 17 years old at the time, West recalled Hurston having "a little feeling about me" due to their age gap. In 1926, Hurston was 35 years old—although she told everyone she was 25—and therefore a more seasoned writer. Despite her initial coldness toward West, Hurston developed such a close relationship with both West and Johnson that she referred to them in her letters as her "little sisters." In one such letter, she addressed the pair with a warm greeting: "Dear Little Sisters D&H." Her next question was less of a request and more of an offering, "Do you girls want my apartment for 3 months?"[29] This was characteristic of Hurston's generosity—she often loaned money to friends with little concern about receiving the funds back. Hurston's travels and her recent marriage kept her away from the Harlem apartment for extended periods. Loaning the apartment to her "little sisters" was simply the right thing to do. West and Johnson took Hurston up on the offer, moving from the Women's YWCA in Harlem to her apartment at West Sixty-sixth Street.[30] As Boston transplants, both West and Johnson were new to New York and had been splitting their time applying for literary prizes and writing. Neither woman relied on the patronage of powerful white benefactors as Hurston and other Black writers did during this time. To pay the bills, they worked odd jobs, all the while surviving on "Nedrick's hot dogs and orange soda."[31] As scholars Verner D. Mitchell and Cynthia Davis explain, "Without established avenues of support, there were, as Nellie McKay points out, few opportunities for African American women to display their work in mainstream (white) journals, and even fewer to publish a book."[32] West and Johnson worked tirelessly to get their works published; however, even when opportunities arose from their efforts, they were faced with the realities of being Black women writers in the 1920s. Shortly after selling one of her poems to *Vanity Fair*, Johnson met with the magazine's editor, Frank Crowninshield. Things quickly went south. At the meeting, Crowninshield sexually propositioned Johnson, promising her a full page in *Vanity Fair* if she acquiesced. Her cousin, West, remembers the aftermath, "She came home in tears. We held hands and got down on our knees to pray. That was the end of her career at *Vanity Fair*." Many years later, in an interview with Deborah E. McDowell, West told her, "You don't know what we had to go through back then and I'm so glad you don't … In those days, women were just like excess baggage or fair game."[33] Under these circumstances, Hurston's offering of her apartment may be thought of as the sisterwork essential for fostering and sustaining the emotional, mental, and spiritual well-being of Black creatives. Indeed, Hurston offered her home to West and Helene again in 1928—the brevity of her writing suggested quickly jotted sentences fired off before departing to another faraway place. "I won't be home for months & when I do, it will be so sketchy that you can just stick me on the day-bed," Hurston writes.[34] But the tenderness with which she regards West is reflected not only in her address to her as "Dear Dot Child," but also in her query: "Did you get the box of pecans I sent you for Thanksgiving?"[35] When Hurston opened up her home to West again in 1931, they would be sharing the space together. To navigate this situation more efficiently, Hurston listed her two conditions: "#1 Please don't expect me to keep a very tidy kitchen. I ain't that kind of a person" and "#2 That you just feel at home & don't expect to be company."[36] Many years later, in an interview with Deborah E. McDowell, West tracked some of her inability to finish her novel to the long hours she worked.

> I got a nine-to-five job at the Gazette, and when you come home after a day's work, you don't always feel like writing. I worked there for two years, and after that, went to work at Harborside [a restaurant on Martha's Vineyard]; I was a cashier. I would go on there at five o' clock

in the afternoon, and, very often, I didn't get home until one o' clock in the morning.[37]

In locating her "nine-to-five job" as forestalling her creative process, West makes clear Black women's limited creative output as an unintended consequence of race- and class-based stress.

The structural economic challenges facing Black women writers determined Wheatley-Peters' career length and productivity. Finding little financial stability as a poet, she worked as a scullery maid. The arduous nature of the labor no doubt worsened her asthma. Performing the backbreaking labor likely contributed to Wheatley-Peters' fatal bout of pneumonia at only 31 years old. The harsh economic realities Wheatley-Peters faced as a free Black woman living in colonial America are in no ways a singular condition.

In 1952, Audre Lorde had not yet ascended to the Black feminist literary icon she would become shortly before her death. The 18-year-old poet accepted a job at Keystone Electronics where she performed "dirty, low-wage work" among other Black and Puerto Rican workers. Alexis De Veaux, poet and Lorde's biographer, speculates that Lorde's frequent exposure to carbon tetrachloride, a chemical agent known for causing kidney and liver damage, may have placed her at increased risk for cancer. Desperate to earn an additional bonus to supplement her low wages, Lorde frequently hid pockets of crystal shards in her socks, "chewing them up and spitting them into the toilet on her breaks" to produce a faster time.[38] While it is impossible to know for certain if the origins of her cancer began with the "dirty, low-wage work" she performed, Lorde's early exposure to the toxic crystals speaks to the risks Black women engage as a means of survival. Therefore, Black women establishing alternative routes to publication cultivate an erotic space where collaboration between women nourishes creative talent, feeding resistance to "terrifying whiteness."[39] This looks like a frustrated Audre Lorde calling her longtime friend and Black feminist activist Barbara Smith, and saying, "We really need to do something about publishing." The pervasive silencing and sidelining of Black feminist and lesbian writers by mainstream white presses had been a problem for both women. For years, Smith and Lorde fought battles in academia and against white presses dismissing the significance of African American literature.

By 1981, they were sick of it and formed Kitchen Table: Women of Color Press. As a Black woman-founded publishing group, Kitchen Table filled the gap in publishing by providing a space for activist-centered scholarship authored primarily by Black lesbians and lesbians of color. Embedded into the name is the warmth and comfort blossoming in the kitchens, nooks, and porches of homes guided by Black women. bell hooks, recalling her grandmother cultivating her home as a space of resistance, defined this as "homeplace." Although surfacing from the sexist divisions of labor, "homeplace" names the radical element of Black women reworking domestic sites into spaces "where we could restore to ourselves the dignity denied us on the outside in the public world."[40] And, Kitchen Table Press also draws attention to Black women's long domestic and economic subjugation. Culinary anthropologist and Geechee Verta Mae Grosvenor's *Kitchen Crisis* outlines the historical trajectory of this issue succinctly:

> it is no accident that in the old old south where they had slaves that that they was eating fried chicken, coated with batter, biscuits so light they could have flown across the mason Dixon line if they had wanted to. They were eating pound cake that had to be beat 800 strokes. Who do you think was doing this beating?[41]

Too often, the archive obscures the recuperative maternal labors required for nurturing and preserving Black female artistry. To render the role of sisterwork in Wheatley-Peters' life more clearly, stretching her humanity beyond the narrow, tightly constricted view typically confining her to that of a child prodigy is necessary. As Bynum reminds us, the "letters make real the fact that Wheatley was not just a lone genius, holed up in a room, writing poems all day long."[42] Wheatley-Peters is often conceptualized as a rarity. One of a kind. The language of white supremacy singularizes her, and marvels at her ability to grasp English. It is almost as if Wheatley-Peters arrived in America with no "mother tongue" of her own. As the archives function as an apparatus of white supremacist power, enslaved Black women "appear as historical subjects through the form and content of archival documents in the manner in which they lived: spectacularly violated, objectified, disposable, hypersexualized, and silenced."[43] This lingering violence consigns "our earliest foremothers to figments of the violent white imagination," significant only through their connections to white men.[44]

In 1772, Wheatley-Peters' authorship was put on trial by a gathering of powerful politicians and authors identifying themselves as "the most respectable characters in Boston."[45] For hours, the teenaged Phillis faced interrogation by 18 white men. Some of them were slaveholders like Cotton Mather and John Hancock. They were not alone in doubting a Black girl—an enslaved Black girl at that—could write such flowing, elegant poetry. Thomas Jefferson unleashed a caustic rebuke of Wheatley-Peters' poetry even after she "passed the interrogation with flying colors."[46] Thus, Tanner-Collins' significance in nurturing Wheatley-Peters' career reflects the extent to which sisterwork revitalizes the legacies of Black women disappeared through white supremacist apparatuses of power.

Therefore, Tanner-Collins' decision to relinquish the letters nearing the close of her life—keeping Wheatley-Peters' correspondence in her possession until a "great shock of the whitest wool" blanketed her head—appears as a final gesture of love.[47] One final attempt to position Wheatley-Peters firmly within American literature as a richly complex figure. One far more intriguing than her portrayal in the eyes of racist patriarchal white men. Shortly after her interrogation, Wheatley-Peters, finding no American publisher willing to publish her book, was forced to secure publishing in England. The final years of Wheatley-Peters' life reflect the extent to which white supremacist state power short-circuited the poet's career. Although she gained fame for penning poetry, claiming a literary career proved far more difficult. Unfortunately, the long shadow cast by powerful white men obscured the more subversive elements of Wheatley-Peters' poetry.

Before Black women writers of the 1970s and 1980s began recuperating Wheatley-Peters, the young poet was largely derided in Black literary spaces. At best, she was nothing more than a mime. Her poems evidence a misguided but perhaps understandable attempt at imitating the elegiac poems she was first introduced to by her slaveholders. At worst, she was a severely compromised poet divorced from any sense of political Black consciousness. But Margaret Walker, perhaps because she was a poet herself, filled in the gaps and silences of Wheatley-Peters' odyssey. Her poem "A Ballad for Phillis Wheatley" initiated the process of literary recuperation. Poet June Jordan continued this critical care work, penning "The Difficult Miracle of Black Poetry in America, Something like a Sonnet for Phillis Wheatley." Musing on Wheatley's improbable though not impossible path towards becoming a poet, Jordan asks,

> Come to this country a slave and how should you sing? After the flogging the lynch rope the general terror and weariness what should you know of a lyrical life? How could you, belonging to no one, but property to those despising the smiles of your soul, how could you dare to create yourself: a poet?[48]

We may locate the beginnings of a response to Jordan's critical line of inquiry via Tanner-Collins' sisterwork. Although the eldest of the pair by a few years, she outlived Wheatley-Peters by nearly 50 years. The two women's lives, beginning sometime around 1750, perhaps somewhere in Senegambia, arch, diverge, and testify to sisterwork's life-affirming potential. Tanner-Collins fostered Wheatley-Peters' connections with a small literate community of formerly enslaved Black people, nourishing her "dear sweet sister's" poetic appetites. In *Trickster Comes West*, Babacar M'Baye cites Tanner-Collins as Wheatley-Peters' "primary link to the Pan-African community in colonial New England."[49] She arranged for Wheatley-Peters to meet with Bristol Yamma and John Quamine, two formerly enslaved

Black men who "had been brought to Newport from Africa as Children."[50] Although they still spoke their native language, Yamma and Quamine studied at Princeton while planning a return to Africa. Because they may have hailed from the same Senegambia region as Wheatley-Peters, their ties to Senegambia establish the presence of a linguistic mother tongue. One that Wheatley-Peters was at least familiar with as girls and boys are taught how to read Arabic at a very young age. In Senegambia, Wheatley-Peters more than likely learned how to read, write, and speak Arabic.

Through Tanner-Collins, the young poet's legacy centers her African heritage as a primary determinant of her creative talents. Indeed, most scholars agree that although her slaveholders believed that the young Phillis had simply been scribbling on the walls, she was more than likely writing Arabic in Boston. Wheatley-Peters connected to a growing population of formerly enslaved Black people producing art, poetry, and other written works. The fact that one of her few poems dedicated to a living person was written to the young Black enslaved artist Scipio Moorhead evidences an emergent Black political consciousness. In "To S.M., A Young African Painter, On Seeing His Works," Wheatley-Peters writes, "How did those prospects give my soul delight, A new creation rushing on my sight?"[51] Some historians also believe that Moorhead painted the cover profile used by Wheatley-Peters in her book of poems. Interactions such as these disrupt the violence of the archives.

Staging mothering between Black women as a garden blooming with tender acknowledgments of admiration and encouragement shifts our understanding of Wheatley-Peters to that of a much more politically conscious figure. Indeed, in 2023, Professor Wendy Raphael Roberts found two new poems believed to have been written by Wheatley-Peters in a commonplace book held at the Historical Society of Pennsylvania. Eighteenth-century commonplace books, the equivalent of a literary scrapbook, typically contained collections of writings, quotes, and works by other authors. As such, the first poem buried within the commonplace book contains the header: "A few lines 'Written by a Negro Girl about 15 years of Age on the Death of Love Rotch her Mistress.'"[52] The poem functions as Wheatley-Peters' standard elegy, a lament for the rich white woman Love Macy Rotch, a Nantucket resident whose family dominated the nearby whaling industry. Most remarkable, however, is the fact that the poem places Wheatley-Peters closer to Tanner-Collins in Newport, Rhode Island. Thus, "On the Death of Love Rotch" may also be a link in the chain of clues connecting Wheatley-Peters to the city's growing Black community.

But the second poem found in the commonplace book radically shifts previous conceptions of Wheatley-Peters. Titled "The Black Rose," the second poem is dedicated to a Black woman named Rose. A glowing header reads, "'The Black Rose.' A Negro woman of that name lately deceas'd being remarkable for her innocent and sincerely pious life Philadelphia 9th month 3rd 1772."[53] Notably, the poem is the only known elegy by Wheatley-Peters that was written for a Black woman. Roberts explains that the unique subject of the poem

> could account for how it differs from the movement common to other Wheatley-Peters' elegies. For instance, the poem does not start with the deceased in heaven. Instead, this is delayed because the poem must first justify the unusual subject of her elegy—a Black woman.[54]

Through this lens, "The Black Rose" is an unmistakably political poem in that it registers the hypocrisy of the local white society for refusing to mourn a Black woman. Praising Rose for exhibiting virtuous morals in a society unwilling to grant Black women respect, Wheatley-Peters uses her words to essentially confer humanity onto another Black woman denied it in life:

> If to be faithful in a low Estate
> Wise without Learning, Without Riches great.
> If where those Relatives united blend;
> The Tender Mother, Daughter, Sister, Friend,
> If where th' harmonious social Virtues meet,
> And Piety untainted with Deceit;
> If in so rich a Garden Honour blows
> Illustrious then the Life of honest Rose.[55]

With the discovery of "The Black Rose," it is much more difficult to whitewash Wheatley-Peters' legacy. In fact, she becomes a decidedly modern figure navigating the same tenor of hatred contemporary Black women face. However, the archive conceals even as it reveals. While "On the Death of Love Rotch" poem has been authenticated as a Wheatley-Peters' poem, the "Black Rose" poem is still a speculative attribution. By establishing an alternative literary tradition for Wheatley-Peters, one rooted in Black creative genius, it seems she never lost these connections to her motherland. And, "her dear friend" Tanner-Collins deemed these connections soul-replenishing for a young woman daring to call herself a poet.

Black Feminist Mothering

Tanner-Collins never wrote a single line of poetry. Yet her nurturing of Wheatley-Peters' poetic talents positions her as a Black feminist literary foremother. Her sagacious eye toward preserving Wheatley-Peters' legacy crystallizes a Black feminist model of recuperative maternal labor. Amid a historical archive silencing Black women, locating this type of labor is paramount in spotlighting Black women's creative legacies. Indeed, the cultural renaissance of Zora Neale Hurston's *Their Eyes Were Watching God* cannot be fully appreciated without first understanding its current popularity as the culminating effect of Black women's sustained efforts at keeping the text alive.

Ubiquitous now in high school and college curricula, the novel had fallen out of print by the late 1980s. But Black women professors and educators, those lovingly photocopying their worn versions and circulating them among each other so that the book could be taught in classrooms, revived Hurston's masterpiece. And Alice Walker's recovery efforts to find Hurston's unmarked grave, documented in her landmark *In Search of Our Mother's Gardens*, speak to the maternal tenderness Black women extend to our literary foremothers. Wandering through the Eatonville swamps to recover Hurston's unmarked grave, Walker called out to the author and anthropologist, fussing at her as if they were long-lost sisters, as in, "Zora! I hope you don't think I'm going to stand out here all day, with these snakes watching me and these ants having a field day. In fact, I'm going to call you just one or two more times."[56] Here, the undeniable tone of maternal care expressed for Hurston exhibits what I have been tracking within Black feminist literary circles as that of an interstellar mother tongue. Across generations, Black women communicate with each other using a sacred mother language anticipating our collective need to be mothered by Black women writers before us. "I became aware of my need for Zora Neale Hurston's work some time before I knew her work existed," Walker explains.[57] In scouring her way through snakes and Lord knows what else, Walker underscores these recovery efforts as a desperate attempt to render Black women in the archives as something other than a catalog of suffering.

Thus, Black women's critical care work is the imaginative labor responsible for conferring humanity back onto Wheatley-Peters. In the 1970s, Margaret Walker and June Jordan laid the early groundwork for this Black maternal care project. Today, in large part due to their efforts, the pendulum has swung toward viewing Wheatley-Peters as a far more sympathetic figure. This cultural resurgence is evident in *The Trials of Phillis Wheatley* as Henry Louis Gates contextualizes the young poet's place within wider discourses of race, colonial America, and American intellectualism. Yet his framing of Wheatley-Peters through the eyes of her powerful interlocutors reinscribes her as white men's intellectual property. Therefore, perhaps no other extended work on Wheatley-Peters has so radically shifted our understanding of her than Honorée Fanonne Jeffers' 2020 poetry collection, *The Age of Phillis*. Following the paths already set by Walker and Jordan, Jeffers imagines a life for Wheatley-Peters that considers how the bountiful, deep, affirming quality of Black women's friendship may well have been the very thing keeping her poetic genius alive.

By reimagining a series of lost letters existing between Tanner-Collins and Wheatley-Peters, Jeffers constructs for the women an intimate space insulated from the closely surveilled slaveholding society. Wheatley-Peters writes first, addressing Tanner-Collins with "Dear Sister of My Nation." It is both a reclamation and acknowledgment of their shared African heritage. In this remixed rendition of history, Wheatley-Peters has a chance encounter with Tanner-Collins in the streets after stealing away from her mistress to breathe in and get some fresh air for her asthmatic lungs. "I shiver at the other chance, that had your master not been visiting those few days in summer ... had I not stolen away there would be no you," a grateful Wheatley-Peters confesses.[58] The two women, standing on a colonial street, craft for themselves what Lorde defines as "the sweetness of womanspace." Away from the prying eyes of slaveholders, their chance meeting invigorates and elevates them so that they may soar beyond their circumscribed position in 18th century America. Jeffers continues constructing for the friends a self-actualized Afrocentric identity in "Lost Letter #7." Here, Wheatley-Peters pays tribute to her friend's homeland: "Your name a comfort, though how should I spell you? Arbour, an astounding, shady grove that protects? 'Obour,' the name of 'stone' in your homeland?"[59] In this poem, both women speak back to each other in call-and-response fashion. Remarkably, for the first time, Tanner-Collins is no longer silenced by the archive. Indeed, in "Lost Letter #8," she speaks in her tender tones, writing, "Spell me how you wish, for you have saved me. Before your letter, no one gave a care for my name."[60] Here, too, Jeffers envisions Tanner-Collins' perilous journey aboard a slaving ship, as "even thoughts of canoes from long ago trouble me." Tanner-Collins tells her "dear friend," "I knew I loved you when you did not speak of ships."[61] From a historical standpoint, the lost letters epitomize what historian Saidiya Hartman calls critical fabulations.

Hartman developed the theory while reviewing the legal documents of a slave ship captain prosecuted for savagely beating and murdering two enslaved Negro girls. Growing frustrated at her inability to tell the story of Venus since she is mentioned only briefly in the slaveholding records and "history pledges to be faithful to the limits of fact, evidence, and archive," Hartman held back from telling Venus' story "because to do so would have transgressed the boundaries of the archive."[62] In effect, she needed "a new story, one unfettered by the constraints of the legal documents."[63] She found that by "playing with and rearranging the basic elements of the story [and] representing the sequence of events in divergent stories and from contested points of view," she could then tell the story of Venus, the other Black girl murdered aboard the ship. That is, the theory of "critical fabulations" freed her from the constraints of the archive. And, Hartman could now also imagine the "friendship that could have blossomed between two lonely and frightened girls."[64] Instead of the Black girl suspended from the air, whipped, and abused by her captors, Hartman put forth a new image—a tender, life-affirming one in which "two world-less girls found a country in each other's arms."[65] Hartman's critical fabulations theory is central as the seeds of this chapter grew from my frustration at the veritable blank surrounding the lack of details about Tanner-Collins' life. I too longed to tell a new story. Did Obour, a few years older than Phillis and perhaps like a big sister, learn of Phillis' fatal pneumonia via letter? Was there enough time to travel to Boston to lay eyes on Phillis one last time? To comfort her through the worst of it? I have asked these questions, despite knowing that the line of inquiry will lead to a dead end. White living and its minutiae are copious in the historical records, while Black living is scant. However, because "so much of the work of oppression is policing the imagination," Hartman's theory of critical fabulation opens up a space for considering a new origin story for enslaved Black women, one untethered from the violence of the white imagination.[66] Guided by the work of Jeffers and Hartman, I began pondering a series of questions: What would it look like to consider Obour's statement that she recognized Phillis from her enslavement on the ship as fact? To imagine Obour as her sister's keeper aboard the ship? While several historians point to evidence of their meeting, we cannot be entirely sure if the pair met in person beyond a handful of times. And while oral accounts suggest Tanner-Collins recognized Wheatley-Peters from aboard the slaving ship, *Phillis*, verifying this as an absolute certainty is difficult. Indeed, as if in response to my musings, I, having never written a poem precisely because the power poets command with fewer words is intimidating, woke up one morning and scribbled the following lines:

> Gap-toothed, raven-haired
> Girls.
> Tender spines curving along a ship named *Phillis*.
> When only God knew ours.
> Sister, I needed you. Dearest Obour.
> You tore the moon from the sky and fed it to me.

Here, I include this poem not because it is singular or even a decent one. Rather, I connect my early morning thoughts and this chapter to the Black feminist mothering labors of Jeffers and Hartman, who engage to render Black women's humanity more thoroughly visible. As with Tanner-Collins, we are collectively involved in examining an interstellar mother tongue, one that allows Black women to communicate across generations.

Because somehow Tanner-Collins knew, before Walker even wrote it that "We are a people. And a people do not throw their genius away."[67] Perhaps most significant is that her thoughtful act exhibits a commitment to recuperative maternal labor not only for Phillis but also for a new generation of Black women that she would not live to meet. In the many years that passed since bidding a final farewell to her "dear sweet sister," Tanner-Collins preserved Wheatley-Peters' letters until she herself was "very old [and] very infirm."[68] Her decision to only relinquish the letters as she neared the close of her life to Harriet Beecher Stowe's sister-in-law underscores her keen understanding of white colonial power and its impact on Black women's literary careers. Tanner-Collins, in other words, placed the letters in the hands of power. Her shrewd decision, perhaps stemming from an awareness that Wheatley-Peters would be far more valuable to history in death than she had been alive, crystallizes Black recuperative care work. In imagining Tanner-Collins as foremother, as keeper of her sister's letters, we may reflect on her as perhaps anticipating Black women eagerly scanning the archives, desperately seeking something other than a catalog of suffering. At another time, she could have been an archivist. Because she could not occupy these professions in colonial New Bedford, I imagine that Tanner-Collins knew that Black women would one day seek out Wheatley-Peters not solely for what she could tell us about the "difficult miracle of Black poetry" but also about sisterhood forged in the wake of dispossession, longing, and loss.

Even more, the batch of surviving letters, six in total, surfacing in the closely monitored colonial America encourages a consideration of the correspondence as signifiers of everything 18th-century Black women could *not* say. To cast off these silences, we may once again turn to the intimate spaces Black women cultivated in letters via the development of a mother tongue. Perhaps one of the clearest examples is the letters between Audre Lorde and Pat Parker.

Written between 1974 and 1988, the back-and-forth exchange offers a bird's-eye view of two artists at various points in their careers navigating racism, homophobia, the publishing industry, and the mundane challenges of balancing family, work, and writing. Writer and professor Mecca Jamilah Sullivan explains that "these letters shape and historicize the building of a black feminist literary politics in the twentieth century" while also making "clear the very personal stakes involved in the building of a black feminist literary politics." In an especially high-stakes letter, Lorde requests that Parker regard her letter cautiously precisely because of their precarious roles as lesbian Black women poets.

> Now. I wish I could have this letter self-destruct like Mission Impossible, but I can't, so don't please leave it laying around. The thing about these Poetry in the Schools gig is this: get in there, give the kids what you

can (and from you that's a lot) make a lot of bread, which is possible if you play it right, but don't stay around too long. AND DON'T TRUST ANYONE IN IT. ... Consider seriously what I've just said, but keep your mouth shut about it to EVERYBODY, or both our asses are liable to wind up in the street.[69]

On one level, Lorde's insistent advice to not trust anyone reinforces the perilous position of Black women in academia. At the time of the writing, Lorde's professional position at Brooklyn College and the numerous battles she fought undoubtedly endowed her with useful insights for steering Parker's career path. On another level, Lorde's "keep your mouth shut about it to EVERYBODY" hints at their forging of a mother tongue. Via letter writing, they encode specific African American language systems and tones to drive home messages to each other. Thus, their letters are preservations of a treasure trove of Black girl sisterways, or the coded double entendres unique to our communities. In one October 1974 letter, this mother tongue flows between the pair as a miffed Lorde chastises Parker's seeming disregard of her professional advice, writing,

Get it together, lady. Of course it's not REALLY important on the cosmic scale of things: we both know it, but like every other kind of grease, it helps to keep the kinks at least manageable and I know you what I mean.[70]

Nearly every Black woman reading this knows what Lorde means—some of us even feel and smell what she means. Thus, their letters call out and respond to us even as the duo cultivates for themselves an intimate space for fostering creativity. In doing so, their letters hearken back to the unbreakable bond between Wheatley-Peters and Tanner-Collins and the barriers they encountered along the way. It is a knowledge Wheatley-Peters shares in her letters, expressing regret when "a variety of hindrances" impedes her ability to write to her "dear friend," saying, "tho' I have been Silent, I have not been unmindful of you."[71] Muffled by American colonial living and its close surveillance of Black female bodies, Wheatley-Peters urges us to imagine what these hindrances may have been.

The letters passing between Black women become a litany for creating when standing outside "the circle of this society's definition of acceptable women."[72] In a July letter dated 1975, Parker addressed the homophobic attitudes she experienced while traveling to Houston for a poetry reading. Despite growing up in Houston, Parker confessed to Lorde that she deliberately read her poems which focused on all "the shit I caught there."[73] She follows up by describing a Black woman radio host interviewing her, noting that "the poor child looked scared to death." The radio host conducting the interview does so from "about three feet away" and holds "the microphone out at arms length." A sarcastic Parker writes, "When she realized I wasn't going to rape her or her arms got tired she moved in closer."[74] Here, Parker names the outsider-within position she occupies as a Black lesbian writing poetry dealing explicitly with her sexual orientation. Although she had been married to Ed Bullins in 1962, Parker divorced in 1966 and embraced her lesbian identity in ways that Lorde had not yet come to terms with until later in her life. Later, when Parker visits a local bar with her partner, Ann, she observes the shock and disgust of the people around them,

> Had the feeling we were definitely in the wrong place. And when we got up and did the bump, I thought the folks were going to faint. In fact, I had the feeling, the fact that Ann and I were together was causing a few mind problems.

On April 29, 1980, Parker seemed to link some of her inability to write to anxiety surrounding the repeated attempts to adopt a child with her partner. Parker confided in Lorde that she hoped the new "young, white, liberal" judge would be less willing to deny their claim based on their lesbian status. "The attorney thinks that we're in a really good position." Parker wrote,

> considering the lack of attention by the natural mother; not doing the two visits, not calling on her birthday, not calling on Christmas, just general shabby, "I don't really give a damn about this kid, but I'm just going to fight you because I don't want you dykes to have her" attitude.[75]

Their correspondence, driven by the desire to carve out a space where they could address their deepest fears and impediments to writing, exemplifies the myriad ways Black women's letters archive the labor, focus, and productivity necessary for maintaining Black feminist literary traditions. In December 1985, Lorde cautioned Parker against spending too much time focusing on housework as it stalled creativity. Even more, she offered explicit rules for surviving a disastrously anti-Black woman world with an empathetic gaze attuned to bearing the weight of homophobia as an out Black lesbian woman.

> Things you must be aware of right now—
> A year seems like a lot of time now at this end—it isn't ... Don't lose your sense of urgency on the one hand, on the other, don't be too hard on yourself—or expect too much.
> Beware the terror of not producing.

Beware the urge to justify your decision.
Watch out for the kitchen sink and the plumbing
And that painting that always needed being done.
But remember the body needs to create too.
Beware feeling you're not good enough to deserve it
Beware feeling you're too good to need it
Beware all the hatred you've stored up inside
You, and the locks on your tender places.[76]

Her "beware all the hatred you've stored up inside you" is a harrowing reminder of the homophobia both women navigated during the early 1970s and 1980s. As tender moments of mothering, their letters emerge as love offerings not only for each other but also for Black women, particularly Black lesbians.

Staging mothering between Black women shifts Black women's truncated legacies from the margins to the center. The sisterwork blooming within these letters sustains Black female creativity beyond the archives. Mecca Jamilah Sullivan perfectly articulates the ability of Black women's letters to connect past and future generations:

Figure 3.1 Child's Drawing of Phillis Wheatley-Peters Sitting in Her Room Surrounded by Books

As black girls, queer kids, trans folks, womanists, lesbians, feminists, and radicals in-becoming, we know that the air between these letters is anything but dead. It breathes life and lives–lives lived fiercely and documented generously so that we may keep them going.[77]

In this light, we may consider Lorde's "Beware the terror of not producing" as a clarion call to Black women poets and writers, but also to the next generation of artists. For example, last August, I taught a class on African American historical figures to a group of my daughter's classmates. Within the small group, ranging from ages 6–8, I introduced them to leading Black abolitionists and orators: Frederick Douglass, Phillis Wheatley-Peters, Anna Murray Douglass, and William Still. Among their favorites, Phillis Wheatley-Peters stood out to them as a kind of modern role model. Perhaps the sketch of her with earrings and a nose ring modernized her before a young audience. Perhaps the fact that I shared with them that young Phillis was likely the same age as my students when she was stolen from her homeland, as evidenced by slaveholders emphasizing her missing teeth. Their fascination with Wheatley-Peters amazed and saddened me. How could slaveholders look at children no older than 8 years old and see property? Despite my own knowledge and expertise in African American history, I was sobered by their child-like innocence and the harrowing reality of a girl named Phillis enduring the Middle Passage when her permanent teeth had not yet grown in. As most educators know, teaching is always a two-way street. A lesson I learned when one student, a little boy named Heru, shared with me his painting of a young Phillis. In Heru's sketch, he imagined her sitting in a room of her own, books and flowers surrounding her. A painting hangs from the wall. The drawing brought tears to my eyes. Because how had this child tapped into what Tanner-Collins and Alice Walker knew?

"We are a people. And a people do not throw their genius away."[78]

Notes

1 M'baby, 2011
2 "History Bytes: Reading between the Lines for Obour Tanner," 2023.
3 Walker, 2003, 233.
4 Walker, 233.
5 Walker, 233.
6 Stover, 140.
7 Melonas, 2021, 38.
8 Bynum, 2014, 43.
9 Wheatley and Vincent, 2001, 176.
10 M'baye, 2011, 50.
11 Walker, *The Color Purple*, 2003b, 1.
12 Walker, *The Color Purple*, 2003b.

13 Hartman, 1997, 87.
14 Jacobs, 1987, 81.
15 Lorde, 2007, 54.
16 Bynum, 2014, 44.
17 Wheatley and Vincent, 2001, 148.
18 M'baye, 2011, 58.
19 Walker, 1982, Preface.
20 Walker, 1982, Preface, 45.
21 Walker, 1982, Preface, 25.
22 Wheatley and Vincent, 2001, 148.
23 Wheatley and Vincent, 2001, 161.
24 Wheatley and Vincent, 2001, 161.
25 Walker, *The Color Purple*, 2003b, 49.
26 Walker, *The Color Purple*, 2003b.
27 Wheatley and Vincent, 2001, 149.
28 M'baye, 2011, 48.
29 Kaplan, 2002, 101.
30 Mitchell and Davis, 2011, 181.
31 Mitchell and Davis, 2011, 181.
32 Mitchell and Davis, 2011, 181.
33 Smith, 1989, 11.
34 Kaplan, 2002, 134.
35 Kaplan, 2002, 134.
36 Kaplan, 2002, 200.
37 West, 1987, 299.
38 De Veaux, 2004, 41.
39 hooks, 1990, 383.
40 hooks, 1990, 384.
41 Smart-Grosvenor, 1970.
42 Bynum, 2014, 43.
43 Fuentes, 2016, 6.
44 Hartman, "Venus in Two Acts," 2008, 3.
45 Gates, 2010, 15.
46 Gates, 2010, 15.
47 Society, 1863.
48 Jordan, 2006.
49 M'baye, 2011, 48.
50 M'baye, 2011.
51 Wheatley Peters, n.d.
52 Roberts, 2023, 161.
53 Roberts, 2023, 172.
54 Roberts, 2023, 173.
55 Roberts, 2023, 176.
56 Walker, 2003, 105.
57 Walker, 105.
58 Fanonne Jeffers, 2020, 77.
59 Fanonne Jeffers, 2020, 77.
60 Fanonne Jeffers, 2020, 78.
61 Fanonne Jeffers, 2020, 78.
62 Hartman, "Venus in Two Acts," 2008, 9.
63 Hartman, "Venus in Two Acts," 2008, 9.
64 Hartman, "Venus in Two Acts," 2008, 8.

65 Hartman, "Venus in Two Acts," 2008, 8.
66 Hartman, "Under the Blacklight: Storytelling While Black and Female: Conjuring Beautiful Experiments," 2020.
67 Walker, 2003, 92.
68 M'baye, 2011.
69 Lorde and Sullivan, 16.
70 Lorde and Sullivan, 25.
71 Wheatley and Vincent, 2001, 162.
72 Lorde, 2007, 112.
73 Lorde and Sullivan, 43.
74 Lorde and Sullivan, 43.
75 Lorde and Sullivan, 56.
76 Lorde and Sullivan, 22.
77 Lorde and Sullivan, 24.
78 Walker, In Search of Our Mothers' Gardens: Womanist Prose, 2003, 92.

Bibliography

Bynum, T. Phillis Wheatley on Friendship. *Legacy*, vol. 31, no. 1, pp. 42–51, 2014.

De Veaux, A. *Warrior Poet: A Biography of Audre Lorde*. New York: W.W. Norton, 2004.

Fanonne Jeffers, H. *The Age of Phillis*. Middletown: Wesleyan University Press, 2020.

Fuentes, M. J. *Dispossessed Lives: Enslaved Women, Violence, and the Archive*. Philadelphia: U of Pennsylvania P, 2016.

Gates, H. L. *The Trials of Phillis Wheatley: America's First Black Poet and Her Encounters with the Founding Fathers*. Frederick: Civitas Books, 2010.

Hartman, S. *Scenes of Subjection: Terror, Slavery, and Self-Making in Nineteenth-Century America*. London: Oxford U P, 1997.

Hartman, S. "Venus in Two Acts." *Small Axe*, vol. 12, 2008, pp. 1–14.

Hartman, S. *Under the Blacklight: Storytelling While Black and Female: Conjuring Beautiful Experiments*, 2020. African American Policy Forum: https://www.youtube.com/watch?v=xGS5aP5Vi7g.

History Bytes: Reading between the Lines for Obour Tanner, 28 July 2023. 1 June 2024, from Newport History: https://newporthistory.org/history-bytes-reading-between-the-lines-for-obour-tanner/.

hooks, b. *Yearning: Race, Gender, and Cultural Politics*. Boston: South End Press, 1990.

Jacobs, H. *Incidents in the Life of a Slave Girl, Written by Herself*. Boston: Harvard U P, 1987.

Jordan, J. *The Difficult Miracle of Black Poetry in America*, 15 August 2006. Poetry Foundation: https://www.poetryfoundation.org/articles/68628/the-difficult-miracle-of-black-poetry-in-america

Kaplan, C. *Zora Neale Hurston: A Life in Letters*. New York: Random House, 2002.

Lorde, A. *Sister Outsider: Essays and Speeches*. Vancouver: Crossing Press, 2007.

Lorde, A., and J. M. Sullivan. *Sister Love: The Letters of Audre Lorde and Pat Parker 1974–1989*. Berkeley: Sinister Wisdom, n.d.

M'baye, B. *The Trickster Comes West: Pan-African Influence in Early Black Diasporan Narratives*. Mississippi: U P of Mississippi, 2011.

Melonas, D. R. "'Hey Mama;' 'Dear Sister;' 'Sister Love': Black Women's Healing and Radical Self-Care through Epistolary Work." *Journal of Women, Politics & Policy*, vol. 42, pp. 38–57, 2021.

Mitchell, V. D., and C. Davis. *Literary Sisters: Dorothy West and Her Circle, A Biography of the Harlem Renaissance*. New York: Rutgers U P, 2011.

Roberts, W. R. "On the Death of Love Rotch," a New Poem Attributed to Phillis Wheatley (Peters): And a Speculative Attribution. *Early American Literature*, vol. 58, pp. 155–184, 2023.

Smart-Grosvenor, V. M. *The Kitchen Crisis*, 1970. Retrieved from Myron Beasley.

Smith, B. "A Press of Our Own Kitchen Table: Women of Color Press." *Frontiers: A Journal of Women Studies*, vol. 10, 1989, pp. 11–13.

Society, M. H. "November Meeting. Death of Lord Lyndhurst; Death of Hon. William Sturgis; Dr. Ephraim Eliot; Diary of Ezekiel Price; Letter of Count de Marbois; Phillis Wheatley; Letters of Phillis Wheatley." *Massachusetts Historical Society*, vol. 7, 1863, pp. 168–279. https://www.jstor.org/stable/25079312.

Stover, Johnnie M. *Rhetoric and Resistance in Black Women's Autobiography*. 2003.

Walker, A. *In Search of Our Mothers' Gardens: Womanist Prose*. Orlando: Mariner Books, 2003a.

Walker, A. *The Color Purple*. Orlando: Harcourt Books, 2003b.

West, D. "Conversations with Dorothy West." (D. E. McDowell, Interviewer) The Harlem Renaissance Re-examined, 1987.

Wheatley Peters, P. *To S. M. A Young African Painter, On Seeing His Works*, n.d. Retrieved from https://www.poetryfoundation.org/poems/52519/to-s-m-a-young-african-painter-on-seeing-his-works.

Wheatley, P., and C. Vincent. *Phillis Wheatley, Complete Writings*. New York: Penguin Classics, 2001.

4 We Can Learn to Mother Ourselves
Sisterwork in the Time of Betty, Coretta, and Myrlie

"Every Black woman," Audre Lorde declares in "Eye to Eye: Black Women, Hatred, and Anger," "has survived several lifetimes of hatred."[1] The origin of this difficult truth is often lodged in painful childhood memories. For Lorde, the memory begins with a Harlem subway ride. At the woman's sudden mouth twitching, a young Audre first believes that perhaps a roach has crawled onto the empty seat—the one nearest to the woman and the seat taken by Audre. "When I look up the woman is still staring at me, her nose holes and eyes huge. And suddenly I realize there is nothing crawling up the seat between us: it is me she doesn't want her coat to touch," Lorde writes.[2] My own exposure to "several lifetimes of hatred" began at the park while I played with my sisters. Two white girls hurled *nigger!* at us. They were probably sisters too. No older than 7. The same age as me. My sisters and I chased after them. What I did not know how to handle, and what continues to puzzle me even today, was the look on their mother's face when she saw us. Her daughters had managed to find her and she, quick as a cat, scooped them up into the waiting minivan. Seven-year-old me had believed that all adults acted like adults. That she would ask her daughters for clarification, encourage them to apologize, and perhaps request to speak with our parents so that there was no lingering confusion. It is what my mother would have done if the roles were reversed. But her cherry-red face, jerky movements, and wide eyes communicated to me a lesson that I have never forgotten: she had not seen a short, little Black girl but something far more monstrous. Worthy of disgust, hatred, and fear.

What 7-year-old me had not known then is the degree to which adults view "Black girls as less innocent and more adult-like than their white peers."[3] Adultification of Black girls, as shown in the research study conducted by Georgetown Law's Center on Poverty and Inequality, may lead to negative outcomes in the areas of education, juvenile justice, and child welfare. As girls, both Lorde and I were grappling with the psychological impact of this adultification. Our experiences may be understood as precursors to grappling with the weight of Black women's racialized violence.

DOI: 10.4324/9781032719993-5

This chapter has been made available under a CC-BY-NC-ND license.

In her landmark *Black Feminist Thought*, Patricia Hill Collins situates Black women's mainstream dehumanization into four major categories: stereotypical mammies, matriarchs, welfare recipients, and hot mommas. These images uphold and maintain Black women's outsider-within position. Under this social theory of power, Black women's lifelong exposure to racialized violence produces, I argue, a mother wound. We may think of this mother wound within a national context in which Black women love and labor for an American nation refusing to love them back. As shown in Chapter 1, Black political and reproductive justice advocate Fannie Lou Hamer worked Mississippi into a more equitable place for disadvantaged populations while living with disabilities sustained from police beatings. Thus, what I am most concerned with in this chapter is Black women forging relationships with each other as an antidote to the lack of mothering we receive from society at large. Like Lorde, I am most concerned with the difficulty of fostering sisterwork among Black women precisely because we tend to unleash our internalized rage onto each other.[4]

In "Eye to Eye: Black Women, Anger, and Hatred," Lorde ruminates on Black women's daily interactions with each other. First, she considers a seemingly mundane encounter between her and an unnamed Black female library clerk. When the woman refuses to look up from her book, Lorde straightens her glasses and jiggles her bangles. At the moment the woman finally assists her, she writes, "Her eyes cross mine with a look of such incidental hostility that I feel pilloried to the wall."[5] This dismissal infuriates Lorde: "What makes her eyes slide off of mine? What does she see that angers her so, or infuriates her, or disgusts her? Why do I want to break her face off when her eyes do not meet mine?"[6] Lorde's desire to physically hurt the woman—and her introspective musings into why this perceived slight rattles her so deeply—renders her complicit in the cycle of Black women's oppression. In a sudden shift, Lorde uses the master's tools and seeks to teach the impudent young Black woman a lesson by "[breaking] her face off."[7] The magnitude of the slight is evidenced by Lorde's desire to physically hurt the woman—the woman's dismissal pitches Lorde back to her girlhood where she endured the twitching woman's disgust on the subway. She is no longer in the library awaiting assistance but back on the subway, vaporized in the "eyes of so many white people."[8] Lorde's intensifying vengeance for the Black library clerk, expressed via her candid desire to teach the young Black woman a lesson by "[breaking] her face off," registers white supremacy's cruel aftershocks.

Because Lorde's relationships with other Black women were fraught, she frequently drew attention to these vengeful dynamics in her writings, letters, and journals. What Lorde offers here is an honest examination of how our continued exposure to "several lifetimes of hatred" disrupts Black women's capacity for forming meaningful bonds with each other. One of my Black female friends pondered this very thing as our children splashed nearby in the pool, asking me, "What is it that makes us so hard on each other?" In "Eye to Eye," Lorde wondered too, "What is the source of that mistrust and distance maintained between Black women?"[9] In response to Lorde, I explore the evolution of Black women's friendships via Myrlie Evers-Williams, Coretta Scott King, and Betty Shabazz. The women, united by their shared experience of widowhood in the turbulent Civil Rights era, provide a model for sisterwork as the mothering, caring, and nurturing of Black women. To render more clearly how we may navigate the barriers to establishing friendships with other Black women in our lives, as my friend asked me on that sunny July day, I begin with an examination of the public's perceptions of each woman and its impact on their early interactions with each other. In the years following the assassinations of Martin Luther King Jr. and Malcolm X, the tenacity of the grieving Civil Rights widow image initially thwarted any potential bonding between Betty Shabazz and Coretta Scott King. Exploring how the pair formed a friendship amid this hostile environment may well serve as a remedy for collapsing the barriers too often holding Black women aloft from each other.

Since the title of this chapter borrows from Lorde's audacious assertion: "We can learn to mother ourselves," Lorde's years-long friendship with fellow Black lesbian poet Pat Parker, maintained and preserved through letters, serves as a guide for contextualizing sisterwork's revolutionary potential.[10]

Sisterwork in the Time of Betty, Coretta, and Myrlie

To help us understand the delay in Betty Shabazz and Coretta Scott King forging a friendship, we must first engage with the American white imagination and its propensity for mythmaking. As public historian Brenda Tindal observes, "one of the most dramatic, albeit tragic, ways in which African American women entered the national imagination during the Civil Rights era was through the mortality and martyrdom of black boys and men."[11] Indeed, *Life* magazine's iconic 1968 photograph of Coretta on the cover froze her into a perpetual state of mourning. In the close-up shot, Coretta's face is partially shielded behind a thin black veil, a weary smile tracing her lips, and her hair falling softly around her shoulders. Beneath her, the white-lettered caption "America's Farewell in Anger and Grief" revises King's grief as a national loss, sidestepping the FBI's surveillance, harassment, and role in murdering King.[12] In evading the white supremacist structures responsible for devastating Black families and communities, *Life* depoliticizes Coretta. She becomes a universalized figure of mourning, plucked away from the racialized violence claiming Martin Luther King's life. Scripting her grief this way displaces white American discomfort, obscuring the racial politics Coretta navigated daily.

Take, for instance, the fact that Coretta was forced to issue an ultimatum to the all-white press pool on the day of King's funeral. If Moneta Sleet, the World War II veteran and photographer responsible for documenting King's historic marches, was not allowed inside Ebenezer Baptist Church and given an optimal photography spot, no one would photograph the funeral.[13] In this racial context, Sleet's photograph visually and rhetorically counters white mainstream narratives by archiving documentation of Coretta's refusal to accommodate racist politics. Indeed, Sleet's Pulitzer Prize-winning photograph defies whitewashing attempts and the transferring of white American culpability.

Figure 4.1 Coretta Scott King Holding Her Daughter Bernice at Martin Luther King's Funeral

Taken from a similar vantage point as *Life*, Sleet firmly ensconces King within the Black Christian community to which she belongs. By panning outward to include King's black-gloved hand clutching her 5-year-old daughter Bernice and the funeral program, Sleet captures Black female grief as a disturbing feature of American life. A somber, pigtailed Bernice looks out from her mother's embrace. The magnitude of King's loss to not only his family but also the Black community is made visible by the three Black women clad in black, seated in church pews directly behind Coretta. Sleet's image may be understood as a visual signifier of Black female resistance.

In contrast, the rhetorical power of *Life*'s grieving widow image locked Coretta into an image of Black mainstream respectability. In public, she was often likened to Jacqueline Kennedy Onassis. One politician described his encounter with King as the equivalent of meeting Mother Teresa. The high esteem with which the public regarded King granted her a *bona fide* celebrity status at events. Heightening her beloved public status was her ability to maneuver deftly in social circles—a skill she likely perfected during her time performing as a singer. She was a favored speaker at women's empowerment conferences, congressional caucuses, and colleges.[14] Therefore, as Betty's biographer Rickford noted, "One obstacle to genuine camaraderie was the disparity of the widows' experience."[15] Although Malcolm X was eventually hailed as Harlem's favorite son, in the immediate aftermath of his assassination, there was an unmistakable air of hatred for the minister, dampening public support for Betty and her children. In the wake of Malcolm X's assassination, she occupied a curious position. As journalist Chuck Stone recalls, "People forget what was being said about Malcolm at the time. They said death was too good for him." *Newsweek* labeled Malcolm X a "desperado."[16] Howard University alumni booed Black Arts poet and close family friend Amiri Baraka for mentioning the slain minister.[17] Betty's close proximity to Malcolm X, despite her grief, did not elicit much sympathy from the public. As Evers-Williams discovered shortly after Medgar's assassination, "Americans find weeping widows and fatherless kids infinitely easier to embrace—and finance—than defiant freedom fighters,"[18] citing the lack of overwhelming support she received following Byron De La Beckwith's 1963 assassination of Medgar. She learned this shortly after Medgar's death when she and her children were initially shunned by the community. The key to securing public and financial support, Myrlie learned, hinged on mobilizing her identity as a grieving widow.

> Once the media gave the public a glimpse of his thirty-year-old widow at the podium a mere twenty-four hours after his death, people wanted more. In short, the children and I became a powerful public relations tool, which was just what the NAACP needed. The organization reprinted a

photograph taken at Medgar's funeral, a close-up of my face, showing a tear running down my cheek. It appeared in train stations and bus terminals throughout the country. Calls and letters poured into the New York office, requesting my appearance at branch offices, at membership drives, and at functions held by all sorts of other organizations and corporations that supported the cause.[19]

Betty, too, was both a "weeping widow" with "fatherless kids," but as her absence from the front cover of *Life* and other magazines suggested, she remained confined to that of a phantom, an unapproachable pariah.

Betty's noticeable absence from any major magazines, in sharp contrast to *Life*'s sympathetic scripting of Coretta in mourning, confirms the venom that America reserved for both her and Malcolm X. As a Black Muslim woman married to a man many regarded as the "Apostle of Hate," her image could not be easily recuperated. Thus, *Life*'s cover displaying the destroyed Mosque 7 and headquarters, where Malcolm X ministered and which had been bombed *after* his assassination, symbolized the adversarial tensions within the NOI and Malcolm X's death as a consequence. The title caption, "A Monument to Negro Upheaval: Death of Malcolm X and the Resulting Vengeful Gang War," further reduced Malcolm X's death to that of a petty turf war between rival Black Muslims.[20] Of course, the FBI's role in sowing dissent among NOI members, infiltrating the organization with informants, surveilling, and harassing the Shabazz family was never mentioned. Rather, inside the magazine were images of a lifeless Malcolm X lining the pages. Betty, kneeling over his lean body sprawled out on the floor, clutched at him in an unsuccessful attempt to staunch the bullet wounds puncturing his bared chest. These gruesome photos, in gratuitous fashion, reflect white mainstream media's fascination with circulating images and videos of Black death, grief, and suffering. Professor Deborah Walker King names this phenomenon *blackpain*, or "the visual and verbal representation of pained black bodies that function as rhetorical devices, as instruments of socialization, and as a sociopolitical strategy in American popular culture and literature."[21] In America, the wanton way in which Black death is displayed in vivid detail works as a unifying tool for those imagining themselves as white, defining and clarifying "true" Americans as those commanding respect both in life and death. Thus, *Life*'s coverage helped cement Malcolm X's early legacy as that of *persona non grata*. As a result, Betty could not be converted into a praiseworthy symbol of Black female suffering.

In the difficult months and years after Malcolm's death, a weary Betty struggled under the weight of this reality. Betty recalled, "A lot of Black people were very much afraid of me when Malcolm was assassinated." Interestingly, she found more public support abroad than in America.[22] For example, during her travels to Mecca for Hajj, Saudi Arabia's Prince Faisal provided chauffeured cars, offered to cover all her expenses, and extended citizenship to Betty and her daughters. Declining the opportunity, Betty returned to America to face an overwhelming air of anti-Malcolm X sentiment. But concerns over how she would take care of her growing family loomed as she was pregnant with twins.

Therefore, the speed with which mainstream media absorbed Coretta into a fabricated American identity while relegating Betty to society's outskirts contributed to the "artificial distances" between the pair. Lorde names these "artificial distances" as the structural barriers, both real and imagined, preventing Black women from acknowledging each other beyond a perceived, heavily distorted image. "We refuse to give up the artificial distances between us or to examine our real differences for creative exchange."[23] The carefully constructed image of the grieving Civil Rights widow conferred onto Coretta King the title of the "right" kind of widow and contrasted heavily against Betty's erasure from public sympathy, effectively severing her from deserving legitimate resources and assistance typically reserved for widows and their families.

Since Medgar, the 37-year-old NAACP field activist, was killed four years before King, Myrlie's extolling as an aggrieved widow modeled the similar treatment Coretta would receive years later. This time, *Life* placed Myrlie Evers-Williams on the cover consoling her distraught son, Darrell Kenyatta Evers. But the small white caption above the grieving widow, "A Martyr—and the Negro Presses On," tacitly affirmed Evers-Williams' suffering as the inevitable and logical condition of Black women in America. And, although she understood the rhetorical value of her image as a grieving widow, in the years following Medgar's death, Myrlie struggled under its weight:

> Sometimes I even smiled at people, acting sweet, appreciative, forgiving. I had to carry on. I feared that if I became too abrasive, expressing the true extent of my deep hatred, my family and I would be shunned. I would not have been seen as the "proper" civil rights widow, and worst of all, Medgar might be forgotten.[24]

Myrlie's understanding of the praise reserved for smiling "sweet" widows in exchange for the public's adulation shrewdly articulates Black women's negotiations in the wake of the white racist imagination. She implicitly connects, in highlighting the psychological impact of this racialized violence, the grieving widow to the slew of fabricated Black female stereotypes lodged within the white mainstream imagination. These stereotypes—Mammy, Black Bitch, and Angry Black woman—constrict Black women's humanity as we often struggle not to appear too angry, too hostile. Doubly burdened, Coretta, Myrlie, and Betty resist white supremacist stereotypes while simultaneously maintaining a veneer of respectability before Black communities. As the trio navigated their new status before a curious public, they were often hailed as a "sacred triumvirate."[25] Hence, the labeling of Betty, Coretta, and Myrlie as "movement widows" by the broader American public confined and restricted their humanity before an American public.[26]

Indeed, even in predominantly Black spaces, the trio was often honored for representing "the finest in black womanhood."[27] This particular emblem of Black womanhood rests on maintaining a cool, poised demeanor at all times. In *Beyond the Black Lady*, Lisa B. Thompson explains that performing middle-class Black womanhood relies "upon aggressive shielding of the body; concealing sexuality; and foregrounding morality, intelligence, and civility as a way to counter negative stereotypes." Notably, Coretta rarely danced. "You won't see Coretta King boogaloo," a friend of hers noted.[28] Neither did she share intimate details about her marriage. Her outward displays of restraint exalted her to a classy, dignified icon in her own right. One example surfaced on April 8, 1968, when Coretta Scott King led three of her young children through downtown Memphis. Just 4 days prior, Martin Luther King had been assassinated at the Lorraine Hotel. James Earl Ray's murder of King came on the heels of his speech supporting Black Memphis sanitation workers. Nearly 20,000 people gathered to silently protest King's assassination and the sanitation workers' low wages and hazardous working conditions. Veiled and dressed in black, Coretta walked arm in arm with her children and Civil Rights activist Ralph Abernathy. She insisted to the audience that the fight for better pay and working conditions among Black sanitation workers must continue. For many Black protesters, Coretta's quiet stoicism tempered the flames smoldering in Memphis. One member of the audience who heard her speech at the City Hall that day, Luella Cook, a Black domestic worker, remembers her poise: "If Mrs. King had cried a single tear, this whole city would have given way."[29] However, Cook's oral testimony also beckons a consideration of the internal battles that the image waged on the trio.

Coretta's carefully constructed image, conferring her with the "right" kind of widowhood, clashed sharply against Betty's less restrictive demeanor. Betty, known for cutting up a dance floor, often told girlfriends of the passion shared between her and Malcolm. Although the pair presented a united front, sharing platforms at the 1972 National Black Political Convention, an executive aide working closely with Betty and Coretta observed that "they had agreed to coexist."[30] In fact, Coretta's prominence in movement spaces "spawned a quiet rivalry with Betty."[31] Her resentment arose from believing Malcolm X's legacy deserved the same halcyon treatment as Martin's. Having no problem "aggressively campaigning to be present wherever [Coretta] was scheduled to appear, Betty felt spurned by most of America as the public seemed to grieve at Coretta's side."[32] Even Myrlie, frequently invited to speak at the same events, noticed that she and Betty seemed to disappear behind Coretta as guests flocked towards her. Even more, the political utility of the trio placed tremendous pressure on the women to "hoist the unity banner."[33] For onlookers, Myrlie, Betty, and Coretta helped ease the tensions rising from the turbulent Civil Rights years. Because Malcolm X and Martin Luther King were often depicted as diametrically opposed, if their widows could come together, however, then the path toward reconciling militant and non-violent activism could also be smoothed. Perhaps even more important, their political utility, emerging at a time when Black women had begun explicitly rejecting white beauty standards, revised co-dependent scripts of Black women as mammies and maids.

Indeed, it is no coincidence that in the years following the Civil Rights era, images of Black sisterhood dominated the mainstream. Movies and shows like *Waiting to Exhale*, *Soul Food*, and *Living Single* often featured a quartet of successful, conventionally attractive Black women. Black audiences eagerly embraced images of Black women's friendship as a testament of our collective value to each other.

As a teenager, I found immense value in the millennial hit television show, *Girlfriends*.[34] Centering on the lives of three Black women and one biracial Black woman, the quartet navigated careers, friendship, and romance. *Girlfriends* seemed to embody what I perceived to be real adulthood.[35] Now that I have returned to the show as an actual adult, I realize that the poor quality of their friendships arose from their internalizations of stereotypes around colorism, sexuality, and class. For example, Joan, a lighter-skinned Black woman with loosely defined curls, symbolized a whiter, more conventionally desirable beauty standard. Her stable career as an attorney—though she faces sexist and racist discrimination—further elevates her to that of a respectable, productive, model citizen. Toni, the other side of the proverbial coin, is equally beautiful and successful in her career as a mortgage broker but, as she constantly reminds Joan, must work harder to uphold an image of perfection due to her darker skin. That means preserving her neatly styled weave with no hint of kink, draping herself in designer labels, keeping a regimented workout plan, and refusing to date men who are not rich. Like Bride from Toni Morrison's *God Help the Child*, Toni's early battles with colorism and poverty cause her to fabricate a public persona for herself.[36] And yet, the duo mirrors each other's insecurities. Joan's emotional, neurotic need to overextend herself to others is in complete opposition to Toni's cold, ruthless goal of acquiring as much money and property as she can to bolster her public persona. Somehow, perhaps impossibly so, they are best friends. But their sisterhood never ascends beyond the ornamental—it is an empty, shallow bond. Because neither woman confronts the other on an "eye-to-eye" level, the dynamic playing out between the two is that of romantic partners locked in an unhealthy, co-dependent relationship. As Lorde warned, "connections between Black women are not automatic by virtue of our similarities, and the possibilities of genuine communication between us are not easily achieved."[37] Yet *Girlfriends* is one of the few depictions of sisterhood on the silver screen addressing the weight of "controlling images" on Black women's relationships with each other. On the friendship between Joan and Toni, show writer and creator Mara Brock Akil explains:

> What was unique about *Girlfriends* that was different than *Sex and the City*, was *Sex and the City* was all about their dating relationships with a girl group to discuss it with. I wanted to shift it to the chosen family of sisterhood and use Joan and Toni as my Carrie and Mr. Big. It was always about that—whether or not that relationship was ever going to make it, and then letting all the other ones wrap around it.[38]

Girlfriends then emerges as the cultural vehicle highlighting the faultiness of equating gender and race as the unifying principle for Black women's friendships.

In the heightened political context of the 1960s, we may wonder how the friendship between Coretta and Betty was even possible. First, we must consider the obstructions preventing Black women from acknowledging each other beyond a heavily distorted lens as both real and imagined. In "Eye to Eye," Lorde notes that these barriers surface when we are unwilling to release the fabricated identities we construct for ourselves. In 1969, Parker and Lorde initially kept their distance from each other as Betty and Coretta had, although they orbited the same spaces. In "For Audre," Parker wrote a poem detailing their frosty encounter and her first impressions of Lorde:

> Who is this bitch?
> I mean really
> who is this bitch?[39]

In these opening lines, Parker archives the weight of tokenized images on Black women's attempts at bonding. At the time of their meeting, Lorde had established herself as a premier poet, one highly sought after for speaking engagements at colleges and universities. However, in Parker's estimation of Lorde, she appears arrogant and disconnected from the actual Black lesbian communities to which she belonged.

> Like where is she from?
> I know literally
> how she got here.
> Been hanging around with East Bay dykes and wants to know
> where the Black women are and to them I am the Black women.[40]

As is common with talented Black women, Lorde had become something of a superstar, a lone Black poet in mostly white spaces. At these events, she often preferred her starry-eyed followers to call her Mother. In some ways, the term was a reminder of Lorde's benevolence as she often served as a mother figure to young poets and activists.[41] Yet, in other ways, her insistence on the term evidenced her growing arrogance and tendency towards disrespect. As Lorde biographer Alexis De Veaux explains in *Warrior Poet*, Lorde's dealings with women sometimes crossed the line into inappropriate, abusive territory.

> Early in her friendship with Barbara Smith, for example, she'd told Smith she was coming to Boston to do a reading and wanted to stay at Smith's house instead of a hotel. Smith agreed to the arrangement, realizing only later Lorde meant to use the opportunity as occasion to seduce her.[42]

With this in mind, Parker's questioning of Lorde's fabricated identity exposes the degree to which Black women may be seduced into embracing a tokenized status, one elevating them for being the first or only Black woman in rooms with few others who look like them. Parker, though younger, refused to "behave like a doting fan, or treat ... Lorde as anything but a peer."[43] A Houston, Texas native, Parker worked as an activist in the Black Panther Party, forming the Black Women's Revolutionary Council, and helping found the Women's Press Collective. For a decade, Parker worked as director of the Oakland Feminist Women's Health Center. When she was not working, she wrote poetry addressing domestic abuse, homophobia, and issues of reproductive violence. Parker, motivated by her sister's murder at the hands of an ex-husband, wrote *Women Slaughter*, her most well-known poetry collection. Between 1972 and 1985, Parker published five poetry collections. Like Lorde, she was lesbian. However, she never quite achieved the same level of popularity Lorde enjoyed during her lifetime and even now her legacy, as Mecca Jamilah Sullivan asserts, "has been even more silenced than Lorde's, even in many feminist circles."[44] However, a measure of Parker's legacy may serve as a guide for Black women seeking to establish solid relationships with each other. Using her working-class activism as a critical base of insight, Parker engaged with Lorde on an "eye-to-eye" level, rejecting her celebrity status to instead situate Lorde as an accomplice of white supremacy, capable of wielding power against other Black women. This honest practice of holding Lorde accountable for recognizing the ways that she may have hurt other Black women by playing into white supremacist forms of oppression breaks ground for an authentic friendship to form. "Tell me the ways that I have hurt you," Lorde writes in "Eye to Eye," "Or the ways that the world has hurt you."⁴⁵ Over the years, as the women's bond grew stronger, Parker would become a source of life-affirming truth for Lorde. "Pat Parker illustrates to me again how much of a sucker harpie blowhard creampuff I really am," Lorde wrote in her journal.⁴⁶

Clearing room in our hearts to love each other requires laying down the burdens we are carrying and speaking the truth, no matter how painful. Had Coretta not first acknowledged the vastly different treatment Betty received in the wake of their husbands' assassinations, the duo may have never launched a friendship. "When Martin died I felt almost like I was embraced by the whole world, and 240,000 people came to Atlanta for the funeral. Betty didn't have that."⁴⁷ Most significant about Coretta's observation is that, in implicitly exposing the white supremacist forces stalling their path toward loving each other, she extends tenderness toward Betty for enduring its uneven weight. Years later, Betty would frame her initial isolation in similar terms. "The world wanted me to be perceived as being alone. I wouldn't get the kind of media support and governmental and organizational support that perhaps [Mrs King] received."⁴⁸ Through their public statements, we may consider how Betty, Myrlie, and Coretta eventually confronted these "artificial distances" head-on, cultivating the heartspace necessary for a blossoming sisterhood.

Cultivating Heartspace

By the mid-1990s, the trio had grown so close that they had begun planning retreats together. Myrlie's description of their retreat as a "get away" where they could tend to their spiritual needs "without any folks listening. Without any witnesses. Just as girlfriends" restructures our understanding of them as Civil Rights widows.⁴⁹ We may think of these retreats as nurturing spaces where the women gathered to disrupt public enshrinements of them as perpetual Black widows.

Their retreats also constitute what Lorde calls "that sweetness of womanspace."⁵⁰ When she went on a women's writing retreat, Lorde expressed contentment for having "4 glorious days on the hill to spend time with other women, writing, reading, conversing."⁵¹ In this "sweetness of womanspace," "the erotic [flowed]" and she emerged revitalized after being in communion with other women.⁵² Speaking fondly of their first retreat, Myrlie characterized these carefully curated moments together as intimate spaces where the trio could lay down the burdens of carrying the image.

"We were all under such tremendous pressure. It seemed like there was nowhere we could let down and be ourselves," Myrlie recalls.⁵³ Perhaps this is why Coretta was the first to propose the idea. In this "sweetness of womanspace," the women permitted themselves to bond "without the façade of our being 'widows of' or what not."⁵⁴ Their friendship, moving beyond that of ornamental, represented a concerted attempt to "get down to the business of living" without the image, without the concerns of motherhood, or the one-dimensional portrayals that even the Black community had come to expect from them. The retreat is for simple pleasures also. Myrlie and Betty walk around without makeup. Myrlie washes her hair and lets it go. "No makeup, no nothing, just free."⁵⁵ Betty and Myrlie tease Coretta, ever the glamorous one, for making "herself up so beautifully every day and [sitting] by the pool."⁵⁶ In July 1975, Parker sent Lorde a letter that speaks to these simple yet tender exchanges of sisterhood:

> Also when you write back tell me about your tomatoes. I've been picking blackberries out off my back yard. Had my first pie. Going to try to can some and if I'm successful I'[ll] save some for you.⁵⁷

However, making room in our hearts to love other Black women requires engaging with all the hate we've internalized and unleashed on each other. Though the trio made a pact not to discuss their "jealousies" and "just to be girlfriends," Myrlie persistently broached the subject of their varying experiences with loss. "At least Coretta was spared," Myrlie said, "She and her children were spared seeing her husband and their father shot down."⁵⁸ Although her three children had not witnessed their father's fatal killing as Betty had when she and her two daughters had been seated in the front row of the Audubon ballroom, Medgar's assassination had occurred with his children close by. "They were awake that terrible night, and heard the thunderous roar of the death shot," Myrlie recounted in an *Ebony* article, "Why I Left Mississippi." The children "saw their father lying in a scarlet pool of blood as his life ebbed away" in much the same way Betty's daughters had, although Betty would later insist that she had shielded them from seeing Malcolm with her body.⁵⁹ Coretta had learned of her husband's death by telephone. Myrlie's demarcation of these events matters. We may think of her attention to detail not as an attempt to measure whose experience was worse, but to bring forth the underlying tensions of their friendship and its potential for disrupting their bond. And Betty's response to Myrlie's probing reveals the difficult, tough moments that sisterwork yields. "When we approached that area, Betty would kind of grab on to me, and we knew each other, and we knew each other's pain, well enough that we also knew enough not to push each other into talking about it."⁶⁰ This kind of nurturing, forged from loving each other through what Lorde called the "tenderest winters," fractures the white supremacist images freezing them into perpetual widowhood. During their retreat, a moment between Coretta and Betty momentarily stunned Myrlie. Observing Coretta and Betty enjoying a basketball game on television, she gazes at the pair in awe. Suddenly, she realizes they are no longer bound to the grief-stricken widow image. Heartspace requires making room for holding other Black women's joy too. "We were seeing sides of each other," Myrlie recalls, "because Betty had the spirit that could make you let go."[61]

Sisterwork in the Tenderest Winters

For much of Lorde's life, meaningful connections with Black women eluded her. In her journal, she writes:

> I have looked and looked for the black woman who would really be my mother—who could tell me how the lies we swallowed in the tenderest winters could be toughened and explored and thrown away, who would name me hers and sanction my suffering not by removing it which she could not because it echoed hers, but by reducing it because within lay the key to all our future powers, but by a recognition that would heal the gaps within my strength. Who would recognize me as both proud and loving.[62]

Paradoxically, Lorde's tensions with other Black women spurred her critical investigations into fraught social dynamics. Moreover, the circuitous path she took to carve out a friendship with Parker highlights the generative practice of sisterwork. We may locate this sisterwork in the letters brimming with tenderness but also gritty honesty. The pair do not shy away from confronting the many artificial distances pitting them against each other. To sustain a meaningful connection, Lorde not only addressed the financial disparity between her and Parker, but she also set out to rectify it. After the pair read their poetry at the University of Oregon, Lorde sent a letter dated February 16, 1983:

> The enclosed check is part of what I feel belongs to you as a sister Poet from what I was paid in Europe, given that you did one reading+I did two. It would be more but I also paid for Barbara's transportation.
> I think the financial matters in Europe were handled very badly, altho I'd like to believe it was bad planning rather than any one person being to blame. So this is the only way I can see to try and make sense of it all.
> I feel it is very important, Pat, for you and I to maintain some kind of clarity between us about such matters, financial+otherwise, since I have

the feeling that this is not the only time we have been used against each other in petty ways.⁶³

Lorde, by engaging in the honest practice of acknowledging white supremacist attempts to wedge a divide between the two, avoided playing into or performing for white structures of power. As their friendship deepened, Parker and Lorde navigated each other through the "tenderest winters" of their lives. Over time, their friendship transitioned away from the defensive "Who does this bitch think she is?" to Parker offering Lorde comfort through her cancer diagnosis and mastectomy.

In "For Audre," Parker's touching prose envelops Lorde in a gentle embrace:

> After I read *The Cancer Journals*
> I made love to you
> touched your body-pressed my hands deep into your flesh and passed my warmth to you.
> I kissed the space where your **right** breast had been
> ran my tongue over your body to lick away your fear to lick away my fear.
> I felt jealous
> wanted to be near you and to hold you
> and to sing you songs
> to say I love you you are not alone.⁶⁴

Parker's poem is particularly resonant as she was diagnosed with breast cancer, passing away only two years after Lorde. Their friendship serves as a powerful testimony for employing Black feminist mothering as an ethic of care for resisting systems of oppression.

In the days after Malcolm's murder, Black feminist mothering helped Betty navigate the "tenderest winter" of her life. Although a registered nurse, she had never worked outside the home as Malcolm X would not agree to it.⁶⁵ In his role as minister, Malcolm X earned a meager stipend, but the deeds to their Elmhurst home belonged to the Nation of Islam. Making the situation even more dire, months before his death, Malcolm lost a bitter court battle with the NOI. The judge ruled that evicting the family from the home was the proper and legal course of action. Days before his assassination, the home had been firebombed while the children slept. Now, with Malcolm gone, Betty had no home and no means to financially support her children.

Out of these conditions, Juanita Porter, Ruby Dee, Shirley Graham Dubois, Betty Lomax, and Florence Kennedy consolidated their labors to form the Committee of Concerned Mothers. Working together in what would become the most effective support group for Betty and her children, Poitier chaired the committee, and Kennedy managed the funds flowing into her New York home and post office.[66] That not all members of the committee knew Betty personally emphasizes the sense of responsibility they assumed over her well-being. "It was something we did out of love and passion for the Movement," Ruby Dee said.[67] Care networks embedded in Black communities rely on this maternal labor. In her autobiography *Watch Me Fly: What I Learned on the Way to Becoming the Woman I Was Meant to Be*, Myrlie Evers-Williams describes this system of communal responsibility:

> No one we knew went hungry when I was growing up, and no one went begging. We didn't wait for someone to say, "I need," or "I don't have any food." Through informal visits and quilting parties, information was transmitted organically; no one specifically asked or offered, you simply cooked a pan of cornbread, say, and took it over. When you baked pies, you baked two; if you could only bake one, you took half of it to your neighbor. Likewise, you handed down clothing and shoes. It was a value system I never forgot. Over the years, whenever I've encountered a single mother who is struggling and striving to make something of herself, I've tried to help.[68]

Similarly, the committee employs this brand of sisterwork on behalf of Betty. In ten days, the committee netted $4,000 and then $6,000 more in a few weeks. They continued organizing concerts, swanky affairs held at Poitier's home. These gatherings, attended by Poitier's white neighbors, clergymen, and college students, did not always raise substantial sums of money. However, they did the work of transforming Malcolm X into a modern but perhaps misunderstood philosopher. As Lomax asserted,

> We'd like to see the white American public show some of the compassion for Mrs. Shabazz that they showed in donating sixty thousand dollars to Lee Harvey Oswald's widow. I personally don't consider Malcolm guilty of anything wrong. But nobody, even his detractors, can equate him with Oswald. Yet Marina Oswald is cared for.[69]

In the end, the committee funneled nearly $20,000 toward Betty's purchase of a "large, beautiful home" in Mount Vernon.[70] Spiriting Betty away from the city that claimed Malcolm and several of his followers to the secluded suburban area did not end the harassing phone calls or FBI surveillance, however. But their efforts did provide the much-needed stability for Betty to raise six young children.

In her autobiography, Myrlie would praise this kind of mothering as "one of the most resonant chords in the symphony of my life has been the support of women."[71] Myrlie continues,

> Many of my female friends have discovered this as well. Long after our mothers are gone, we get mothering from one another. We seem to have the power to reach into the deepest parts of our sisters—parts we rarely if ever allow men to see—and find solace in our common threads.[72]

When Betty was badly burned in a house fire, Evers-Williams no doubt offered this mothering to Betty's daughters. Years after Betty's passing, when news of a feud between six siblings reached Coretta, she was so deeply disturbed by it that she worked toward facilitating a reunion among the daughters. These extensions of tenderness by a Civil Rights icon, performed in service to young Black women, show the perseverance of Black women's sisterly bonds. In moving beyond the image of them solely as grieving widows, the trio's political salience to Black female friendship is clear. They gift us with the tools for learning how "to mother ourselves."[73]

Myrlie too offered comfort to Betty when she arrived at the hospital, praying that the Lord would take her so that she did not have to suffer. Although she survived the incident, Betty languished in pain before eventually succumbing to her injuries. Back home after visiting Betty, Myrlie looked at the mountains, her favorite place, and listened to "the sound of the wind blowing, the peace, the quiet, the serenity." Only then was she able to say, "Go, sister, go. It was like I was setting her free in my heart."[74]

Sisterwork's generative potential, long after Betty's and Coretta's passing, sustains another generation. As COVID-19 shuttered businesses around the world, two legendary daughters gathered for a virtual discussion hosted by GirlTREK, a Civil Rights-inspired campaign established to foster "life-saving sisterhood" among Black women.[75] During the nearly two-hour chat, Bernice King offered tender memories of her mother, Coretta Scott King, singing around the house. Recalling her mother's zest for fashion, Ilyasah Shabazz also praised Betty Shabazz for whipping up a mean mashed cauliflower dish. At times, the women sounded eerily similar to their fathers. When asked about gun ownership, Bernice dismissed the use of guns while Ilyasah insisted upon the need for self-defense. However, the bulk of the conversation spotlighted King's and Shabazz's friendship. Over the years, the pair had grown so close, Bernice revealed, that "they could probably look at each other and know what the other one was going through."[76] Celebrating vivid memories of their mothers as three-dimensional figures, Ilyasah and Bernice unseated Betty and Coretta from visual iconographies of mourning. In expressing her gratitude for their friendship, Ilyasah tells Bernice, "I'm so grateful, Bernice, that they had a sisterhood. Along with Myrlie Evers-Williams. They knew they could lean on each other. They knew they could trust each other 100% percent."[77] In a particularly tender response, Bernice shares how troubling Coretta found Betty's untimely death. "I don't know if I told you this but when your mother passed it really affected my mother."[78] In the wake of Betty's passing, Coretta routinely checked in on Betty's daughters, with Ilyasah tenderly referring to her as "Aunt Coretta."

The friendship between Bernice and Ilyasah testifies to the care work forged by their mothers in the wake of tremendous loss compounded by white supremacy's dehumanizing force. Their sisterhood also rewrites the divisive portrayal of their fathers as enemies, diametrically opposed in their struggles. While the private nature of Betty's and Coretta's friendship makes it impossible to know the degree to which they learned to mother each other, humanizing them beyond the role of Civil Rights widows harnesses the political power of Black women's friendship.

Notes

1 Lorde, 145.
2 Lorde, 147.
3 Epstein, Blake, and Gonzalez, 1.
4 Collins, 71.
5 Lorde, 154.
6 Lorde, 154.
7 Lorde, 154.
8 Lorde, 154.
9 Lorde, 157.
10 Lorde, 173.
11 Tindal, 260.
12 "America's Farewell in Anger and Grief."
13 Moneta Sleet: "The great Black photographer you've never heard of."
14 Rickford, 402.
15 Rickford, 402.
16 Rickford, 249.
17 Rickford, 274.
18 Rickford, 259.
19 Evers-Williams, 121.
20 "A Monument to Negro Upheaval: 'Death of Malcolm X and the Resulting Vengeful Gang War.'"
21 Walker King, 16.
22 Rickford, 275.
23 Lorde, 169.
24 Evers-Williams, 121.
25 Rickford, 404.
26 Spillers, 65.
27 Rickford, 404.
28 Rickford, 404.
29 "King's Last March: Black Reaction to King and/or his Death."
30 Rickford, 404.
31 Rickford, 403.

32 Rickford, 404.
33 Rickford, 404.
34 Akil.
35 In the show, thehe fictional Lynn emphasized her biracial identity.
36 Lorde, 153.
37 Parker, 68.
38 Betancourt.
39 De Veaux, 38.
40 Parker, 69.
41 De Veaux, 38.
42 De Veaux, 241.
43 De Veaux, 14.
44 Lorde and Sullivan, 14.
45 Lorde, 173.
46 De Veaux, 169.
47 Rickford, 404.
48 Rickford, 404.
49 Brown, 18.
50 De Veaux, 222.
51 De Veaux, 223.
52 De Veaux, 223.
53 Brown, 18.
54 Brown, 18.
55 Brown, 18.
56 Brown, 18.
57 Sullivan, 44.
58 Brown, 12.
59 "Why I Left Mississippi."
60 Brown, 12.
61 Brown, 12.
62 De Veaux, 127.
63 De Veaux, 59.
64 Parker, 70.
65 Rickford, 406.
66 Rickford, 252.
67 Rickford, 262.
68 Evers-Williams, 135.
69 Rickford, 264.
70 Rickford, 263.
71 Evers-Williams, 36.
72 Evers-Williams, 36.
73 Lorde, 173.
74 Brown, 22.
75 "Dr. Bernice King and Ilyasah Shabazz Live Discussion with GirlTrek."
76 "Dr. Bernice King and Ilyasah Shabazz Live Discussion with GirlTrek."
77 "Dr. Bernice King and Ilyasah Shabazz Live Discussion with GirlTrek."
78 "Dr. Bernice King and Ilyasah Shabazz Live Discussion with GirlTrek."

Bibliography

"A Monument to Negro Upheaval: 'Death of Malcolm X and the Resulting Vengeful Gang War.'" *Life*. 5 March 1965.

"America's Farewell in Anger and Grief." *Life*. 19 April 1968.

Akil, Mara Brock. "Just Say No." *Girlfriends*, Golden Brooks, Jill Marie Jones, Tracee Ellis Ross, Persia White, Season 2, Episode 2, UPN, 2001.

Betancourt, Bianca. *Mara Brock Akil on the Everlasting Influence of Girlfriends*. 11 September 2020. 1 September 2023. https://www.harpersbazaar.com/culture/film-tv/a33970111/mara-brock-akil-influence-of-girlfriends-interview/.

Brown, Jamie Foster. *Betty Shabazz: A Sisterfriend's Tribute in Words and Pictures*. New York: Simon and Schuster, 1998.

Collins, Patricia Hill. *Black Feminist Thought: Knowledge, Consciousness, and the Politics of Empowerment*. New York: Routledge, 2000.

De Veaux, Alexis. *Warrior Poet: A Biography of Audre Lorde*. New York: W. W. Norton, 2004.

Dr. Bernice King and Ilyasah Shabazz Live Discussion with GirlTrek. 2020. 2023. https://www.youtube.com/watch?v=05eewWu2QOY&t=2400s.

Epstein, Rebecca, Jamilia J. Blake, and Thalia Gonzalez. "Girlhood Interrupted: The Erasure of Black Girls' Childhood." Center on Poverty and Inequality: Georgetown Law. 1 March 2023. https://www.law.georgetown.edu/poverty-inequality-center/wp-content/uploads/sites/14/2017/08/girlhood-interrupted.pdf.

Evers-Williams, Myrlie. *Watch Me Fly: What I Learned on the Way to Becoming the Woman I Was Meant to Be*. Boston: Little Brown and Company, 1999.

King's Last March: Black Reaction to King and/or his Death. n.d. 1 March 2023. https://features.apmreports.org/arw/king/c3j.html.

Lorde, Audre, and Jamilah Mecca Sullivan. *Sister Love: The Letters of Audre Lorde and Pat Parker 1974–1989*. Dover: Sinister Wisdom, n.d.

Lorde, Audre. *Sister Outsider*. New York: Crossing P, 2007.

Moneta Sleet: The Great Black Photographer you've Never Heard of. 27 October 2019. 1 October 2023. https://www.bbc.com/news/stories-50186270.

Parker, Pat. "For Audre." *Callaloo*, 2000, pp. 68–72. https://www.jstor.org/stable/3299520.

Rickford, Russell J. *Betty Shabazz: A Remarkable Story of Survival and Faith Before Malcolm X*. Chicago: Sourcebooks, 2003.

Spillers, Hortense. "Mama's Baby, Papa's Maybe: An American Grammar Book." *Diacritics*, 1987, pp. 64–81.

Tindal, Brenda. "Configuring America: Iconic Figures, Visuality, and the American Identity," edited by Rieser, Klaus, Michael Fuchs and Michael Phillips. *Intellect*, 2013. p. 260.

Walker King, Deborah. *African Americans and the Culture of Pain*. Virginia: University of Virginia P, 2008.

"Why I Left Mississippi." *Ebony*. March 1963. https://magazine.pomona.edu/2013/spring/myrlie-evers-williams-68-and-her-time-in-claremont/.

5 I Am Not My Brother's Keeper
Black Women M(o)thering Themselves

Years ago, while teaching an African American literature course in New York, I received a request for a meeting from two of my Black female students. As I made my way across the icy campus to the library, I was slightly nervous. This was my first tenure-track appointment and, like most newly minted PhDs, I worried that my class wasn't progressing as smoothly as it should. Had I put too many readings on the syllabus? Was I moderating class discussions adequately? To my surprise, the young women wanted to discuss the Black male students in the class. We had just wrapped up our discussion on *Their Eyes Were Watching God*. In class, students had been grappling with Hurston's now-famous quote, as in, Nanny's warning to her granddaughter Janie: "De nigger woman is de mule uh de world so fur as Ah can see."[1] A heated discussion ensued, one splintering the class along gender lines. For most of the young Black men, the quote seemed inaccurate, an overblown exaggeration that they waved away as one might a pesky fly. To the Black women in the class, the quote held valuable insight into not only the injustices that they faced but also how Black men contributed to these injustices. Their concerns were largely met with groans and apathy, however. My Black female students wanted strategies for navigating this. "What can we do," they asked, "and why don't they care about us like we care about them?" Their questions cut deeply. Because I had been pondering these same issues, it was difficult for me to answer adequately.

In the same year that I began teaching in New York, Korryn Gaines was shot and killed by the Baltimore police. Her son, 5-year-old Kodi, was close enough for a police officer's bullet to critically injure him. Gaines' murder in her own home with her son as a witness, transpiring only six days before the loss of my son, rocked me. The fact that police officers had known of Kodi's presence in the home yet still proceeded to shoot Gaines further unnerved me. Had they at least thought of protecting his welfare first? From his hospital bed, Kodi recalled a harrowing scene, "They saw me run and they hurt my arm."[2] In my classes, my students, many of them young Black women, invoked Gaines' name often. Complicating their sorrow

DOI: 10.4324/9781032719993-6

This chapter has been made available under a CC-BY-NC-ND license.

was their growing anger at the onslaught of public criticism skewering her as a bad, ignorant mother who got what she deserved. Incredulous, my students asked, "Isn't she like Mike Brown?" In 2014, two years before police killed Gaines, they had watched the Black Lives Matter protests unfold after Darren Wilson killed 18-year-old Michael Brown in Ferguson. Why, they wanted to know, was there so little outrage for Gaines?

This chapter, in some ways, is an attempt to provide my students with a more adequate response. By connecting Black feminist literature of the Black Power Era to contemporary Black feminists addressing the plight of Black girls and women, I resituate the discourse around Gaines as a call for what Christina Sharpe defines as "wake work."[3] Public protests eulogizing the dead operate as "wake work," or rituals of mourning declaring the inherent value of Black life. "How might," Sharpe asks us, "we stay in the wake with those whom the state positions to die ungrievable deaths and live lives meant to be unlivable?"[4] To stay with Gaines "in the wake" is to acknowledge the devaluation of her as an unworthy victim.

Empathy, care, and mercy are often in short supply for Black women and girls. Therefore, in the pages that follow, I explore gendered ideologies of victimhood as a means of providing Gaines, and other Black women and girls, the mercy denied to them in life and death. What these gendered ideologies of victimhood produce is Black patriarchal stealth. For Black men and boys, Black patriarchal stealth is the phenomenon by which an overabundance of concern shields Black men from accountability. My definition of Black patriarchal stealth resists naming the interplay between violence and gender as privilege or power, though Black feminist scholarship has unearthed various configurations of the violence Black women endure at the hands of Black men by lensing it through such terms as Black patriarchy, Black male heteropatriarchy, and Black male privilege.

The utility of patriarchal stealth lies in moving beyond the question of whether Black men may exercise privilege toward examining how Black men's gender affords them a modicum of stealth at Black women's expense. I first diagnose Black patriarchal stealth's function within families and its spawning of a mother wound. Black women's unfulfilled yearnings for reciprocity within our communities create this deep spiritual wounding. In *Crunk Feminist Collection*, Brittney Cooper sums up Black women's fierce but unrequited loyalty and its effects eloquently: "I wish there were more examples of Black men fiercely loving, fiercely defending, and fiercely holding down Black women who didn't carry them in their wombs, but do carry them on their backs sometimes."[5] In seeking to be mothered within the communities that birthed us, we are also seeking to be cherished, to be tended to as one might comfort a child. Therefore, in attending "to Black life and Black death,"[6] this chapter offers Black feminist mothering as the process by which we memorialize Black female lives beyond the headlines.

In the chapter's final sections, I examine Tory Lanez's 2020 shooting of Megan Thee Stallion as a struggle to make visible Black women's pain at the hands of Black men.[7] In exploring the varied dimensions of her initial loyalty to Lanez, I juxtapose Megan's attempt to make visible her victimhood with Zora Neale Hurston's experience of intimate partner violence and her subsequent depiction of it in *Their Eyes Were Watching God*.

Gendered Ideologies of Victimhood

Before she was shot and killed by the police, 23-year-old Korryn Gaines had a pending lawsuit against the Baltimore landlord who owned the two homes she lived in as a child. Gaines described the homes as filled with a "sea of lead" paint in the 2012 lawsuit. Legal documents reveal that the doctor examining Gaines found she displayed "signs of neurocognitive impairment" and "lost significant IQ points as a result of that exposure."[8] The doctor's assessment aligns with the Centers for Disease Control's warnings on lead: "Even low levels of lead in blood are associated with developmental delays, difficulty learning, and behavioral issues." The expansive definition of reproductive justice by the SisterSong Women of Color Reproductive Justice Collective includes "the human right to maintain personal bodily autonomy, have children, not have children, and parent the children we have in safe and sustainable communities," reframing Gaines' lead poisoning as an American reproductive healthcare crisis.[9] One largely ignored because Black children are the primary victims.

While lead paint was banned in 1978, most low-income houses built before the ban have not been upgraded. Black children, according to the CDC, are most at risk precisely because their families tend to live in low-income, affordable housing. Baltimore lawyer and founder of a firm exclusively representing children suffering from lead poisoning, Saul E. Kerpelman confirms, "Nearly 99.9 percent of my clients were Black."[10] Freddie Gray, the 25-year-old Black Baltimore man so violently mishandled by police that they severed his spine filed a lawsuit against former landlords for lead exposure. Gray's exposure to lead began early. At just 22 months old, his blood tests revealed elevated levels of lead, which would signal the impending behavioral and cognitive crisis befalling not only him but his twin sister too.[11] In his 2009 deposition, Gray noted that his sister, Fredericka, struggled with aggression: "She still got problems like that. She still do. She always was the aggressive one. She liked to fight all the time and all of that."[12] Like his twin sister, Gray's exposure to lead had a disastrous impact on his education: "All the schools that I went to, I was in special education."[13] His frequent absences and suspensions no doubt affected his ability to graduate.

Gray and Gaines, linked together through their untimely deaths at the hands of police officers and childhood exposure to lead, reveal the degree to which reproductive violence converges on the bodies of Black boys and girls. Their exposure to lead paint may be understood as one of the many "slow deaths" blocking Black girls and boys from becoming healthy, self-actualized adults. But despite the state's clear interference in their lives, exposing both Gray and Gaines to premature death, dying, and disease, only one could be mourned as a victim.

In the wake of Gaines' murder, social media users took to the platform formerly known as Twitter to blame Gaines for her own death. Some accused Gaines of deliberately putting her son in harm's way. A smattering of tweets reflected the general apathy with which the public regarded Gaines: "It's looking mighty justifiable right now." "Korryn Gaines deserved to die." "She decided to be reckless with her son and her own life."[14] This marked apathy for Gaines during the Black Lives Matter era was significant on two levels. One, Twitter had been instrumental in rallying protesters to action in the early hours of Darren Wilson's shooting of Michael Brown, the 18-year-old unarmed Black boy from Ferguson, Missouri. Black social media users from all over America connected with each other to mobilize their outrage after Ferguson residents shared video of Brown's body lying in the road for hours after his death. My own knowledge of Twitter's efficacy for organizing protest rallies occurred after George Zimmerman's 2012 killing of Trayvon Martin. When I learned from Twitter—not local media as they had not yet even picked up the story—that no charges had been filed, I joined a group of local activists to travel from Fort Lauderdale to Sanford, Florida. At least half of the people in attendance, all of whom I had not met before, had made connections with me on Twitter in the wake of Trayvon's killing.

The second, more troubling, aspect of the criticism aimed at Gaines is that the harshest rebukes came from mostly Black men. Journalist and editor Bené Viera took to her personal blog to observe that "all black lives are not mourned equally." In "For Colored Girls Like Korryn Gaines and the Black Men Who Hate Us," Viera marveled at the speed with which "Black men will adopt the language of our oppressors to blame her for her own murder."[15] The flood of criticism aimed at Gaines may be best understood as a symbolic tug-of-war over the right to claim the victim label and the marshaling of resources and emotional labor that come with it. This last point is crucial since her perceived negative image impeded the public from engaging in wake work.

At play here is the slanted perception of victimhood toward a decidedly male purview. Prevailing images of Black men as an "endangered species" emerged in the 1970s, with Black men magnifying their plight through liberation organizations like the Black Panther and Black Liberation Army. The "endangered species" narrative took shape as an effective political strategy. When Howard professor Justine Rector established the African

American Male Resource Center, her central mission was "to bring to the attention of the public the plight of the Black male in America."[16] In 1978, while holding a conference on issues specifically addressing Black men, Rector promoted the event with flyers featuring the heading, "Black Males, An Endangered Species?"[17]

The flyer spelled out the issues impacting Black men in a lengthy list: lower life expectancies, higher homicide rates, lung cancer, and prison

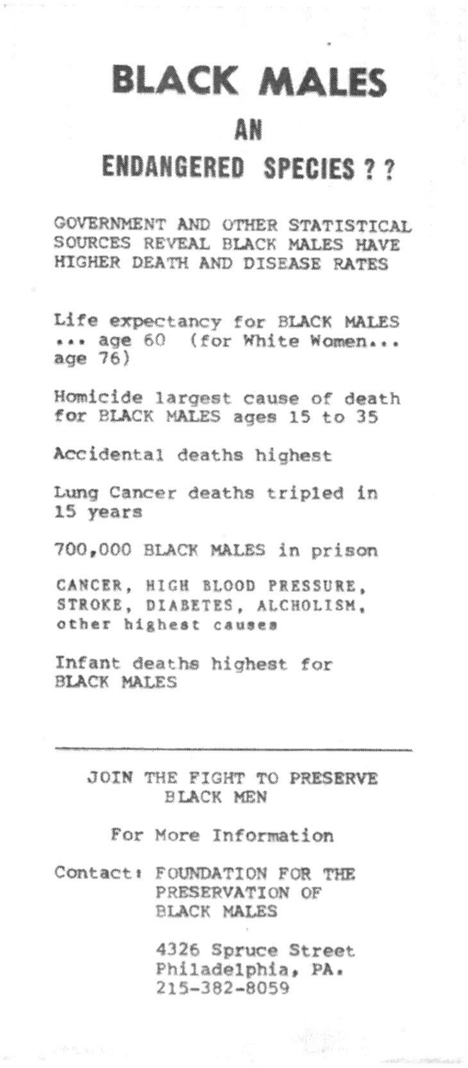

BLACK MALES

AN
ENDANGERED SPECIES ? ?

GOVERNMENT AND OTHER STATISTICAL
SOURCES REVEAL BLACK MALES HAVE
HIGHER DEATH AND DISEASE RATES

Life expectancy for BLACK MALES
... age 60 (for White Women...
age 76)

Homicide largest cause of death
for BLACK MALES ages 15 to 35

Accidental deaths highest

Lung Cancer deaths tripled in
15 years

700,000 BLACK MALES in prison

CANCER, HIGH BLOOD PRESSURE,
STROKE, DIABETES, ALCHOLISM,
other highest causes

Infant deaths highest for
BLACK MALES

JOIN THE FIGHT TO PRESERVE
BLACK MEN

For More Information

Contact: FOUNDATION FOR THE
PRESERVATION OF
BLACK MALES

4326 Spruce Street
Philadelphia, PA.
215-382-8059

Figure 5.1 1978 Flyer Listing Various Statistics Concerning African American Men

incarceration rates. At the bottom, the call for action further entrenched the image of Black men as a steadily declining population with the capitalized words, "JOIN THE FIGHT TO PRESERVE BLACK MEN." Although Rector's flyer and other calls to mobilize for Black men amplified the troubling impact of race-based oppression on Black men's lives, their heightened visibility as chief victims of structural oppression has, for decades now, dwarfed other pressing issues within the fight for Black liberation.

In movement spaces, the sloganeering rhetorical power of depicting Black men as endangered resurfaced in the Black Panther Party. Centering the image of the black leopard due to its rare, endangered species designation, the Party tethered Black male identity to that of the perpetually oppressed while simultaneously obscuring the violent interplay of Black men staking claim over Black women's bodies. In 1974, this would become a chief point of contention between Black Panther Minister of Defense Huey P. Newton and Black Panther Chairwoman Elaine Brown. In the same year that Newton fled murder charges in America and traveled to Cuba for a years-long self-exile, he selected Brown as Chairwoman of the Black Panther Party. Her leadership of the Party proved successful, including her political inroads to broadening the Party's legislative legitimacy, strengthening Black neighborhoods with Black Panther-oriented schools, and increasing financial gains. However, in her autobiography *A Taste of Power*, Brown recalls the men rankling at Newton's embrace of an egalitarian model of leadership: "A gang had formed at Huey's door and called him out. Nobody said it, but it was understood that the Panther was a man."[18] Gendering the panther mirrors the defensive masculinist stance championing armed resistance and is prominently displayed in the organization's promotional materials.

Posters of Newton seated in a rattan throne-like chair while holding a shotgun in his right hand and a spear in his left hand reinforced armed resistance as the primary form of revolutionary struggle—despite the Black Panther Party's numerous welfare programs promoting mutual aid and communal activism. Directly beneath Newton's outstretched foot was a small image of a black panther, with the accompanying text: "The racist dog policemen must withdraw immediately from our communities, cease their wanton murder and brutality and torture of black people, or face the wrath of the armed people." In *A Taste of Power*, Brown alludes to the infamous photograph, portraying Black male Party members' anger as a result of "Huey's postexile pronouncements that he was not climbing back into his poster image."[19] Not only had Newton relinquished this "poster image" of virulent masculinity but he had also handed over the reins of the kingdom to a Black woman. The men regarded this decision as a betrayal. And they set out to test the limits of Brown's reach by carrying out brutal acts of physical abuse against female members.

106 Black Feminist Mothering in 21st Century Literature

Figure 5.2 Huey P. Newton Seated in a Rattan Chair, Holding a Gun and Spear

As the rising dissatisfaction among male members reached a fever pitch, men in the Party brutally beat a female assistant so severely that they broke her jaw. For Brown, the beating was not an anomaly; it was a homosocial rallying point. "The beating of Regina would be taken as a clear signal that the words 'Panther' and 'comrade' had taken on gender connotations, denoting an inferiority in the female half of us," Brown writes.[20] At its core then, the refusal to see Black women as victims may be understood as a unifying practice cementing Black male constructions of identity.

If we begin to consider the organizing principle for Black male identity formation as bound up and tied to gendered oppression, then we may also conceive of the process as producing a kind of Black patriarchal stealth, positioning Black boys and men as the most deserving of support, mercy, and emotional labor.

Often, Black women's first encounter with Black patriarchal stealth begins in girlhood. Not until reading Alice Walker's *In Search of Our Mothers' Gardens* as an undergraduate college student did I register the family as a type of cocoon, shielding Black boys from accountability. Walker's 1983 text, with its blend of essays, speeches, poetry, and memoir, gave me the language for naming the gender imbalances within my own family. My awakening came while reading a pivotal scene near the end of the text. Notably, Walker returns to her girlhood to tell the story of how she lost sight in her right eye.

> Then my parents decide to buy my brothers guns. These are not "real" guns. They shoot "BBs," copper pellets my brothers say will kill birds. Because I am a girl, I do not get a gun. Instantly I am relegated to the position of Indian. Now there appears a great distance between us.[21]

The game positions a young Alice as an outsider within—a gun-less Indian defending herself against gun-toting cowboys. Her parents' refusal to equip Alice with a BB gun widens the "great distance" between her and her siblings. In fact, this widening creates the perfect circumstances for her brothers to perceive her as weak and defenseless. An easy target. *A girl*. Her brothers, indeed, already taking on the role of conquerors, are poised to test the limits of their authority. One day, while playing, Alice feels an "incredible blow" in her eye and looks "down just in time to see my brother lower his gun."[22] In her retelling, Walker repeatedly characterizes the loss of sight in her eye as an "accident." Her use of quotation marks, however, implicitly challenges her brothers' actions as an innocent mistake. Even more troubling, her parents' response opens Alice up to further injury. Alice develops a high fever, for which her dad wraps lily leaves around her head to break it. Her mother attempts to feed Alice soup. But even after learning of what happened, her parents let a week pass before they took the young girl to the doctor. The delay vexes the doctor precisely because it places Alice's eyes at further risk. "Why did you wait so long to come?" he asks, looking into my eyes and shaking his head. "Eyes are sympathetic ... if one is blind, the other will likely become blind too."[23] That her parents do not act swiftly diminishes her body to that of a testing ground. For their part, her brothers measure their concern for her through her ability to assist them in skirting accountability. And in their immediate attempts to coax Alice into saying that she stepped on a piece of wire, they further subjugate her. Even as her eye fills with blood, they say, "If you tell we will get a whipping. You don't want that to happen, do you?"[24] Here, Alice learns a profound lesson: Becoming a woman may well mean surrendering ourselves to becoming a perpetual daughter, responsible for laboring on behalf of the community and Black boys and men. That there is no mention of Walker's parents doling out any repercussions for her brothers is a curious omission—one instantly unlocking a core memory of mine.

My three older brothers had not experienced any consequences from my parents when they, tasked with babysitting me, "wrestled" with me. For what felt like an eternity, my brothers practiced all the "wrestling moves" we had seen our father watch on television: slamming me against the floor, elbowing me, and jerking me every other way. When my body grew hot and my eyes felt like they might burst, I managed to climb on top of the couch to become taller than them to scream for them to stop. They laughed. "Her eyes are so red," one brother observed. They stopped only when the blood began oozing down my scalp.

I did not think of the incident again until the summer of 1999, the same year Lionel Tate brutally murdered 6-year-old Tiffany Eunick in his mother's South Florida home.[25] I was in high school at the time. Because it was a local story, my friends and I occasionally discussed it in class. At home, my family and I often engaged in heated discussions about the particulars of the case and how the 12-year-old boy had not noticed something wrong with the little girl he had killed only 30 minutes away from our home. During Tate's trial, defense attorneys argued that he was simply copying wrestling moves he had seen on television and, therefore, since he did not intend to hurt Tiffany, he should not be held accountable for her death. Her cracked skull, broken rib, lacerated liver, hemorrhaged kidneys, brain bleed, and dozens of other injuries were simply evidence. They had played a game that had gotten a bit out of hand. At home, while my family and I spoke about Tate's guilt, we did not, even when he was convicted, mention the time my brothers "wrestled" with me. Or the fact that I was only a year or two older than Tiffany when she died.

The next time I hear of a Black girl being killed by boys babysitting her, I am a mother. The story of 3-year-old Blessing Buckles is forever etched into my mind.[26] Twenty-four years after Tiffany's murder, she enters the news stream as a victim killed by two young boys in charge of taking care of her. Like Tiffany, Blessing endured injuries so severe that the bleeding on her brain and bruising to her face and body were consistent with blunt force trauma. This time, however, paramedics were only able to briefly resuscitate her. Blessing died from her injuries on February 14, 2024.

At one level, the loss of Blessing and Tiffany points toward a diminished social safety net and the failure of the state government in assisting caregivers with affordable childcare options so that young boys are not tasked with caring for even younger children. On another level, though their deaths have largely faded from the mainstream, excused away as unfortunate accidents by society at large, Blessing and Tiffany indicate the parasitical gendered hierarchies at play within Black family dynamics.

Black feminist writers sounded the alarm on these toxic familial structures as early as the 1970s. Activist and author Toni Cade Bambara's *The Black Woman: An Anthology*, released during the height of the Black Power Era, notes in the introduction that the new wave of voices tackle "the relationship between Black men and women, with the revolutionary Black women of the current period, with the Black abolitionists, with the whole question of Black schools."[27] Compiled works from Black women across the country, the anthology's varied list of contributors, ranging from Audre Lorde, Nikki Giovanni, Verta Mae Smart-Grosvenor, and Alice Walker, spotlight the *The Black Woman* as a time capsule of sorts, an archive preserving the most compelling voices on the Black liberation struggle. Unsurprisingly, a consistent point of critique for contributors is the family unit. For poet Kaye Lindsey, the family operated as a staging ground preparing Black girls for their eventual sexual and economic exploitation precisely because

> it is immediately within the bosom of one's family that one learns to be female and all that the term implies. Although our families may have taken a somewhat different form from that of whites, the socialization that was necessary to maintain the state was carried out.[28]

Writing nearly a decade after the chorus of Black women in Bambara's anthology, Michele Wallace characterized the family as a "torture chamber designed to oppress and repress women."[29] As her controversial *Black Macho and the Myth of the Superwoman* was widely panned as a vengeful, solipsistic creed, particularly against Black men, the more salient observations of her argument have been overlooked. Today, with hindsight and time, *Black Macho* emerges, as Jamilah Lemieux asserts in the 2015 Foreword, articulating the depths of Black girl pain and its ontological origins within the family.

As so much of the literature produced during the Black Power Era stages the family as a space in which Black girls cannot survive whole, the literature of the era is primed for examining the degree to which Black patriarchal stealth produces a mother wound. Engaging Black women and men as mirror images of each other highlights the gendered hierarchies at play. In Toni Morrison's 1977 novel, *Song of Solomon*, she engages Black women and men as mirror images of each other to underscore these gendered hierarchies at play. There is no doubt that Milkman, the titular character, is made whole by the women around him. At the novel's start, he is an uncertain, unsteady man-child who has stretched his boyhood out to 33 years. Each woman in his life—from his mother to his aunt—propels him toward self-actualization. Early critics of the coming-of-age novel did not shy away from hinging Milkman's growth on "the fluid constellations of black women loving him, supporting him, guiding him and even rejecting him."[30] Reflecting on her writing process during a 1988 interview, Morrison contextualized the novel as an examination into the relationships among Black men and women.

> I'm interested also in the relationships of black men and black women and the axes on which those relationships frequently turn, and how they complement each other, fulfill one another or hurt one another and are made whole or prevented from wholeness by things that they have incorporated into their psyche.[31]

If Morrison registers Black men's nurturing through Milkman's relationships with women, then it is through Hagar that she centers Black women's unmet need for communal recognition. Lovelorn and long-suffering, Hagar endures under the weight of Milkman's apathetic disregard for her. For him, she is "the third beer, the one you drink not because you want it but because it's there."[32] Their toxic relationship, evidenced by Hagar's desire to kill Milkman after she sees him with another woman, becomes a euphemism for the shaky coalitions Black men and women managed to build during the height of the Black Power Era.

As if to illustrate this, Morrison presents Milkman and Hagar's relationship as not only toxic but incestuous, as they are second cousins. What their incestuous bond seems to expose is Morrison's tacit critique of the Black Power Era's mobilizing of familial rhetoric hailing Black women as "sisters" to their "brothers." In her contribution to Bambara's anthology in "Dear Black Men," Fran Sanders questioned the familial use of "sister" and "brother" as a greeting. After being street-harassed by a Black man, who first greets her with "Hey soul-sister" and then immediately threatens to shoot her if she does not acknowledge him quickly enough next time, Sanders asserts, "I am not, and have never been a sister to any man except my brother, Danny, and feel that the whole thing is about to go too far."[33] Beneath the "soul-sister" greeting, Sanders suspected hostility lurked there. "Talk to me like the woman I am and not to me as that woman who is the inanimate creation of someone's overactive imagination," she writes.[34] Her rejection of Black Power Era language underscores the use of the family as a tool for imposing strict loyalty codes upon Black women. The intimacy of the moment—the man's use of soul-sister and his subsequent degradation of Sanders' afro hairstyle as an indication that she should have responded immediately to his greeting because of it—renders Black men's abuse as a wound capable of cutting so deeply precisely because of our shared heritage and culture.

Indeed, in *Song of Solomon*, the internecine strife between Hagar and Milkman eradicates any chance for unity. Milkman's rejection of Hagar represents a wholesale repudiation of her gendered Blackness, one rooted in her not having the "right" skin tone, hair type, and features. Dying, quite literally, from a lack of love, Hagar pleads with her mother and grandmother for understanding, "Why don't he like my hair?" Though Pilate insists that "he got to love it" since it's "the same hair" growing "out of his own armpits," Hagar dies convinced that Milkman does not love her because she does not have silky, "penny-colored hair," "lemon-colored skin," and "gray-blue eyes."[35] Her death, precipitated by a descent into temporary madness, explicitly critiques the community's inability to extend care her way even as Milkman, her male equivalent, soars to unfettered heights. "While he dreamt of flying, Hagar was dying."[36] It would not be an exaggeration, however, to say that all the women in the novel are dying. Pilate, Milkman's guiding light, is shot down by another Black man—one she cared for and fed as a boy. But it is through Hagar that Morrison reveals the depths of the mother wound. Hagar "needed what most colored girls needed: a chorus of mamas, grandmamas, aunts, cousins, sisters, neighbors, Sunday school teachers, best girlfriends, and what all to give her the strength life demanded of her—and the humor with which to live it."[37] Lacking this intracommunal support, Hagar is felled by a community withholding tenderness from Black girls most in need of it.

The Politics of Refusal, or Toward a Language of Care

In the wake of our community's failure to wrap its arms around Black women and girls, healing this mother wound is possible when engaging in the process of finding "the words that will articulate care."[38] Today, Black women striving to articulate for themselves and Black girls "a language of care" have begun advancing a politics of refusal. On its surface, this politics of refusal is often dismissed as cold, selfish, and harmful to the revolutionary struggle itself. Take, for instance, Kimberly Nicole Foster's 2014 opinion piece, "Why I Will Not March for Eric Garner." The article, published shortly after Daniel Pantaleo put Eric Garner in an illegal chokehold as he repeatedly told officers, "I can't breathe," sparked a round of heated intracommunal debates. In it, Foster admitted that while "images of murdered black men haunt my thoughts ... I am reserving my mental and emotional energy for the women, the Black women, no one will speak for."[39] Here, Foster struck out against the enshrining of Black women's labor as a boundless resource for the movement. However, she was chided, by Black men and women, for her seemingly cruel and careless position. Some felt it was simply not the time to articulate such thoughts in the wake of Garner's untimely passing. Others pointed out that Garner had left behind daughters. What the public furor over Foster's article reveals, however, is the presumption of Black women's labors as a limitless resource. The links

Foster makes to her own emotional labors emphasize the degree to which the Black liberation struggle pivots on Black maternal care work.

Imagined and implemented largely by Black women, this kind of maternal care work surfaces in the rent strikes organized by Afeni Shakur to secure housing for Black residents in the South Bronx and Harlem. Black maternal labor, implemented by Assata Shakur's coordination of the Free Breakfast for Children program, is one of the most tangible indicators of the lingering success of the Black Power Era. In disadvantaged communities today, Black women marching, organizing, and protesting highlight "wake work" as the unpaid labor performed on behalf of the slain no longer among us. Through the lens of Christina Sharpe's "wake work," these communal performances of mourning seek to "sound an ordinary note of care" for Black people living and dead.[40]

However, the toll that "wake work" takes on those advocating for the lost is rarely discussed. Years before becoming a mother, I attended a local bus ride from Fort Lauderdale to Sanford, Florida, for Trayvon Martin.[41] The 16-year-old boy from Miami seemed familiar to me in the sense that he could have been my brother, except he had been killed by George Zimmerman, an overzealous neighborhood watchman, on his way back from the store. As the details of Trayvon's killing trickled out, my rage intensified. Tracy Martin, Trayvon's father, was only notified of his son's murder after filing a missing person's report, even though Trayvon was shot in his father's complex. George Zimmerman had not been arrested. On the four-hour bus ride to Sanford, I had a sense of hope as we steeled ourselves for whatever awaited us by listening to Curtis Mayfield's "People Get Ready." In Sanford, my hope shifted to a crushing sense of dread. I could not escape the feeling that despite our chants of "No Justice, No Peace," George Zimmerman would walk free among us—free to terrorize another kid. After news of his acquittal broke, I could not speak.

Now, I understand that the weight of history extinguished me that day. In Sanford, a town less than 30 minutes from Eatonville, I understood how out of place a kid from Miami must have felt walking to the store. I had felt it marching down the streets as the residents stood outside the storefronts, gawking at us with a kind of ancient hate. I had not known it then but sensed that the ancient hate was the kind that killed Harry T. Moore and Harriette V. Moore, the couple murdered by the Ku Klux Klan who tossed a firebomb into their home.[42] Sanford was still drenched in their blood, and you could feel it. Mourning our dead takes a psychological toll—an element of "wake work" not often discussed. Even less attention is paid to the emotional burdens "wake work" places on Black women gathering and organizing protests for slain Black women and girls when so few show up to #SayHerName. In 2014, the African American Policy Forum and Center for Intersectionality and Social Policy Studies launched the #SayHerName campaign to bring "awareness to the often invisible names and stories of Black women and girls who have been victimized by racist police violence, and provides support to their families."[43] For Black women involved in the liberation struggle, this "wake work" may feel as if we are witnessing our own loss.

Thus, lodged in the dissent for Foster's article was her explicit withdrawal of care as an automatic service to be paid out to Black men. In expressing her decision to redirect her labor, she articulated the painful wounding that these unbalanced dynamics caused: "I could not refrain from comparing the empathy shown him, particularly by Black men, to that which is heartbreakingly absent when Black women attempt to discuss the everyday terrors we experience both in the world and at their hands."[44] In the Black Lives Matter era, Black women's unrequited labor has tipped toward a growing sense of disillusionment. In recent years, the predominance of Black women-led protests and the virtual erasure of Black women's victimhood from public concern have widened the gaps between Black men and women in ways too difficult to ignore.

In the online spaces where Black women mobilize for social change, social worker and writer Feminista Jones amplified these concerns with the #YouOKSis? hashtag on the platform formerly known as Twitter.[45] Spurred by noticing a man harassing a young woman pushing a stroller, Jones intervened and asked the woman, "You OK Sis?" As a challenge to street harassment, the #YouOKSis hashtag outlined Black women's unique oppression as targets of state and gender-based violence. The hashtag drew attention to the ways in which street harassment operates as a male bonding ritual even as it encodes Black girls' and women's bodies as accessible. In many ways, then, Foster and Jones were involved in the project of recuperating Black women's humanity—their varied approaches reflecting larger social justice attempts to increase Black women's visibility as victims of gender-based violence. We may think of how this labor, in grappling with Black women's vulnerability as both victims of police and gender-based violence, requires re-thinking our investment in Black liberation movements. This too is "wake work."[46] In addressing the thornier, complex issue of "internecine strife" within our communities, Black women assert our right to mother ourselves, defending ourselves against anyone preventing access to healthy, oppression-free lives.

I Am Not My Brother's Keeper: Black Women Mothering Ourselves

In 2020, Megan Thee Stallion's public plight for justice called attention to what Moya Bailey defines as misogynoir or the "vexing crossroads" Black women find themselves at when we are "hyper-visible in media through misogynoir and invisible when in need of life-saving attention."[47] Shortly after leaving a house party in Hollywood Hills and climbing into an SUV, the Houston rapper began arguing with fellow rapper and friend-turned-enemy Tory Lanez. The heated discussion between the two quickly soured, with Lanez calling Megan and her friend Kelsey "bitches and hos."[48] In response, Megan chided him for his less-than-stellar musical career. Although peers, Megan cast a much larger net of success than Lanez had and in a much shorter time span. By 2020, she had become something of a rap darling, collaborating with industry heavyweights like Nicki Minaj and Beyoncé. She had not yet cinched a Grammy Award for Best New Artist and Best Rap Song at the time of the shooting. However, the viral sensation of her hit song "Hot Girl Summer" as a catchphrase secured her mainstream chart-topping success. Lanez enjoyed nominal success, whereas Megan's star was rising, and his was likely fading. Therefore, Lanez firing at Megan as she exited the vehicle signaled an attempt to also reclaim rap as the exclusive territory of men. Violence as a symbolic tool of territorial power has long been wielded by men in the rap industry.

Dr. Dre's 1991 brutal beating of television host Dee Barnes followed an interview she conducted with bandmate-turned-rival Ice Cube for the popular rap series, *Pump It Up*. In recalling the harrowing details of the attack at an album release party in L.A., Barnes remembers Dre picking her up and "slamming her face and the right side of her body repeatedly against a wall near the stairway."[49] Yet the staggering difference between Barnes' and Dr. Dre's versions of events exposes Black patriarchal stealth's conversion of the abuser to that of a victim:

> People talk all this shit, but you know, somebody fuck with me, I'm gonna fuck with them. I just did it, you know. Ain't nothing you can do now by talking about it. Besides, it ain't no big thing—I just threw her through a door.[50]

To shrink such a heinous act into "no big thing" requires that Dr. Dre mobilize the language of spontaneity to portray his beating of Barnes as a sporadic, one-off occurrence. His "ain't no big thing" obscures not only the savage details of the beating but also the many other women he physically abused in a similar fashion. In this way, his beating of Barnes appears less an indication of his larger investment in pervasive systems of dominance over women and more a momentary lapse in judgment for which he need not apologize. Social constructions of Black men's violence as spontaneous eruptions stave off engagement with gender-based violence as the pervasive force shortening Black women's lives.

Wielding this kind of Black patriarchal stealth allows violent Black men to escape accountability by foregrounding Black masculinity as unassailable. In the aftermath of the Lanez shooting, Black male rappers struck a similar note. They ridiculed, questioned, or outright denied that Megan had been shot. Although 50 Cent would later apologize, the retired rapper shared an Instagram meme riffing on the *Boyz in the Hood* scene to depict Megan running away from Lanez as he aimed his gun at her from the passenger side of a car. In his "Circo Loco" song, rapper Drake sprinkled seeds of doubt onto Megan's version of events, rapping a line alluding to both the shooting and plastic surgery: "This bitch lie 'bout gettin' shots, but she still a stallion."[51] Legendary Houston rapper Bun B's public defense of Megan, in which he denounced Lanez by insisting Houston "would have rode" for Megan, was one of the few vocal displays publicly defending Megan. Most of her male peers, even those she had collaborated with previously, were largely silent. Even Lanez's 2022 conviction of assault with a semiautomatic firearm, discharging a firearm with gross negligence, and carrying a loaded unregistered firearm in a vehicle—and the subsequent 10-year prison sentence—did not stop rappers like Fivio Foreign and The Game from proclaiming Lanez's innocence. Despite aerial footage capturing a visibly pained Megan hobbling from the truck, hands raised at the command of the Los Angeles Police Department with blood trickling down her feet and trailing onto the sidewalk, she was not seen as a victim.

To better contextualize Lanez's shooting of Megan Thee Stallion, returning to the difficult paths Black women tread before us yields crucial insight. Because Zora Neale Hurston's experience with intimate partner violence served as her inspiration for *Their Eyes Were Watching God*, the novel and Hurston's creative process behind the novel serve as one of the most culturally relevant tools for mining gendered ideologies of victimhood, Black patriarchal stealth, and misogynoir. In her 1942 autobiography, *Dust Tracks on a Road*, she describes a volatile romance with a man referred to only as P.W.P. Loving him for his ability to stand "firmly on his own two feet," Hurston observes that whenever literary events and business affairs called for her attendance, P.W.P. would fall into a sulking mood, "and then he would make me unhappy."[52] Tellingly, she does not reveal what he would do to make her unhappy. But Hurston does reveal her lover's list of demands: give up writing, marry him, and leave New York. At his insistence that she abandon her writing career, Hurston writes, "I really wanted to do anything he wanted me to, but that one thing I could not do."[53] P.W.P's manipulative tactics—his seeking to isolate her from friends and community in New York—reflect typical abuser dynamics. Yet, Hurston, when recalling his abuse against her, portrays herself as the chief actor in the abuse. Not only does she admit to slapping him in a fit of jealousy, but she then goes on to portray P.W.P's hitting of her in ambiguous terms. On one level, she implies that his beating of her was severe, "He paid me off then and there with interest."[54] On another level, Hurston downplays the violence in the very next sentence, "No broken bones, you understand, and no black eyes."[55] Early biographers and critics immediately picked up on the contradictions in Hurston's autobiography. Mary Helen Washington defines Hurston's *Dust Tracks* as a "study in the art of subterfuge."[56] Kathleen Davies argues that the "doubleness" of the text speaks to the difficult position Hurston occupied as a Black woman writer in the 1930s, putting to paper the "things clawing inside of [her] that must be said."[57] In grappling with the varied contours of Black women's dilemma as victims of racism and sexism, Hurston exposes Black women's divided loyalties along race and gender lines. "Anticipating racist appropriation of a Black woman's description of abuse by a Black man," Davies argues, "she can both tell what happened and protect the Black man."[58] That Hurston—a woman who once responded to a man's unwanted advances by coldcocking him "with a roundhouse right that left him sprawled on the elevator floor"—felt compelled to protect her ex-lover's image before the public renders Black women's predicament more clearly. Though Hurston wrote her autobiography over 100 years ago, her desire to protect her ex-lover parallels the very real conundrum facing Megan Thee Stallion. That is, Megan initially resisted telling police officers the truth about what happened the night she was shot because of the immense pressure to protect Black men.

Days after the shooting, Megan expressed a desire to "spare" Lanez from criminal prosecution.[59] As Megan later testified, her hesitancy to give police the full story stemmed from concerns about police violence against Black people.

> I didn't want them to kill any of us, or shoot any of us. So I just said I stepped on glass. For some reason, I was just trying to protect all of us, because I didn't want them to kill us. Even though this person just did this to me, my first reaction still was to try to save us. I didn't want to see anybody die.[60]

Megan's initial decision to tell detectives that she had not known Lanez shot her implicates our collective traditions conditioning Black women to shield Black men from accountability even when our lives are in jeopardy. The price for telling the truth is quick vilification by the community at large. As Barnes later explained when discussing her treatment by the public:

> Women survivors of violence are expected neither to be seen nor heard, and the pressure increases when it involves celebrities. No one wants to see their heroes criticized. And if they are African American, the community at large becomes suspicious of an underlying motive to tear down a successful Black man.[61]

Therefore, the haste with which Black men mobilized a defense of Lanez reflects the homosocial bonding rituals arising from Black women's abuse.

I Am Not My Brother's Keeper 117

As in *Their Eyes Were Watching God*, the men band together at Janie's trial for shooting Tea Cake in self-defense, becoming as united as "a choir" with "the top parts of their bodies moved on the rhythm of it."[62] To condemn Janie, the Black men in the community gather in the courthouse and paint a portrait of Tea Cake so at odds with his previous treatment of Janie:

> Tea Cake was a good boy. He had been good to that woman. No nigger woman ain't never been treated no better. Naw suh! He worked like a dog for her and nearly killed himself saving her in the storm, then soon as he got a little fever from the water, she had took up with another man. Sent for him to come there from way off. Hanging was too good. All they wanted was a chance to testify.[63]

Black men defending Lanez is the means by which he becomes a victim, a symbol of an endangered Black man even as Megan's path toward victimhood is blocked. In *Their Eyes Were Watching God*, Hurston depicts the community's fawning response to Tea Cake's violence as a kind of disease that spreads from the women to the men:

> Everybody talked about it next day in the fields. It aroused a sort of envy in both men and women. The way he petted and pampered her as if those two or three face slaps had nearly killed her made the women see visions and the helpless way she hung on him made men dream dreams.[64]

Once again, Tea Cake's reasoning for beating Janie portrays him as a victim with a bruised ego employing violence spontaneously because he had to do it. He tells the men,

> Ah didn't wants whup her last night, but ol' Mis' Turner done sent for her brother tuh come tuh bait Janie in and take her way from me. Ah didn't whup Janie "cause she done nothin." Ah beat her tuh show dem Turners who is boss.[65]

His decision, calculated and methodical, comes after overhearing Mrs Turner disparage his darker skin and lower social class. However, even today, scholars still tend to use love to define the fraught relationship between Janie and Tea Cake. In "Love in Hurston's Art and Life," Patterson situates her article as an examination of the "power of love to both liberate and suffocate Black women's lives and sensibilities."[66] Bealer argues that the "story arc of Janie and Tea Cake's courtship and marriage suggests that Tea Cake is both Janie's 'great and selfless love' and susceptible to the 'diverse nuances' that 'destroy' romantic relationships between African

Americans."⁶⁷ Some of this is due to Hurston's successful shrouding of Tea Cake's abuse in a romanticized lens. In fact, when I first encountered *Their Eyes Were Watching God* in high school and then again in college, I do not recall either my teacher or professor paying much attention to Tea Cake's abuse. We often discussed the novel through the lens of a love story. Once I began teaching the text, I would pose a question to my students: "Can love exist in the presence of abuse?" The simple question typically spurs discussions on how Hurston seems to point out the structural underpinnings of systemic, pervasive abuse in the lives of Black women. Its development first as a "brainstorm" in the mind of Tea Cake, then a fully realized event that goes unchecked by an entire community championing it, implicates Black men's protective shielding from accountability as an endemic force thwarting Black women's claims for justice.

When Megan testified against Lanez, she called out the presence of this "boys club" in hip hop as one of the main reasons she knew that public support would be withheld as she was "telling on one y'all's friend."⁶⁸ Tearfully confessing to the jury, Megan explained how the consequences of public scorn contributed to her suicidal thoughts, "I don't wanna be on this Earth. I wish he would have shot and killed me if I knew I would go through this torture."⁶⁹ Her positioning of the rap industry as a boys' club and her ostracism within it as a "torture" worse than the shooting itself reveals the psychological toll that patriarchal codes impose upon Black women. Echoes of her confession surface in *Their Eyes Were Watching God*. As Janie stands trial for the self-defense shooting of Tea Cake, she thinks, "It was not death she feared. It was misunderstanding."⁷⁰ Like Megan, Janie understands that the boys' club prevents her from being seen as a victim. We may think of the community's refusal to mourn with either woman as further entrenching the mother wound. It is, as Hurston describes, "a mass cruelty."⁷¹

Healing the Mother Wound

In the opening pages of *Their Eyes Were Watching God*, Janie's return to Eatonville is anything but triumphant. Gone is her fancy dress. Instead, the overalls she now wears symbolize her working alongside Tea Cake down in the Everglades. And Tea Cake? He is gone too. His death has transformed her into a woman content to seek her own company. Janie returns, after shooting her lover in self-defense, as a woman "come back from burying the dead."⁷² She has not buried the "sick and ailing" but "the sodden and bloated; the sudden dead, their eyes flung wide open in judgment."⁷³ Tested by the fire, Janie's "burying the dead" is also a metaphor for killing off communal expectations of solidarity. Janie has managed to heal herself. Freed from their judgment, she thinks little of the townspeople watching her from their porches as they make "burning statements with questions and killing tools out of laughs."[74] Telling her friend Phoeby that the community's "mass cruelty" no longer affects her, Janie says: "Ah don't mean to bother wid tellin' 'em nothin', Pheoby. 'Tain't worth de trouble. You can tell 'em what Ah say if you wants to. Dat's just de same as me 'cause mah tongue is in mah friend's mouf."[75] There, in Janie's home with Pheoby's heaping plate of rice as an offering, the two friends cultivate what Lorde calls "the sweetness of womanspace."[76] Talking late into the night, Janie testifies to her membership in the "big 'ssociation of life." This intimate moment between two friends serves as a touchstone for considering Megan Thee Stallion's transformation away from sparing Black men to cultivating sonic performances of "wake work" for Black women.[77]

In her 2021 Saturday Night Live performance, Megan Thee Stallion performed her viral single "Savage." As she rapped the song's "sassy, moody, ratchet" refrain, large white words appeared behind her, "Protect Black Women."[78] Halfway through the song, the music abruptly stopped, and Megan and her dancers stood silently. The moment of silence cleared a proverbial space for Megan to recall the night she was shot as a screen riddled with images of gunshots appeared. The rapid pop of gunfire which followed, however, suggested that this time Megan would tell her story on her own terms. Laced in between the dramatic pause, a voice recording of Malcolm X crackled over the air, saying,

> The most disrespected person in America is the Black woman. The most unprotected, neglected person in America is the Black woman. Who taught you to hate the texture of your hair, the color of your skin, the shape of your nose? Who taught you to hate yourself from the top of your head to the soles of your feet?

In transitioning toward the 1962 audio, Megan curated a space for her performance to serve as a testimonial, a mourning song for Black women to name their pain and its source. As one of my students observed when we revisited this moment in class, "It was very hard to watch and kind of awkward. I could hear it in her voice—her trying to be brave, push through the performance." As my student would explain to me later, Megan had attempted to shine a spotlight on Black women's pain while performing before a mainstream audience. Prior to being shot, the rap starlet had maintained an upbeat aura and encouraged women to embrace joy through twerking. Yet here she was, symbolically returning to the scene of the shooting, revisiting it for the whole nation to see the depths of her pain. In Ntozake Shange's 1975 choreopoem, a lady in brown delivers what has become something of a Black girl's anthem: "Somebody, anybody, sing a black girl's song."[79] Therefore, perhaps the "awkward" note of Megan's performance stemmed from her singing a Black girl's song, not only for herself but for Breonna Taylor, the 26-year-old Black woman killed by Louisville police officers during a no-knock raid. As Megan and her dancers stood still with bowed heads, activist Tamika Mallory's voice boomed over the speakers, "Daniel Cameron is no different than the sellout negroes who sold our people into slavery."[80] Attorney General Daniel Cameron, a Black man who announced that no significant charges would be brought against the officers that shot and killed Taylor, faced sharp criticism from Taylor's family and activists.[81] In using Mallory's words to call out Cameron, Megan rips away the veil shielding Black men from accountability. Her unapologetic call-out of Cameron's complicity renders him an agent of white supremacy. In naming names, and specifically paying tribute to Breonna Taylor, Megan participates in the "wake work" central to Black rituals of mourning.

Homecomings filled with grand pronouncements of a life well-lived, a rest well-deserved, capture these mourning songs. In the 1977 *Song of Solomon*, Pilate rewrites the script, diminishing Hagar's life as meaningless. Bursting through the doors of Linden Baptist Church shouting "Mercy!," Pilate's emotive performance at Hagar's funeral demands the tenderness for her granddaughter denied to her in life. Sometimes whispering, sometimes begging for mercy, Pilate makes her way up the church aisle, demanding that the community answer her call, to which the mothers and daughters respond by singing:

> In the nighttime.
> Mercy.
> In the darkness.
> Mercy.
> In the morning.
> Mercy.
> At my bedside.
> Mercy.
> On my knees now.
> Mercy. Mercy. Mercy.[82]

Here, Morrison seems to say, is a Black girl's song. As the song comes to a close, Pilate issues a resounding, "And she was *loved!*" Tributes such as these are far too difficult to locate in our communities. But we find them in the songs written for us by our foremothers.

These mourning songs, a form of "wake work," stanch the wound. In a world where Black women are frequently denied justice and blamed for our own suffering, examining the gendered dimensions of our pain may prove healing. As Bambara reminds us in *The Black Woman*, "if we are serious, we shall have to check out everything that is characteristic of the Black community and examine it for health or disease."[83] In calling out this "disease," we may unburden ourselves from carrying trauma that was never ours to begin with. However, while the "uptown mamas" pushed Bambara to finish *The Black Woman: An Anthology*, insisting that she "just set it down in print so it gets to be a habit to write letters to each other, so maybe that way we don't keep treadmilling the same ole ground," young Black women today are still deeply wounded from the dehumanizing effects of Black patriarchal stealth. In 2025, what new songs of freedom are available for Black girls to sing?

We must first begin with cultivating mothering beyond its narrowly conceived functions. Former Black Panther Chairwoman Elaine Brown offers a possible path forward. In July 2024, Brown realized a decades-long dream with the opening of The Black Panther, a 100% affordable housing project for low-income and formerly incarcerated residents. Situated in West Oakland, California, and in a historically Black neighborhood known as the Harlem of the West, The Black Panther offers residents the opportunity to co-own businesses within the complex. The fully furnished dwellings follow a communal living format, housing a restaurant, gym, urban farm, shops, and offices. It extends the legacy of the original Black Panther Party's ten-point plan in which they demanded the right to affordable, decent housing. Brown's efforts to bring the complex to West Oakland fulfill a promise made to her daughter decades ago. When Brown fled the Black Panther Party and boarded a plane to take her away from California, she recalled the bittersweet moment in *A Taste of Power*. Thinking of Oakland as the birthplace of so many of her comrades, she is overcome with the feeling that there is still "so much work undone."[84] Aboard the plane, she gazes at her sleeping daughter's face, realizing, "I was abandoning something, but I was saving something." Brown, a singer, writes a song for her daughter.

> One night just before bed
> She shocked me when she said,
> What would happen if I died
> 'Cause no one cared
> When black girls cried—
> Oh, Ericka, my little baby,
> Ericka, my little child,
> Ericka, there is no maybe,
> I'll change the world for you
> In just a little while[85]

If we permit Black girls the space to sing songs of rage and pain, then we may prepare the foundation for them to soar above anything and anyone holding them back.

Notes

1 Hurston, 14.
2 Gaspard.
3 Sharpe, 14.
4 Sharpe, 22.
5 Cooper, 20.
6 Sharpe, 22.
7 Sharpe, 22.
8 "Korryn Gaines Believed She Had Lead Poisoning. In Black Communities, It's Very Common."
9 "Sistersong."
10 "Freddie Gray's Life a Study on the Effects of Lead Paint on Poor Blacks."
11 "Freddie Gray's Life a Study on the Effects of Lead Paint on Poor Blacks."
12 "Freddie Gray's Life a Study on the Effects of Lead Paint on Poor Blacks."
13 "Freddie Gray's Life a Study on the Effects of Lead Paint on Poor Blacks."
14 Qtd. in Viera.
15 Viera.
16 Rector.
17 "Black Males: An Endangered Species??"
18 Brown, 441.
19 Brown, 441.
20 Brown, 445.
21 Walker, 363.
22 Walker, 363.
23 Walker, 363.
24 Walker, 363.
25 The Associated Press.
26 Lambe.
27 Bambara, 6.
28 Bambara, 106.
29 Wallace, xxxiii.
30 Reed, 54.
31 Davis, 149.
32 Morrison, 91.
33 Qtd. in Bambara, 93.
34 Qtd. in Bambara.
35 Morrison, 317.
36 Morrison, 333.
37 Morrison, 307.
38 Sharpe, 19.
39 Foster.
40 Sharpe, 19.
41 CNN.
42 "The Story of the Moores."
43 The African American Policy Forum.
44 Foster.
45 Springer and Ehrenreich.
46 Sharpe, 19.
47 Bailey, 6.
48 Cineas.
49 Barnes.

50 Light.
51 Cineas.
52 Hurston, *Dust Tracks on a Road*, 208.
53 Hurston, *Dust Tracks on a Road*, 208.
54 Hurston, *Dust Tracks on a Road*, 208.
55 Hurston, *Dust Tracks on a Road*, 208.
56 Washington, 135.
57 Hurston, *Their Eyes Were Watching God*, 208.
58 Davies, 148.
59 Cineas.
60 Barnes.
61 Barnes.
62 Hurston, *Dust Tracks on a Road*, 187.
63 Hurston, *Their Eyes Were Watching God*, 187.
64 Hurston, *Their Eyes Were Watching God*, 147.
65 Hurston, 148.
66 Patterson, 79.
67 Bealer, 312.
68 Cineas.
69 Cineas.
70 Hurston, *Their Eyes Were Watching God*, 189.
71 Hurston, 1.
72 Hurston, 1.
73 Hurston, 1.
74 Hurston, 1.
75 Hurston, 5.
76 De Veaux, 222.
77 Sharpe, 19.
78 Pete.
79 Shange.
80 NowThis Impact.
81 Schreiner and Dylan.
82 Morrison, 319.
83 Bambara, 129.
84 Brown, 449.
85 Brown, 450.

Bibliography

Bailey, Moya. *Misogynoir Transformed*. New York: NYU P, 2021.
Bambara, Toni Cade. *The Black Woman: An Anthology*. Washington: Pocket Books, 1970.
Barnes, Dee. *"This Is Bigger Than Me and Bigger Than Hip-Hop": Dee Barnes Responds to Dr. Dre's Public Apology*. 24 August 2015. https://web.archive.org/web/20150824223513/http://gawker.com/this-is-bigger-than-me-and-bigger-than-hip-hop-dee-b-1726114418.
Bealer, Tracy L. "'The Kiss of Memory': The Problem of Love in Hurston's 'Their Eyes Were Watching God.'" *African American Review*, 2009, pp. 311–327.
"Black Males: an Endangered Species??" 24 June 1978. *National Museum of African American History and Culture*. 24 June 2020. https://nmaahc.si.edu/object/nmaahc_2012.114.4.

Brown, Elaine. *A Taste of Power: A Black Woman's Story*. New York: Anchor, 1993.
Cineas, Fabiola. *Megan Thee Stallion, Me Too, and Hip-hop's Cycle of Misogynoir*. 9 December 2022.
CNN. *Trayvon Martin Shooting Fast Facts*. 14 February 2014. 2022. https://www.cnn.com/2013/06/05/us/trayvon-martin-shooting-fast-facts/index.html.
Cooper, Brittney C. *The Crunk Feminist Collection*. New York: The Feminist Press at CUNY, 2017.
Davies, Kathleen. "Zora Neale Hurston's Poetics of Embalmment: Articulating the Rage of Black Women and Narrative Self-Defense." *African American Review*, 1992, pp. 148–159.
Davis, Christina. "Interview with Toni Morrison." *Présence Africaine*, vol. 145, 1988, pp. 141–150.
De Veaux, Alexis. *Warrior Poet: A Biography of Audre Lorde*. New York: W.W. Norton, 2004.
Foster, Kimberly Nicole. "Why I Will Not March for Eric Garner." *For Harriet*. 22 July 2014. https://www.forharriet.com/2014/07/why-i-will-not-march-for-eric-garner.html.
Freddie Gray's Life a Study on the Effects of Lead Paint on Poor Blacks. 29 April 2015.
Gaspard, Whitney. *Korryn Gaines' 5-Year-Old Son Recalls His Mother's Death in New Video*. 27 October 2020. Essence. 24 February 2021.
Hurston, Zora Neale. *Dust Tracks on a Road*. New York: Amistad, 2006.
Hurston, Zora Neale. *Their Eyes Were Watching God*. New York: Harper Perennial, 1937.
Korryn Gaines Believed She Had Lead Poisoning. In Black Communities, it's Very Common. n.d. 4 August 2020.
Lambe, Jerry. *"Ignored her Children's Pleas for Help": Mom and Friend Charged after 3-year-old Beaten to Death by Other Kids While Adults Were at Casino, Police Say*. 19 February 2024. 19 February 2024. https://lawandcrime.com/crime/ignored-her-childrens-pleas-for-help-mom-and-friend-charged-after-3-year-old-beaten-to-death-by-other-kids-while-adults-were-at-casino-police-say/.
Light, Alan. *N.W.A.: Beating Up the Charts*. 8 August 1991. 8 August 2023. https://www.rollingstone.com/music/music-news/n-w-a-beating-up-the-charts-100915/.
Lopez, German. *Korryn Gaines Believed She Had Lead Poisoning. In Black Communities, It's Very Common*. 4 August 2016.
Lorde. *Sister Outsider*. Crossing Press, 2007.
Merrit, Candice. "Lest We Forget Black Patriarchy; or, Why I'm Over Calling Out White Women." *South Atlantic Quarterly*, 2023, pp. 485–503.
Morrison, Toni. *Song of Solomon*. New York: Penguin Random House, 1977.
NowThis Impact. *BLM Activist Tamika Mallory Slams Kentucky AG Daniel Cameron | NowThis*. 2021. 8 February 2022. https://www.youtube.com/watch?v=islXphyHJNk.
Patterson, Tiffany Ruby. "Love in Hurston's Art and Life." *The Langston Hughes Review*, vol. 26, no. 1, 2020, pp. 77–93. https://www.jstor.org/stable/10.5325/langhughrevi.26.1.0077.
Rector, Justine. "Justine J. Rector Papers." *Historical Society of Pennsylvania: Philadelphia's Library of American History*. n.d. 9 September 2020. https://www2.hsp.org/collections/manuscripts/r/RectorMSS076.html.
Reed, Harry. "Toni Morrison, 'Song of Solomon' and Black Cultural Nationalism." *The Centennial Review*, 1988, pp. 50–64.

Savage Remix. Perf. Megan Pete. Saturday Night Live, New York. 2021. https://www.youtube.com/watch?v=CTpilDQXYr0.

Schreiner, Bruce, and Lovan Dylan. *Breonna Taylor Supporters Launch Campaign Against GOP Gubernatorial Nominee in Kentucky*. 5 June 2023.

Shange, Ntozake. *For Colored Girls Who Have Considered Suicide When the Rainbow Is Enuf*. New York: Scribner, 1997.

Sharpe, Christina. *In the Wake: On Blackness and Being*. North Carolina: Duke University Press, 2016.

Sistersong. *SisterSong: Women of Color Reproductive Justice Collective*. n.d. 16 September 2020. https://www.sistersong.net/.

Springer, Aisha, and Kelly Ehrenreich. *#YouOkSis Challenges Street Harassment, Starts a Movement*. 11 August 2014. 1 August 2018. https://www.hashtagfeminism.com/youoksis-challenges-street-harassment-starts-movement.

The African American Policy Forum. *#SAYHERNAME: Black Women Are Killed By Police Too*. n.d. 9 February 2020. https://www.aapf.org/sayhername.

The Associated Press. *Lionel Tate Pleads Guilty in 6-year-old's Death*. 29 January 2004. 29 January 2020.

The Story of the Moores. 2021. 8 February 2022. https://www.harryharriettemoore.org/the-moores.

Viera, Bene. *For Colored Girls Like Korryn Gaines And The Black Men Who Hate Us*. 3 August 2016.

Walker, Alice. *In Search of Our Mothers' Gardens: Womanist Prose*. Orlando: Mariner Books, 2003.

Wallace, Michelle. *Black Macho and the Myth of the Superwoman*. New York: Verso, 1979.

Washington, Mary Helen. "Zora Neale Hurston: A Woman Half in Shadow (Reprint)." *The Scholar and Feminist Online*, vol. 16, no. 2, 2020. 1 March 2023. https://sfonline.barnard.edu/zora-neale-hurston-a-woman-half-in-shadow-reprint/.

6   I Am Not Your Mammy
Kamala Harris and the Politics of Refusal

In 21st century America, Black women's political strivings for power have taken center stage. During her 2017 questioning of Treasury Secretary Steve Mnuchin about President Trump's financial ties to Russia, California State Representative Maxine Waters unwittingly went viral. As Mnuchin attempted to evade Waters' questions, she calmly stated, "Reclaiming my time. Reclaiming my time."[1] Waters, utilizing the House's procedural rules for allotted time, redirected Mnuchin's stonewalling attempts. Her staunch determination quickly gained the admiration of social media users. For Black social media users especially, the moment emphasized the perverse racial dynamics at play. The hashtag #ReclaimingMyTime trended on X, the online platform formerly known as Twitter. Black Lives Matter activist Deray Davis tweeted, "Reclaiming My Time: The Story of a People." Black PhD student A.D. Boynton II tweeted, "Reclaiming My Time: A Collection of Essays on Black Women Who Are Sick of White Men's Mediocrity."[2] Waters' bespectacled face emblazoned on shirts and mugs with the phrase "Reclaiming My Time" appeared online for purchase. The National Museum of African American History and Culture curated the "Reclaiming My Time" exhibit as the phrase entered the cultural lexicon as a mantra for Black "resistance and refusal."[3] Although she had not been trying to do so, Waters joined a growing cultural trend among Black women visibly and audibly rejecting white supremacist claims on their emotional, physical, and mental labor.

Take, for instance, Arkansas Senator Stephanie Flowers' impassioned speech against the 2019 "Stand Your Ground" laws. Fueled by righteous anger, Flowers' voice rose as she explained her position as the only Black person on the panel: "My son doesn't walk the same path as yours do, so this debate deserves more time."[4] When her white colleague, Senator Alan Clark, interrupted Flowers, insisting that she stop, Flowers retorted, "No, I don't. What the hell you going to do? Shoot me?! Go to hell!" Shouting back to the committee, Flowers insisted that she would not be silenced, neither by the NRA bills nor the bullet of a gun.[5] Her impassioned speech,

DOI: 10.4324/9781032719993-7

This chapter has been made available under a CC-BY-NC-ND license.

expressing dread for "other little Black boys and girls," advanced an audacious politics of refusal.

In *We Refuse: A Forceful History of Black History*, historian Kellie Carter Jackson situates this refusal as a powerful demand for "setting the terms for how humanity should be understood and treated with dignity, respect, and decency."[6] A politics of refusal is key to Black women reclaiming their political efforts, thereby countering the "mammy" figure eager to lavish her labor onto white families. In this shifting political arena, Black women's visibility in American politics presents an opportunity to explore the alacrity with which the United States recruits Black women into white capitalistic empire. As Carol Boyce Davies asserts, "Since the new millennium, a number of Black women have played influential roles in spheres hitherto defined as wholly male and white."[7] Therefore, by analyzing political heavyweights Shirley Chisholm, Condoleezza Rice, and Kamala Harris, I consider how their political maneuvering rejects traditional conventions surrounding Black women's labor.

However, this chapter is not a hagiography. I investigate our collective investment in scripting Black women as morally upright and impervious to corrupting forces by focusing on the less savory aspects of each woman's political career. I consider how these major political figures sometimes played the role of token or engaged in harmful acts against Black and disadvantaged people. Because Toni Morrison so often trained a critical eye on the gritty underbelly of Black women's agency in her novels, *Sula* serves as a guide for understanding how these Black women commandeer political power amid their gendered and racialized subjugation. Asked about the central role women play in her works, the late Morrison responded,

> Well, in the beginning, I was finally placing Black women center stage in the text, and not as the all-knowing, infallible Black matriarch but as a flawed here, triumphant there, mean, nice, complicated woman, and, some of them win and some of them lose.[8]

Morrison's words serve as a guide for considering Black women's complex humanity. As modern Black women living in the United States, our dueling and intersecting identities are now on full display, but we have always known that "we are beautiful. And ugly too."[9] Like Morrison, I explore Black political figures as complicated women navigating life as flawed individuals, swayed by ambition and yearnings for power and belonging.

Shirley Chisholm, Unbought and Unbossed

In 1972, Barbara Lee was worried that she might fail her politics course at Oakland's Mills College. None of the leaders discussed in the "Candidates, Campaigns, and Constituents" course interested her.[10] At 19, she was already championing Black feminist ethics calling for affordable housing, childcare, healthcare, and education. While the white male trio of Democratic presidential hopefuls—Hubert Humphrey, Edward Muskie, and George McGovern—ran on platforms with an eye toward ending the Vietnam War, they offered little indication that they understood the needs of marginalized communities.

Shirley Chisholm's arrival on campus as a speaker for the Black Student Union changed everything. Lee attended the event with fellow classmate Sandra Gaines. The two young women connected Chisholm's targeted campaign against poverty and increased educational funding to their own goals. Immediately after the event, Lee approached Chisholm to start a campaign organization for the presidential candidate. Working on a limited budget, one partially financed by Chisholm herself, the congresswoman replied,

> If you really believe in me, and believe in what I stand for, you'll go out and make it happen. We don't have a lot of money. We don't have a national campaign, and so, for those who care about me, we go out and do it.[11]

Lee and Gaines, with their professor's guidance, went out and did exactly that. They launched successful Oakland campaign fundraisers via fashion shows, dinners, and teas. Lee used her local connections with the Black Panthers to help secure Chisholm a broader base of support. We may conceptualize all this unpaid labor as Black feminist mothering since their targeted labors helped usher in a new era of Black women's political strategizing: one in which Black women stopped parceling off their labors to support other candidates, choosing instead to harvest their energies to form their own self-made political agendas.

Because slavery's gendered structures converted every inch of Black women's bodies into fuel for American capitalism, Black women's labor is often conceptualized as the property of everyone else but our own. Notions of Black women as perpetual laborers, confined to subservient roles, persist even when we assume leadership positions. For example, when Wilson Riles, a paid campaign staffer from the National Organization for Women, showed up at Chisholm's campaign headquarters in the Black Fillmore district of San Francisco, noting the "shabby office furniture and a handful of phone lines," he implied that Lee and Gaines should do something about the lack of curtains.[12] To which Lee and Gaines replied, "Buy them yourself."[13] Any working Black woman recognizes this gendered microaggression. My own professional experience with moments like these, arising from the expectation that I perform managerial tasks in spite of my educational qualifications or place myself in the proverbial line of fire for colleagues hesitant to do the same, informs my structuring of Black feminist mothering as the investment Black women make to achieve their own political ends. Black women like Lee, Gaines, and Chisholm investing their money, energies, and labors toward themselves disrupted centuries of deeply entrenched racial and gender paradigms in America.

The "controlling images" of "mammy" and matriarch cast a long shadow over Chisholm's presidential bid. The dueling images are best thought of as two sides of the same coin, in that the matriarch or "Big Mama" plays a vital role by caring for and nurturing both children and men within our communities. In her landmark *Race, Women, and Class*, Angela Davis notes that "the enormous space that work occupies in Black women's lives today follows a pattern established during the very earliest days of slavery."[14] Black women taking on the role of "Big Mama" may elevate their social currency within Black communities. "Mammy" works similarly, except in this configuration laboring on behalf of white people obscures Black women's exploitation. Black women betting on themselves unseat these parasitical configurations of labor.

Thus, Chisholm's 1972 presidential bid exposes the degree to which white supremacist racism impoverishes the collective Black male imaginary, confining Black women to "de mule uh de world." As a euphemism for America's gendered racist imaginary, the mule imagery supplied by Nanny to Janie in *Their Eyes Were Watching God* is perhaps the most succinct summation of oppression's diminishing effects. Scooping her young granddaughter into her lap, the old woman says:

> Honey, de white man is de ruler of everything as fur as Ah been able to find out. Maybe it's some place way off in de ocean where de black man in power, but we don't know nothin' but what we see. So de white man throw down de load and tell de nigger man to tuh pick it up. He pick it up because he have to, but he don't tote it. He hand it to his womenfolks. De nigger woman is de mule uh de world so fur as Ah can see.[15]

Nanny's "Maybe it's some place way off in de ocean where de black man in power, but we don't know nothin' but what we see" stages Black men's limited access to power as the impetus behind their inability to imagine alternative, healthier relationships with Black women. A profound analysis of the gendered hierarchies of power, Nanny's observation lays bare the correlation between Black men's oppression and Black women's continued exploitation of labor. Through her lens, Black women daring to restrict Black men's access to their labor brands them as disloyal subjects.

Indeed, in Chisholm's memoir *Unbought and Unbossed*, the congresswoman asserts, "Of my two 'handicaps' being female put many more obstacles in my path than being Black."[16] On one level, Chisholm's assertion reflects her experiences in Congress and the period in which she wrote the book. Written two years before her historic presidential run, the memoir features a blend of social commentary and political analysis, with her insight paralleling the Black Power Era writing that Black women were producing during the 1970s. As Black feminists theorized on the dueling structures of racism and sexism, one of the rising concerns within Black liberation movements centered on the question of whether one was Black first and a woman second. Therefore, Chisholm's splitting of her race and gender anticipates the hard-fought battles she would endure not only from white and non-Black audiences but also from Black male colleagues during her 1972 presidential bid.

Derision from Black congressmen in reaction to Chisholm's presidential bid was swift. U.S. Representative Louis Stokes of Ohio shrugged and laughed off her announcement. Congressman Clay quipped, "Who's Shirley Chisholm?"[17] Georgia State Representative Julian Bond was incensed. Seeking to assert a solid political Black base, Bond and other Black male political leaders had been deliberating on the best path forward. Their caution was part strategy. Among the most fractured periods in American history, the 1970s plunged American morale into despair and discontent. With the Vietnam War raging on and the bloody aftershocks of the Civil Rights movement still roiling the nation, Black politicians were keenly aware of white America's fears that the nation might crack from within. They sought to leverage their political capital by selecting local Black leaders to run for the state primaries and then pushing a "favorite son" from each state to establish a national source of Black political support. But they could not agree, as some favored nominating Carl Stokes, the former Cleveland Mayor.

However, it was not simply that Chisholm leapfrogged her way onto the presidential stage, but that she threatened gendered ideologies of labor. Inexplicably, she had imagined for herself a role other than that of a loyal helpmate standing beside, but never in front of a Black male leader. She would not be, as Nanny tells Janie, "de mule uh de world." If, as Benjamin reminds us in *Imagination: A Manifesto*, "radical imagination can inspire us to push beyond the constraints of what we think, and are told, is politically possible," then Chisholm's presidential bid may be contextualized as a radical display of imaginative resistance. One primarily concerned with breaking free from the traditional political machine already in place.[18] Therefore, Chisholm's adoption of a "lone wolf" strategy rendered her as a body out of order. Bond's response to a Chisholm aide characterizing Black men within the Democratic Party as "standing around, peeing on their shoes," before "Shirley finally said the hell with it and got a campaign going," confirms her defiance of this pecking order. "We may have been peeing on our shoes," Bond retorted, "but if we were, she wasn't around to get splashed."[19] Within the Black boys' club, Black politicians expected her to mobilize her gendered identity as a woman to garner support for male candidates approved, of course, by Black political leaders. Privately and publicly, Black congressmen seethed at her betrayal. "She had not taken any of us into her confidence and never discussed her plans for seeking the highest office."[20] Another Black congressman confessed, "A great many Black politicians resented it. She went off entirely by herself."[21] These remarks from leading Black politicians at the time reveal uneasiness with Chisholm daring to be guided by her own political strivings and ambitions. Though the leading Black politicians did not outright say it, and though some did, they had implicitly tagged Chisholm with that of a selfish matriarch—one of the most pernicious labels reserved for Black women violating communal expectations of loyalty. So strong was the fervor of hatred from Black male politicians that Chisholm confided to her campaign staffers that "they were going to kill me."[22]

To understand how deeply Black political leaders' rejection cut, their dismissal of Chisholm must be contextualized with the Black Power Era in mind. Although a period of rapid reform, Black women navigating the gendered tiers within the Black liberation movement frequently called out the expectations that they offer both their bodies and labor to Black men without hesitation. This is highlighted by the number of works by notable writers challenging the burdens that the family placed on young Black women. At the end of Toni Morrison's 1981 novel *Tar Baby*, the beautiful model and orphan, Jadine Childs, clashes with her aunt over what constitutes a real woman. Standing in the kitchen, the older Ondine doles out advice that she intends for Jadine to live by, insisting that

> if a girl never learns how to become a daughter, she can't never learn how to be a woman. I mean a real woman: a woman good enough for a child; good enough for a man—good enough even for the respect of other women.[23]

By attaching labor to the role of daughter, Ondine defines a real woman through her service to others. Her implicit chastising of Jadine for refusing to care for others—even if this care work comes at the expense of her own needs—reveals the underlying function of daughter as a title earned through labor. Like Nanny, who cannot imagine another path for Janie other than that of a mule because no other models exist for colored women, Ondine confines Jadine to that of laborer for an imagined husband, child, and community.

If Black women explored the pernicious construction of the family in the Black Power Era, then they also sought to cast off the imposed solidarity via an embrace of Black feminist mothering. In her 1974 choreopoem *For Colored Girls Who Have Considered Suicide / When the Rainbow Is Enuf*, Ntozake Shange depicted a lonely child as the epitome of unfulfilled longing and pain. "I wuz cold / I wuz burnin up / a child and endlessly weaving garments / for the moon with my tears." The protagonist recognizes that she is "missing something / somethin promised / somethin free."[24] But she does not seek this "missing something" from a man or even her mama "holdin me tight / sayin I'm always gonna be her girl." Rather, the protagonist searches herself and locates value within: "I found god in myself / and I loved her / I loved her fiercely."[25] In what would become a litany for Black women's healing, these three lines encapsulate Black women's spirited determination to cast off the lingering remnants of slavery's racialized and gendered hierarchies.

Amid this Black cultural zeitgeist, Chisholm's presidential campaign became a benchmark for the very difficult process of Black feminist self-making. For her stance, she was branded a traitor by both Black politicians and white feminists. Paradoxically, Black male politicians balked at Chisholm's attempts to build bridges with white feminists. "She was spending so much time with women's lib and gay lib that she was forgetting all about Black lib here in Bedford-Stuyvesant," a former supporter complained.[26] Dean of Contemporary Studies at Brooklyn College, Carlos Russell, went even further, condemning Chisholm for espousing what he called "vaginal politics" in which "almost every issue is reduced to male vs. female."[27] But Chisholm, perhaps understanding how quickly Black solidarity collapsed all differences, turned her energies toward coalition building among marginalized people of all races and sexualities, with a particular emphasis on poor working-class women. Complicating matters, Chisholm resisted yielding her political labors to white feminists. White feminist leaders, while praising Chisholm publicly, never endorsed her presidency. As organizers of the National Women's Political Caucus, white feminists Bella Abzug and Betty Friedan maintained their commitment to the "equal representation of men and women in political party conventions" but their overt racism would eventually splinter any attempts at bridging the gap between Chisholm's campaign and the white feminist movement.[28] For instance, Friedan planned a fundraising party but shared none of the proceeds with Chisholm's campaign. In a move putting Friedan's clear racism on display, she arranged a "Traveling Watermelon Feast" campaign event to hand out free watermelons to the mostly Black Harlemites.[29] The event was swiftly canceled, but the damage to Chisholm's reputation and campaign lingered. As she had written 2 years ago in *Unbought and Unbossed*, Chisholm realized that white feminists often reserved a double dose of enmity for Black women venturing "outside the limits of the role men have assigned to females: that of toy and drudge."[30] In the end, she broke with white feminist leaders and most of them, including Gloria Steinem, went on to support George McGovern despite the glowing adulation they heaped on Chisholm. This racial calculus doomed any attempts at Chisholm securing a broad base of women's support and exposed the contradictions of a white women's movement that lauded Chisholm as "far and away the best candidate" but deemed her white male competitor a better representation of women's interests.[31] In essence, Chisholm's presidential campaign broke with an American racist imaginary determined to capitalize off the sustained exploitation of Black women's labors.

Ushering in this new era of Black women's politics, Chisholm stamped her political posters with an air of unmistakable trust in her ability to lead.

Sharply outfitted in a white suit coat with the words "BRING U.S. TOGETHER" above her head and "VOTE CHISHOLM 1972" below her, the congresswoman fashioned for herself a modern, progressive image of leadership with a sole Black woman at the helm. But the image also sought to incorporate Chisholm into an American body politic as she is centered as the political force capable of bringing the United States together. At the

Figure 6.1 Bring U.S. together. Vote Chisholm 1972

bottom of the poster image, her unforgettable tagline, "UNBOUGHT and UNBOSSED," made clear her refusal to serve as a mascot for interests other than her own. Over time, the "Unbought and Unbossed" slogan emerged as a refusal to be pigeonholed into anyone else's imagination. However, perhaps the rhetorical power of her campaign paraphernalia has led to Chisholm's halcyon portrayal. Posthumously, she has risen to a heroic status cemented by Shola Lynch's 2004 documentary *Chisholm '72: Unbought and Unbossed* and Netflix's recent *Shirley*. Filmmaker Lynch characterizes Chisholm as "essentially Afro futuristic," citing her ability to "believe that something is possible that no one around you believes is possible" as proof. But as History Professor Anastasia Curwood argues in her biography, *Shirley Chisholm: Champion of Black Feminist Power*, the tendency to romanticize Chisholm obscures "the true dimensions of her heroism ... behind our reflexive worship of her accomplishments."[32] We must juxtapose her pursuit of power with her longings for belonging and power to avoid flattening Chisholm into a one-dimensional figure. In attending to her crafting of herself as separate and apart from any expectations of racial or gender loyalty, we must also engage her espousal of anti-Black views and support of anti-Black candidates. To render Chisholm less of a heroic figure means we may see more clearly the ways in which she was not immune to embracing pathological views.

In 1974, Chisholm faced her fair share of criticism for cozying up to white supremacist segregationist George Wallace. After the "segregation now, segregation forever" governor was hospitalized following an attempted assassination, Chisholm visited him in the hospital. Recalling the backlash, Chisholm said:

> Black people in my community crucified me. But why shouldn't I go to visit him? Every other Presidential candidate was going to see him. He said to me: "What are your people going to say?" I said: "I know what they're going to say. But I wouldn't want what happened to you to happen to anyone." He cried and cried and cried.[33]

It is difficult to square Chisholm's pattern of aligning herself with white patriarchal power and her "Unbought and Unbossed" mantra. Returning to the intellectual brilliance of the 1977 Combahee River Collective statement reveals how the unbearable pressures of racism and sexism may well produce the perfect conditions for Black women's pursuit of power. The statement's pioneers, Demita Frazier, Audre Lorde, and Barbara Smith, authored a liberation manifesto so commanding in its articulation of Black women's strategizing against sexism, racism, and classism that I may have held my breath when reading the document for the first time in college. Never had I felt a text so perfectly encapsulate the hope, persistence, and fear swirling around inside me as a Black woman. In imagining Black women's revolutionary potential forged from our marginalization at large, the statement recasts Black women as visionaries with a specific line of sight for creating more just worlds. "We might," the Black feminist luminaries write, "use our position at the bottom, however, to make a clear leap into revolutionary action."[34] Hope, a key element for any revolution, surfaces throughout the statement with the signatories asserting,

> Although our economic position is still at the very bottom of the American capitalistic economy, a handful of us have been able to gain certain tools as a result of tokenism in education and employment which potentially enable us to more effectively fight our oppression.[35]

For me, a burgeoning Black feminist with only a dim goal of becoming an African American literature professor, their words quieted my worry that such a career served no real purpose for my community.

However, in my first tenure-track position, I would often quote the statement's concluding assertion: "If Black women were free, it would mean that everyone else would have to be free since our freedom would necessitate the destruction of all the systems of oppression."[36] To imagine Black women's oppression through a prism linking and tethering the health of the world to ours seemed a revolutionary concept. In the years since, I have returned to this sentence to ponder how structuring Black women's oppression as the bedrock upon which society's collective liberation pivots may also foreclose possibilities for examining power's seductive appeal to Black women in particular. Or, put another way, how might Black women's pursuit of power spring from sustained disenfranchisement, giving way to a dogged determination to never be on the bottom again?

With this question in mind, we may begin conceptualizing Chisholm's visit to Wallace as both a political power play and an attempt at belonging. In positioning herself in close proximity to white male power, Chisholm seized power's residual effects. Years after her presidential bid, Chisholm's support of Wallace yielded political dividends as she could call on the governor to flex his political muscle on her behalf. In 1974, Wallace helped Chisholm secure support from Southern members of Congress to get legislation extending the minimum wage to domestic workers. In the years following her presidential bid, Chisholm would go on to make a series of political maneuverings distancing her from more progressive policies aimed at helping Black voters. She shrugged off criticism from Black voters and politicians questioning her support for Mayor Koch in New York's Democratic gubernatorial primary instead of Mario Cuomo.[37] Responding to the backlash, Chisholm chided Black people, "Blacks are always putting their eggs in one basket. They are not politically sophisticated enough to understand the pragmatic reasons behind my moves."[38] Speaking on why she supported Daniel Patrick Moynihan over Bella Abzug in the 1976

Democratic Senatorial primary in New York, Mrs Chisholm asked: "Where was Abzug when I ran for President? Why didn't the reporters ask why a lot of women didn't support me for the Presidency?"[39] The pit of bitterness lodged in Chisholm's dismissal of Abzug is perhaps understandable. Later, Chisholm would also express initial hesitation for Jesse Jackson's presidential bid. Her complex political legacy encourages a consideration of how Chisholm's exclusion from both white and Black political spaces spurred her determination to seize a modicum of power via proximity to white men. Although she would tout herself as a Black woman who "won public office without selling out to anyone," her political maneuverings challenge easy constructions of her as impervious to power's tantalizing appeal.[40] Rather, her insistence that she could not be bought or sold obscures her need for acceptance along a white male axis of power. Echoes of this need for power would surface again in Condoleezza Rice's rise to the White House.

Condoleezza Rice, an Ideology of Power

In 2004, an audience member attending the Society for Ethical Culture event asked Toni Morrison what advice she would give then Secretary of State Condoleezza Rice. The Pulitzer Prize-winning author laid bare the gritty underbelly of Black women's agency that is at once predictable, pathological, and parasitical:

> Oh, I would strongly suggest that Condoleezza Rice get another job. I know how seductive power is. She is an educated woman. She's a gifted woman. She's a talented woman. And she has a lot of attributes. Why trash them? In an area—and I know that she has benefited time and time again from that part of the political spectrum, and particularly that family, but loyalty is not all there is in life. There is something called real integrity. And I don't think she not understands that.[41]

Morrison's frank assessment of Rice humanizes her as a distinguished career woman possessing talents easily co-opted for white heteropatriarchal power—an entity Morrison implicitly rebukes in her dismissal of President Bush and his oil tycoon legacy as "that family." Neither does she ignore the Secretary of State's clear investment in cozying up to this rich, wealthy, white family. In typical didactic fashion, Morrison details power's tantalizing qualities, practically irresistible in its attraction. Rice emerges not simply as a morally bankrupt figure via Morrison's observations but as a cautionary tale of how the once disenfranchised, persistently marginalized, quickly seize oppressive forms of control. As so many of Morrison's novels depict Black women seeking power or something akin to it, her 1973 novel, *Sula*, contextualizes Rice's pursuit of power as the likely path for a young Black girl bearing the weight of Southern white people's segregationist policies. If Rice appears as Morrison constructs her—a morally bankrupt figure whose loyalties lie outside the Black communities to which she belongs—my aim is to use Sula's individual strivings as a signpost for exploring Rice's navigation through power, tokenism, and racial loyalty. Therefore, both Sula and Rice, finding no tangible power or protection in being a Black girl, distance themselves from their communities and their racialized and gendered identities.

Rice's pursuit of power begins in an unlikely place, her hometown of Birmingham, Alabama. However, the denial of power gives rise to her rabid pursuit of it. When 8-year-old Condoleezza Rice learned of the Sixteenth Street Church bombing, she could not believe it. Through tears, she asked, "Why? Why?"[42] Because white supremacists set off the bomb only 2 miles away from her father's church, Condoleezza had attended kindergarten with Denise McNair, the 11-year-old who liked watching *Beverly Hillbillies* with her sister. Cynthia Wesley frequently attended youth fellowship classes hosted by Condoleezza's father, Reverend John Rice, Jr. And 14-year-old Addie Mae Collins had been a student in Alto Rice's social studies class. For years after the bombing, Alto, Condoleezza's uncle, cried whenever he discussed the bombing. Though Condoleezza did not know 14-year-old Carole Robinson, she had likely seen her around town and perhaps knew that the two girls shared a passion for music. For Condoleezza, the piano. For Carole, the clarinet. Her close proximity to the church and the threat of racial violence perpetually linked Condoleezza's childhood to Denise, Addie Mae, Cynthia, and Carole.

In the year of the church bombing, terror had become so ingrained in Birmingham, Alabama, that it had spread into nearly every aspect of Alabamans' lives. Bomb plantings in the stores, churches, and homes of Black people were so common that locals bitterly referred to the town as, "Bombingham."[43] Condoleezza's family narrowly escaped terror when white supremacists planted a shrapnel bomb in the area ten days after the four girls had been killed in church. Another bomb destroyed the store near her father's church. As a Black minister in the South, John Rice was a primary target despite his lack of interest in the Civil Rights movement itself. Emboldened by the police's refusal to take John Rice's concerns seriously, white supremacists tossed a bomb into the next-door neighbor's home. Years later, in a 2000 interview with a reporter, John Rice would remember driving his wife and 8-year-old daughter to his mother-in-law's house to avoid the stench of the exploding gas bomb next door.[44] With his wife and daughter safe, John Rice mobilized a local group of men armed with shotguns to patrol the neighborhood at dusk, as white supremacists favored terrorizing Negro neighborhoods under the cover of night.[45] Thus,

Condoleezza's world was that of a pressure cooker, with tensions bubbling over right as she prepared to enter her adolescent years.

But when asked about her childhood, Rice maintained a cold distance. While admitting to an interviewer that she was "kind of scared" by the Sixteenth Street church bombing, Rice insisted that the Cuban Missile Crisis was far more terrifying: "I'll tell you, funnily enough, what scared me more was the Cuban Missile Crisis. We all lived within range [of the Soviet missiles based in Cuba]."[46] To engage with the terror unfolding in Birmingham would require confronting the limitations of her own power. Thus, her fascination with political affairs in faraway lands became a vessel for Rice to disconnect from her own subjugated status. Adopting the bird's-eye viewpoint of a casual observer to the events unfolding around her, Rice crafts for herself a script to repudiate her powerlessness as a young Black girl growing up in the Deep South.

Meditations on Black girls' restricted access to power surface in *Sula* during Nel's and Sula's early encounter with white boys who frequently pester the best friends on their way home from school. The scene hints at Nel's and Sula's potential sexual violation by the boys who imagine themselves overpowering the girls and possibly "get an arm around one of their waists, or tear."[47] Perhaps one of the most chilling scenes in African American fiction is what Sula does in response to the boys' attempted violation:

> Sula squatted down in the dirt road and put everything down on the ground: her lunchpail, her reader, her mittens, her slate. Holding the knife in her right hand, she pulled the slate toward her and pressed her left forefinger down hard on its edge. Her aim was determined but inaccurate. She slashed off only the tip of her finger. The four boys stared open-mouthed at the wound and the scrap of flesh, like a button mushroom, curling in the cherry blood that ran into the corners of the slate. Sula raised her eyes to them. Her voice was quiet. "If I can do that to myself, what you suppose I'll do to you?" The shifting dirt was the only way Nel knew that they were moving away; she was looking at Sula's face, which seemed miles and miles away.[48]

Forced to confront the fact that her community cannot keep her safe, she appears "miles and miles away." Her seeming calm before the boys is a veneer—a concentrated effort to muster up the courage to slice her own finger. Through Sula's self-mutilation, Morrison exposes the lack of tangible options available to Nel and Sula for protecting themselves. The scene is also, in some ways, an indictment of the community. Consider how differently a similar scene plays out in the real-life one Myrlie Evers-Williams recalls when a "courthouse gang" of white boys who "seemed to make it their life's work to threaten us, spit on us, call us names, hurl rocks and sticks at us, shove and hit us."⁴⁹ Although Evers-Williams walks with her girlfriends for safety as Sula and Nel do, the situation only comes to a resolution when "disgusted and tired of running" they concoct a plan with some of her girlfriend's older brothers and their friends. The importance of community in banishing the white boys from harming Evers-Williams and her friends is central to affirming Black girls' worth in Jim Crow Mississippi:

> On the specified day, we walked by the courthouse as usual, but this time, when members of the gang taunted us, we taunted back; we even threw rocks at them. Naturally, they took off after us. We ran as fast we could and lured them into an enclosed courtyard behind a store, where the older Black boys—brothers, cousins, and friends—were waiting for them.⁵⁰

In *Sula*, the absence of communal protection forces Black girls to over-rely on themselves. They must resort to their own defenses. Sula's face, "which seemed miles and miles away," reveals her act as a distancing technique to mask her seeming calm and lack of concern for her own well-being.

The obvious contrast between Shadrach and Sula emphasizes the community's lack of tools available for nourishing Black girls. Through Shadrach, Morrison lodges an implicit critique of gender norms and its tendencies to shroud Black men in impenetrable shields of stealth. That Shadrach's plight opens the first two chapters of the novel indicates his place as an anchor to both the Bottom and the novel itself in a way that Sula, despite her name spotlighted in the novel's title, never achieves. As Morrison explains, Sula and Shadrach are near doubles of each other, which mirrors what she calls Sula's "genuine classic evil."⁵¹ Like Sula, Shadrach is fascinated, perhaps obsessed, with death. But only one of them is allowed to set down a path of creative expression. Shadrach institutes Suicide Day as a means of balancing out the uncertainty and fear of death. On its face, the day sounds farcical. But the people of the Bottom, starved for order and bounds, begin planning their events around Suicide Day: "Easily, quietly, Suicide Day became a part of the fabric of life up in the Bottom of Medallion, Ohio."⁵² Beyond a display of Morrison's sardonic genius, Shadrach's Suicide Day, although well-intentioned, signifies a Black patriarchal stealth granting Black men copious amounts of freedom to freely explore any number of morbid peccadilloes of their choosing. That Shadrach ambles around the neighborhood striking a cowbell and holding a hangman's rope while insisting that "this was their only chance to kill themselves or each other" but is never expelled from the community or even rejected by those within it speaks to the ways in which Black men's less than stellar actions are often dismissed as harmless or comical despite the imminent harm that these actions may pose to the community.[53] People do, in fact, die during Shadrach's Suicide Day death march.

Unsurprisingly, Sula is blamed for the carnage. Though a lie, the opprobrium for Sula reveals the degree to which the Bottom impoverishes Black girls' radical imaginations. Sula's creative spirit unfed, she becomes menacing:

> Had she paints, or clay, or knew the discipline of the dance, or strings; and her gift for metaphor, she might have exchanged the restlessness and preoccupation with whim for an activity that provided her with all she yearned for. And like any artist with no art form, she became dangerous.[54]

Thus, the narcissistic turn Sula takes incriminates the Black Bottom, Ohio, community.

Similarly, the rigid structures constricting Black life in Birmingham profoundly impacted a young Condoleezza. In her childhood, her parents blanketed her in a world of their own creation. While John Rice met with Martin Luther King and Fred Shuttlesworth, he disdained the marching and protesting and would offer no support beyond that of a listening ear. Her parents instilled in her the belief that racism was not her burden to bear. So they nurtured her talents, taking out loans to buy her a piano and encouraging her dreams of becoming a pianist. Years later, in a 2000 interview, John Rice would insist that the Church Street bombing had little effect on his daughter. She had shed "no tears" and felt "no terror." "She grew up in the era and knew how to handle it. She had faith that we would protect her, and we would."[55] Still, John Rice's recollection reveals a parent perhaps unable to fully grapple with the limits of his own power. By constructing Condoleezza as a stoic child, unmoved by the murder of four Black girls, John Rice invents for his family an alternative historical legacy. One rooted in power, freedom, and choice. And not the bloody and, what he deemed undignified, battle for basic human rights. Under their fierce and narrow protections, Rice cultivated a decidedly individualistic identity.

As Rice's national profile grew in prominence, she too would erect distance between herself and the plight of Black people fighting for equal rights. In interviews, Rice situated 1968 as a significant year due to the assassinations of Martin Luther King and Bobby Kennedy, but her empathy seemed to be reserved most for the Czech people enduring the Soviet invasion of Czechoslovakia: "I can still feel the strong sense I had of remorse and regret that a brave people had been subdued."[56] In a way, Rice's empathy for Czech protesters is understandable. She likely aligned her own family's subjugation with theirs. Yet her years as a Stanford provost and National Security Advisor, in which she maintained a cruel distance from those suffering even when they looked like her, suggest that the beginnings of a pathology developed here. In fact, throughout the course of her political career, Rice's inability to empathize with Black people on issues of race-based oppression tainted her legacy.

When Hurricane Katrina ravaged the South, leaving many Black residents homeless or dead, she claimed that Bush's slow response had little to do with race, calling the accusation absurd. While touring her native Alabama, Rice insisted that President Bush's lack of response had nothing to do with the races of the people being affected. "How can that be the case? Americans don't want to see Americans suffer," Rice said. "Nobody, especially the president, would have left people unattended on the basis of race."[57] Predictably, President Bush used Rice as a buffer against his disastrous response to the 2005 storm wreaking havoc in Louisiana, Mississippi, and Alabama. Indeed, Rice's staunch defense of President Bush's policies throughout her tenure undoubtedly served the purpose of steering the American public away from President Bush's long record of violence against Black people and people of color. During Bush's presidential terms, Americans, all too familiar with this historical narrative, largely relegated Rice to nothing more than a political plaything at best, Bush's secret lover at worst. Rumors of an affair between the two floated around, with Rice inadvertently stoking the flames by mistakenly referring to Bush as her husband during a briefing. But it is too easy to reduce Rice to that of a political token. As the hurricane prepared to make landfall, Rice was wrapping up a nine-month traveling vacation to 46 countries. Yet when she arrived back home in the United States, she, according to her own accounts, did not "think much about the dire warnings of an approaching hurricane called Katrina."[58] Her decision to attend a musical comedy and then go shoe shopping at Ferragamo as the storm hit came *after* she phoned Homeland Security Secretary Michael Chertoff and learned that the situation was "pretty bad." In her memoir *No Higher Honor*, Rice admits recognizing the magnitude of her error while watching the storm coverage: "the airwaves were filled with devastating pictures from New Orleans. And the faces of most of the people in distress were black. I knew right away that I should never have left Washington."[59] Rice's seeming lack of concern for those displaced by Hurricane Katrina, many of them Black residents from her home state, reveals Black women's investment in white capitalistic regimes of power.

In 2004, the year Morrison made her comments, Rice was a staunch defender of the 2003 invasion of Iraq and the use of waterboarding, a torture technique of pouring water over the captive to initiate drowning sensations. Rice, Vice President Dick Cheney, and Attorney General John Ashcroft approved this method, along with sleep deprivation, forced nudity, and other stress-inducing positions. That her status as a Black woman from

Alabama raised under Jim Crow rule did not imbue her with any resistance to these oppressive tactics renders more clearly Morrison's cautions against the seductive element of power. As Ruha Benjamin reminds us, "Our Blackness and our womanness are not in themselves trustworthy, if we allow ourselves to be conscripted into positions of power that maintain the oppressor."[60] We may extend Benjamin's observations to Sula's mishandling of her family and friends as a method for unveiling the psychology behind Rice's strivings for power.

Having no one to mother her, and nowhere to safely express her pain, Sula channels her energies toward hurting those closest to her. So liberated from any expectations of fealty is she that after sleeping with Nel's husband, she expresses no regret for hurting her best friend, but instead condemns Nel as "one of them."[61] Sula reigns as one of literature's most daring figures. She is deliciously wicked. And yet, her rugged individualism prevents her from acknowledging the ways she hurts those closest to her. Her return to the Bottom is punctuated by a contentious argument between Sula and her grandmother, Eva Peace. During their *tête-à-tête*, Eva insists that Sula get married and have babies as it will "settle" her.[62] As David Ikard argues, Eva "is so deeply invested in self-sacrifice that she cannot conceptualize a viable model of womanhood outside the domain of marriage and mothering."[63] The praise and seeming respect heaped onto Black women as a result of shoring up their labors for Black men and children often conscripts older Black women into recruiting younger Black women into the position of "Big Mama." In response to Eva's unwavering defense of matrimony and maternity, a defiant Sula declares, "I don't want to make somebody else. I want to make myself."[64] A courageous declaration, but Sula's decision to throw Eva out of her own house and place her in the Sunnydale nursing home—"she didn't even have time to comb her hair before they strapped her to a piece of canvas"—underscores the degree to which making herself requires Sula to mistreat other Black people in her life."[65] That the novel hints at Sula assuming guardianship over Eva to ensure that she receives her grandmother's social security benefits resists categorizing Sula as the self-made woman of her own dreams.

Like Sula's harming of herself before the white boys, her interactions with Eva and Nel expose the gendered dimensions of her powerlessness. Sula cannot go out into the world and seize power, so she must claim it within the bounds of the Bottom. Incapable of confronting the limitations of her own power and the subsequent pain that this knowledge produces, she sets out to hurt others without ever needing to recognize their pain and her part in causing it. She becomes, in effect, pathological.

I do not make this argument lightly. For one, *Sula* is a favorite novel of mine. And two, when I first declared my thoughts on Sula during a panel discussing Morrison's works, the co-panelist, a respected scholar whose work I deeply admire, was shocked. She took great care gently vocalizing her disagreement. In that record-scratching moment, I briefly reconsidered my reading of Sula as perhaps misguided. The community, as my co-panelist pointed out, had indeed villainized Sula, pillorying her until she had little option but to become a pariah. This community is, of course, the all-Black, tightly knit Ohio town, known simply as the Bottom. In this insular enclave, Black women cling to their "jobs" of wife and mother. They can offer Sula little support as her belief system does not align with these values. However, while my argument implicates the community and its attempt at locking her into either the role of mother or wife, I am most concerned with how these conditions fertilize the grounds for a pathological Black woman to emerge. With no communal guardrails guiding them, Black girls may come to crave power along a decidedly white male axis. Indeed, the childhood bond between Nel and Sula first develops over their shared realization of the extremely disadvantaged position they occupy as Black girls coming of age in the 1920s. "Because each had discovered years before that they were neither white nor male, and that all freedom and triumph was forbidden to them, they had set about creating something else to be."[66] The passage, describing the journey toward self-discovery, also opens up a space for considering how Black girls' yearnings for self-creation remain bound up and tied to traditional constructions of white heteropatriarchal power.

Notably, Rice accepted the National Security Advisor role not out of need. Her distinguished career as a Stanford political science professor and provost certainly qualified her for the high-ranking position within Bush's cabinet. But her maneuverings in academia were perhaps inflected by, but not subsistent on, emulating heteropatriarchal constructions of power. As Stanford provost, Rice ruled with an iron fist, leading to her rising reputation on campus as an autocrat. Any hint of disagreement from faculty could land them in Rice's office, where she told one professor complaining of a university ad campaign, "Either you're a member of the team, or you're not a member of the team."[67] When a staff member pushed back on Rice's understanding during a meeting, the next week he and his entire unit was fired.[68] At meetings, colleagues observed "a coldhearted, merciless way of dealing with people ... There was so little compassion, so little humanity ... It was a major mistake to disagree with her. People who were not aware of that danger generally paid a price."[69] Rice's rise to power as Stanford's first Black woman president no doubt rankled some feathers. However, her tyrannical approach also set the staging grounds for her to claim the kind of power often associated with white men. As one African American colleague at Stanford observed, Rice had developed an "ideology of power."[70] In meetings, she presided with a steely, cold mask of power, insisting to the Faculty Senate Women's Caucus that there were no issues in hiring and retaining women faculty on campus.[71] Though Rice would admit some errors, she ultimately opposed affirmative action guidelines that would have increased the number of women on campus. Her position represented a break with traditional Stanford policies, but she insisted that she would not back down from it, saying, "I'm the chief officer now, and I am telling you that, in principle, I do not believe in, and in fact will not apply, affirmative action criteria at the time of tenure."[72] In a 2001 interview with *Newsweek*, Rice depicted Black Stanford students as recipients of lowered expectations from professors who "[pulled] punches with Black students about low-quality work, even though these were kids who had gone to Exeter."[73] Defending herself against claims of unfairly treating Black students and faculty of color during her tenure as Stanford provost, she said, "I've always said I can't go back and re-create myself as a white male."[74] It would become a common refrain for Rice whenever she found her authority challenged. Over time, as she accumulated more power, Rice created a buffer of protection around herself to head off criticism. By implicitly lamenting her perceived powerlessness as "neither white nor male," she could distance herself from the very real power she had attained over the years. From a psychological standpoint, Rice's emulations of power may be understood as posturing, a defensive measure for inventing a narrative of power frequently denied to Black women. In her professional career, as she had done as a child, Rice would observe the growing racial and gender tensions on Stanford's campus from a bird's-eye view, telling one friend that the hunger strikes of Chicano student protests happening on campus were their decision because "I'm not hungry. I'm not the one who's not eating."[75] As such, Rice's steady embrace of power reveals the degree to which Black women incorporate themselves into an American body politic eager to capitalize on their labors.

Kamala Harris, a Politics of Refusal

Amid a cultural revamp of the mammy myth, Kamala Harris launched her 2020 presidential campaign. Narratives praising Black women as political saviors first took shape during Alabama's 2017 Senate election. Following Democrat Doug Jones' sound defeat of Republican Roy Moore, Democratic National Committee Chairman Tom Perez tweeted: "Let me be clear. We won in Alabama and Virginia because #Blackwomen led us to victory. Black women are the backbone of the Democratic Party and we can't take that for granted."[76] Exit polls indeed confirmed that 98 percent of Black women supported Jones. Without Black women's high voter turnout, he would not have been able to secure his Senate seat as 68 percent of white voters cast their votes for Moore. No Alabama Democrat had held the Senate seat since 1992. By voting against him, Black women made history and sent a clear message disavowing Moore's history of sexual assault allegations. Thus, Perez's attempt at acknowledging Black women's political significance emerged from a sincere and truthful place. Yet his bypassing of interrogating white voting habits evaded larger questions of their clannish support of white men unfit for leadership—Moore was a two-time expelled judge. Instead, the higher voter turnout among Black women symbolized a perceived inherent morality rather than informed political strategy.

This scripting of Black women as morally superior reached a fever pitch three years later, with Former First Lady Michelle Obama delivering an impressive speech at the Democratic National Convention. Mexican ambassador Jorge Guajardo adopted language similar to Perez, declaring in a tweet, "Black women will save the United States."[77] While Guajardo later apologized after mostly Black women rejected this deification, venerating Black women as political saviors had become such a common refrain that shortly after Amanda Gorman recited her poem at Joe Biden's inauguration, political sketch artist Andy Marlette drew her smiling and hoisting a beleaguered Uncle Sam in her arms with the cartoon title: "Poet Amanda Gorman to the Rescue."[78] The image of a young Black woman carrying a cartoon version of an old white man recalled the narratives white women tapped into following the Confederacy's Civil War loss. In 1923, a group of white women calling themselves the Daughters of the Confederacy were so eager to memorialize the "happy mammies" laboring in their homes for free that they proposed the passage of a bill to erect a Washington monument to their "faithful-colored mammies." Confederate monuments had already begun appearing along the Southern landscape, and the bill would have likely passed if Mary Church Terrell, Hallie Quinn, and other Black women from the National Association of Colored Women had not mounted such strong opposition that the bill failed in the House.

Try as it might, America still has not rid itself of the very real monetary profits and labor that the "mammy" image provides. The success of films like *The Help*, Aunt Jemima pancake and syrup line, and the popularization of chain restaurants like Popeyes emphasize the hold with which the mammy retains on the American imagination. Scripting Black women as perpetual sources of labor is reflected in the marketing strategies of billion-dollar companies like Popeyes. The fried chicken conglomerate branded itself as the soul of the South by hiring Deidrie Henry to star in commercials as "Annie the Chicken Queen." Her affected southern drawl (Henry is originally from Barbados) flattens Black women's complex humanities. Similarly, the political trope of Black women saving America repackages Black women's labor as the exclusive property of the white American empire. Scholar Brittney Cooper defines this political labor as the "custodial work of democracy."[79] The United States, Cooper explains, "has this deep sense of Black women as people who come in to clean up the mess that they make. That has historically been our position."[80] As such, Harris' repeated embrace of a politics of refusal telegraphed to the American public her rejection of "custodial work," positioning Black women as the clean-up crew to democracy. Ultimately, this would be a key factor in dooming her 2020 presidential bid and nearly costing her the vice-presidential spot.

Harris, though Black and Indian, was consistently subjected to the impossible demands often foisted on Black women suspended, as Chisholm noted, "between that of toy and drudge." At the 2019 Democratic primary debates, Harris' storied run for President of the United States mobilized a series of racialized and gendered scripts surrounding Black women's perceived incompatibility as leaders. Though Harris had worked closely with Biden's late son, Beau, on the 2011 and 2012 national mortgage settlement, she expressed little hesitation when campaign staffers suggested she target Biden's busing stance. It mattered even less to her that her husband, Doug Emhoff, still had a voicemail he saved from Biden congratulating them on their engagement. In what would become a lightning rod moment, Harris turned to Biden and first approached with what seemed a compliment, "I'm going to now direct this at Vice President Biden: I do not believe you are a racist, and I agree with you when you commit yourself to the importance of finding common ground." Then she pounced as only a former prosecutor could:

> But I also believe, and it's personal—it was hurtful to hear you talk about the reputations of two United States senators who built their reputations and career on the segregation of race in this country. And it was not only that, but you also worked with them to oppose busing. And, you know, there was a little girl in California who was part of the second class to integrate her public schools, and she was bused to school every day. And that little girl was me.[81]

What she directly challenged was Biden's sudden shift away from praising segregationists, downplaying his sponsorship of the 1994 crime bill, and evading his role in spearheading the sexist and racist interrogation of Anita Hill. However, what viewers, media pundits, and Biden aides saw was a Black woman attacking a white man. Caught off guard, Biden struggled to respond before eventually piecing together a defense. As the moderators paused for a commercial break, Biden leaned over to Pete Buttigieg and said, "Well. That was some fucking bullshit."[82] Former First Lady Jill Biden would express far harsher words for Harris during a phone call with supporters, saying, "With what he cares about, what he fights for, what he's committed to, you get up there and call him a racist without basis? Go fuck yourself."[83] In the days following the debate, the media relied on words like "ambush" and "attack" to make visible Harris' betrayal. The coded language obscured the racist and sexist leanings of their expectations. Namely, they had expected a Black woman to automatically defer to white male leadership. Among Biden's campaign staffers, Harris' decision to go straight for the "jugular" outraged them. In effect, she had upset the American body politic enshrining white men into unassailable patriarchs. In their emergency meeting, top aides expressed their fear that Harris had successfully altered this perception of Biden, exposing him as "old, angry, spiteful." For Harris, the moment had been a strategic means to an end. Her campaign had been floundering financially, raising only $12 million of their $15 million goal. Politically, her path toward the presidential nominee was narrowing each day. The only chance at victory was to "take down Biden for any of that money to matter."[84] It was a gutsy move, one that almost torpedoed her chances at becoming Biden's vice-presidential pick. In 2020, with soaring cases of COVID-19 plunging the nation into an economic healthcare crisis and descending toward an economic depression, Harris could potentially emerge as a top pick if, they mused, she knew how to play second position. Prior to her takedown of Biden, campaign staffers had assumed her presidential run was simply a thinly veiled campaign for vice-presidential nominee. Now they expressed confusion at the targeted "attack."[85]

Harris, in vying for the top spot, marked a fundamental shift away from Black women's traditional political strategizing. Shirley Chisholm had launched her campaign with the clear purpose of pushing cautious Americans toward reconceiving leadership as belonging in the hands of someone other than white men. She understood that the symbolic power of her presidential bid was for those coming after her, not herself. Chisholm explained:

> The next time a woman runs, or a Black, a Jew or anyone from a group that the country is "not ready" to elect to its highest office, I believe he or she will be taken seriously from the start. The door is not open yet, but it is ajar.[86]

Before her, Charlotta Bass had staged her 1952 run for vice president along similar lines. Editor and publisher of the Black newspaper *The California Eagle*, Bass' campaign slogan reflected an attempt to bring visibility to specific policies affecting Black Americans: "Win or Lose, We Win by Raising the Issues."[87] As historian Martha S. Jones argues in *Vanguard: How Black Women Broke Barriers, Won the Vote, and Insisted on Equality for All*, "She was trying to shape the political agenda more broadly."[88] Harris' presidential run represented the culminating labors of Bass and Chisholm. Speaking to a crowd in Des Moines, Iowa, Harris made clear her intent to claim the presidential mantle, posing to the few hundred people gathered under an Iowa flag, "Is America ready for that? Are they ready for a woman of color to be president? I'm ready for it. But I don't know if other people are."[89] Harris, striding through the door Bass and Chisholm left ajar, planned to collect her inheritance in full.

But Harris, branded as a disloyal Black woman audacious enough to challenge traditional modes of fidelity to both Black and white voters, found herself in a quagmire. During the vice president vetting process, a contingent of Democrats lobbied privately and publicly against selecting Harris for the role as they felt she could not be trusted.[90] Former Senator and member of Biden's vice-presidential search committee Chris Dodd urged Biden to pick California Representative Karen Bass instead, as "she's a loyal No. 2. And that's what Biden really wants."[91] Scripting Bass, a Black woman, as a "loyal No. 2" exposes the United States' recruitment of Black women into white capitalist empires based on parasitical performances of loyalty. In 2020, former counsel to Biden Symone Sanders-Townsend displayed this kind of "fall on your sword" fealty in consistently providing tailor-made responses dismissing criticism of Biden's patronizing tone toward Black voters suspicious of his congressional track record on racial issues. In a stunning moment captured on camera, Sanders tackled protestors storming the stage during Biden's Super Tuesday speech, essentially blocking Biden from harm. The optics of a Black woman willingly sacrificing herself for a white man split public opinion along racial lines. Sanders earned a round of approval among her mostly non-Black colleagues and the white mainstream media. But in virtual spaces, some Black social media users leveled the "mammy" epithet at Sanders for seemingly cozying up to white supremacist patriarchal power. Unfazed, Sanders seemed to brush off both the criticism and heroism, responding with a flippant, "I think I broke my nail."[92] But her steady defense signaled more than an unwavering loyalty to Biden. She had hopes that her political maneuverings would result in her quid-pro-quo hiring as the first Black woman press secretary. Her unequivocal defense of Biden and the subsequent aftermath only further expose the racialized and gendered ideologies at play in the United States. As Black women's loyalty is rarely reciprocated in kind, Jen Psaki, a white woman and former secretary to President Obama, snagged the job with considerably less effort. As custodians of democracy, Black women are frequently denied visible positions of power even when they labor on behalf of white American empire.

Therefore, Harris' bold strivings for power stand in stark contrast to an American body politic confining Black women to carrying out the dirty work for democracy. When questioned by Dodd about her "attack" on Biden, Harris simply laughed, saying, "That's politics."[93] Stunned by her seemingly callous behavior, Dodd could not believe that she had no remorse. The degree to which Harris appeared cavalier, emotionally distant, and wholly disinterested in publicly performing a maternal persona contributed to perceptions of her as a menacing figure for both Black voters and voters of color.

Days after announcing her presidential run, damning evidence against Harris surfaced in a 2010 video of her speech before a Commonwealth Club audience. As the then District Attorney of San Francisco, Harris explained that because she believed so strongly that "a child going without an education is tantamount to a crime," the best way to remedy the situation was to begin charging parents with truancy laws.[94] Under her truancy law, parents of truant children faced a fine of up to $2,500 or one year in jail. Harris' hardened stance, and her seeming lack of empathy for parents, broke with the concerns of marginalized communities. Contrary to her public endorsement of threatening parents with jail time, Harris had not arrested or jailed any parents during her time as a district attorney, though she had issued citations for parents to come to court to avoid the fine. Once there, they discussed targeted plans for improving their child's attendance. And yet, perhaps confoundingly so, Harris effusively championed jailing parents, publishing op-eds and articles defending her position over the years. Her performative display of power traded on parents' trauma to cement Harris as a self-proclaimed "Top Cop."[95] Harris' posturing, like that of Sula attempting to portray a tough exterior before the white boys, belied the fact that white colleagues considered her too soft on crime. Thus, we may consider Harris' ill-conceived truancy record not as the final nail in sinking her trust with Black voters. Rather, the seeming glee with which Harris reveled in while recounting the terror etched across parents' faces when they showed up to her office worked to position her as a traitor. Worse still, her laughter, though tongue-in-cheek, signaled an abrupt break from expectations of Black communal care.

As outlined in earlier chapters, Black women are often celebrated in direct proportion to the labors that we perform on behalf of our communities. Therefore, Harris' 2020 presidential bid also revealed how stealthily the "Black Women Will Save Us" narrative infiltrates our communities. White people, in other words, are not the only ones in need of this myth. In *Black Women Will Save the World*, April Ryan reflects on Judge Ketanji Brown Jackson's nomination to the 2022 Supreme Court and thinks, "All my life, I have known and embraced—even if, at times, unconsciously—the undeniable fact *that Black women will save the world.*"[96] Ryan pins this core belief on the notion that Black women stand poised to make the world right again because our unique worldview imbues us with a particular insight. "Well, we are magic," she writes, "Juggling it all and helping everyone, including and especially the times when no one notices."[97] The familiarity of Ryan's words echoes the Combahee River Collective. And, although her sentiments are not untrue, they express the depths of a perhaps desperate desire to belong. To be seen. To be valued. This is the seductive appeal of mythmaking. By positioning our labors as integral to America's success and our communities, we snatch for ourselves a kind of political utility, a visibility that renders us something other than mere footnotes to history. Embracing the rhetorical power of savior and magic myths is the phenomenon by which we incorporate ourselves back into the American body politic.

However, Harris' refusal to pledge allegiance to the community to which she belongs threatens this construction of Black women's labor as communal. In *Sula*, this is the very thing that the community uses to condemn her as "she lived out her days exploring her own thoughts and emotions, giving them full reign, feeling no obligation to please anybody unless their pleasure pleased her."[98] Harris' unapologetic commitment to herself renders her particularly loathsome, out of sync with notions of Black womanhood as that of endless public service. Harris, in explicitly rejecting the savior mantle and choosing for herself a "Top Cop" bravado, divorced herself from any communal responsibilities. Liberated from the burdens of Black womanhood, Harris, however, becomes menacing. She is Sula come to life.

Cast out of her community, Sula is first branded as menacing because Eva notices her "standing on the back porch just looking" as her mother, Hannah, burns and dies from a house fire. In Eva's eyes, this looking constitutes the crime. Indeed, when Eva speaks about this moment to friends, she remains "convinced that Sula had watched Hannah burn not because she was paralyzed, but because she was interested."[99] Eva's insinuation depicts Sula's look as the gaze of an unconcerned child, unfazed by witnessing her mother's terrifying death and only "interested." It is a curious moment and one that counters Black social codes. Growing up, I heard different variations of the Black American aphorism "Stop looking in my mouth, child" more than I can count. bell hooks recalls "being punished as a child for staring, for those hard intense direct looks children would give grown-ups, looks that were seen as resistance, challenges to authority."[100] In simply looking, Sula refuses to perform the expected ritual of care on her mother's behalf. Her menacing stare unnerves Eva in the same way that Harris' giggling while talking about imprisoning parents took on sinister implications.

Harris' recall of the parents' fear when they showed up to her office registers a kind of experimental glee at the supposed success of her scare tactics. As voters began digging into her prosecutorial background, they unearthed the story of Cheree Peoples, an Orange County resident arrested after District Attorney Tony Rackauckas used Harris' truancy law to round up parents.[101] In a deliberate public perp walk orchestrated by Rackauckas, six parents were handcuffed before a nearby camera crew. Peoples was shocked. Her daughter had sickle cell anemia, and the school was well aware of how her medical diagnosis affected her attendance because she had registered her disability with the proper paperwork. "This is a young woman who spends a lot of her life in the hospital. How is it that she's giving off the impression of being a gang member? ... Why," Peoples wondered, "are they coming after me?"[102] The racialized implications of Harris' crackdown on parents, though she had not arrested any parents during her tenure, bear out in Peoples' experience as a Black mother since the highest percentage of truancy rates are among Black and Native students of color. Thus, Harris effectively ruptured Black voter trust by divorcing herself from any expectations of Black solidarity. Her gleeful chuckles would not be seen as a political gaffe or hot mic moment but rather indisputable evidence of her alignment with naked power.

Harris would continue to be viewed as a traitor to Black communities in particular, and the most pressing question facing Harris, one that would eventually doom her presidential bid, was why she had chosen to become a prosecutor. On its face, the question seemed benign enough. But it implicitly drew attention to America's incarceration of nearly 2.3 million people, driven by the over-policing of Black and Latinx populations. How could, interviewers seemed to ask, a Black and Indian woman sleep at night knowing she had contributed to locking up people who looked like her? In op-eds, articles, and tweets, prison abolitionists, legal scholars, and voters vocalized their discomfort. In "Many Americans Are Ready for a Black Woman President. Just Not Kamala Harris," social movement lawyer Derecka Purnell plainly stated the limitations of identity politics for initiating progressive change. Purnell writes:

> As a Black woman and lawyer, I did not even see myself in Harris, but instead found myself in solidarity with the people who suffered while she was a prosecutor and Attorney General of California and would have suffered under her administration, had she won the election. While she was the little girl who rode the desegregated school buses that Biden threatened, I was the little homeless girl struggling with absenteeism whose parent Harris would have threatened.[103]

Law professor Lara Bazelon refuted Harris' claims that she was a "progressive prosecutor," noting, "time after time, when progressives urged her to embrace criminal justice reforms as a district attorney and then the state's attorney general, Ms. Harris opposed them or stayed silent."[104] Black social media users took to the platform formerly known as Twitter to fire off a round of memes, videos, and tweets envisioning Harris as gleefully locking up Black people. She became "Copmala Harris." On one level, this labeling was the result of Harris inventing for herself a swaggering tough-on-crime professional identity, as in, she often referred to herself as a "Top Cop." At one level, Harris' embrace of the "Top Cop" moniker explicitly rejected the burden of racial solidarity typically imposed on Black women. She would not, as her Top Cop gloating proved, be saving anyone. On another level, the public criticism, if viewed through the long gaze of history, law, gender, and race, though valid, forestalled a legitimate engagement with the legal system's centuries-long erasure of Black women and girls' sexual abuse.

Erased before the eyes of antebellum law, Black women were denied legal protection from slaveholders. One such woman was a young enslaved Black woman named Celia. In 1855, when her slaveholder, Robert Newsom, attempted to rape her as he had done since she was 14 years old, the then 19-year-old Celia struck Newsom upside the head twice, killing him. Despite Missouri law stating that "homicide shall be deemed justifiable when committed by any person resisting" a felony such as rape, the all-white jury promptly convicted Celia of first-degree murder. At only 19 years old, Celia was executed by hanging as the Missouri courts held that "a slave woman had no virtue that the law would protect against a master's lust."[105] Remnants of Celia's struggle for justice linger on today. In 2014, former police officer Daniel Holtzclaw deliberately preyed on poor uneducated Black women to rape, targeting those with past sex work and criminal records. Despite Holtzclaw's conviction and 263-year prison sentence, victim testimony illuminates Black women's fight to obtain even a modicum of legal protections. S.H., a survivor, first told her mother about Holtzclaw's abuse but she could not bring herself to tell the police "because I didn't think that no one would believe me."[106] I had hoped that Harris' prosecutorial background might lead to discussions about how violence circumscribes nearly every aspect of Black women's lives and our invisibility before the criminal justice system as victims and hypervisibility as perpetrators. A serious discussion on her decision to focus on sexual assault cases, I believed, might also lead to a conversation about some Black women's hesitancy at embracing prison abolitionist frameworks or rehabilitative models of care precisely because the system so often denies Black women justice. However, the silence surrounding these thornier, perhaps irresolvable issues, was loud.

The few insightful takes on the issue came from an unlikely source: prison reform advocate, poet, and felon, Reginald Dwayne Betts. In his *New York Times* article, "Kamala Harris, Mass Incarceration and Me," Betts details his incarceration at 16 for carjacking a man and attempting to rob two women at gunpoint. He would plead guilty, serving his 9-year sentence at Virginia's Southampton Correctional Center. Betts watched Harris' presidential run closely. "I thought the country might take the opportunity to grapple with the injustice of mass incarceration in a way that didn't lose sight of what violence, and the sorrow it creates, does to families and communities," he writes.[107] One of those families would be his own. After he returned home from prison at 24, his mother shared with him that just weeks before his arrest, a man yanked her away from the bus stop and raped her at gunpoint. Betts' mother held off on telling him for years to protect him. When asked about the experience of attending her son's trial, his mother revealed, "I was raped by gunpoint. It happened just before he was sentenced. So when I was going to court for Dwayne, I was also going for a court trial for myself."[108] The relationship between his mother's rape by a Black man and her teenage son facing life in prison resists the neatly constructed binaries of prosecutors as bad, defense attorneys good. In fact, Betts' mother registers the degree to which prosecutors, even when securing convictions, fail to render justice for victims. Despite raping two other women, the man submitted a guilty plea, and the judge's acceptance of it led to his significantly reduced sentence. When asked by her son what she would have wished happened to her rapist, Betts' mother replied, "That I'd taken the deputy's gun and shot him."[109] Her response underscores the path toward legal retribution as inadequate in a system not built to account for victims, especially not Black ones.

Unsurprisingly, Harris' decision to pursue the path of prosecutor was repeatedly discussed within the context of her locking up Black men. In the 2020 Vice President Debates, Tulsi Gabbard insinuated heavily that Harris had imprisoned close to 1,500 poor Black and Latinx people for marijuana offenses.[110] But the accuracy of Gabbard's claim proved suspect. During her tenure as California attorney general from 2011 to 2016, the percentage of Black male inmates did not increase from the 29 percent figure when Harris became attorney general.[111] In fact, it dipped slightly to 28.5 percent during her time as attorney general. The 1,974 inmates convicted during Harris' tenure represent the total sum of all inmates, not solely Black men.[112] Nonetheless, constructing Black men as the biggest victims "suffering under" Harris' prosecutorial reign tainted her run for president. And lodged in the fierce disavowal of Harris as a prosecutor was the mobilizing of the endangered Black men narrative. Though many of the claims would later prove to be false, the damage severely tarnished Harris' trust with Black voters.

On December 3, 2019, Harris withdrew from the 2020 presidential election. Despite the historically diverse array of 2020 Democratic presidential candidates featuring women and men of color, a white man would be the last candidate standing in the end. That Biden emerged as the top pick when Harris, arguably the most experienced person for the job, dropped out of the race early, exposes America's penchant for white male patriarchs and calling on Black women to perform democracy's dirty work.

A Note on the 2024 Presidential Election

In a 2024 interview with Vice President Kamala Harris, television host Drew Barrymore clutched Harris' hand before looking deeply into her eyes, saying, "We need you to be Momala of the country."[113] The strange moment came after Harris shared that her stepchildren affectionately call her "Momala." White women's perverse investment in claiming Black women's maternal labors is made plain by the speed at which Barrymore repackaged Harris' familial love for her stepchildren into providing comfort to an entire nation. The optics of a younger white woman insisting an older Black woman—arguably the most powerful woman in the nation, if not the world—mother the country back to health recalls white women's long, parasitical history of whittling Black women's labors down to their own needs. Barrymore's desire to remake Harris into Momala recalls a harrowing fact of the slave market economy: "In bids to grant their children uncontested access to Black women's bodies, milk, and maternal labors, white women routinely sought 'a healthy Black wet nurse, without a child.'"[114] By requesting childless wet nurses, often those whose children had either been lost through separation or death, white women could more effectively seize Black women's labors as their own. Therefore, Barrymore's remixing of the mammy myth demonstrates the persistent power of mythmaking at a moment when many Americans feel like the country is in need of saving.

Following a series of poor debate performances, charges of Biden looking too old, and facing pressure from his own party to step down, President Biden announced his decision not to seek re-election. And, by informing the American people that his decision to pick Kamala Harris as vice president has "been the best decision I've made," Biden began the process of actively shaping his legacy. Future historians would no doubt analyze his surrender of power to a Black and Indian woman as courageous.[115] Like white abolitionists authenticating narratives written by formerly enslaved Black people, Biden's presidential statement supporting Harris legitimized her before American voters.

With Harris once again seeking the highest office in the land, public opinion shifted toward declaring Harris "ready" to lead. However, Harris' sudden "readiness" was likely informed not only by her close proximity to President Biden and his subsequent endorsement of her candidacy but also the tumultuous state of the country.[116] Increasingly unpopular sentiment for American involvement in Gaza and Ukraine roiled the nation. College campuses were transformed into political hotbeds with students and professors peacefully protesting only to be forcefully detained. Splintering American voters further were issues of immigration, inflation, and reproductive rights. A divisive former president, Donald Trump's nomination as the Republican candidate was met with fierce dissent from his former Cabinet members and other high-ranking officials. In the run-up to the 2024 presidential election, John Kelly, Trump's former White House Chief of Staff and Secretary of Homeland Security, called Trump a fascist, recalling how Trump praised Hitler. Mark Milley, Trump's chair of the Joint Chiefs of Staff, echoed these sentiments, declaring Trump "the most dangerous person to this country." In the months before the 2024 election, a growing list of prominent Republicans, including former Vice President Mike Pence and Dick Cheney, publicly vocalized their opposition to Trump's re-election bid. Fears of Trump plunging America into war or a fascist state led to Harris receiving endorsements from Trump's previous cabinet officials, among them Vice President Mike Pence and former Department of Homeland Security General Counsel John Mitnick. This groundswell of support was as much about preventing Trump's path to power as acknowledging Harris as a capable, steady leader. In fact, Harris' 2024 presidential bid and subsequent loss exposed the degree to which American voters continue to find power comforting when located within the body of white male patriarchs.

Neither white nor male, Harris hinged her success on smoothing over her glaring abnormality as the first potential Black and Indian woman president. Her selection of Tim Walz, a hearty and virile white man, for vice president attempted to tacitly neutralize her visibly Black and female body. In their first television interview together, Harris and Walz sat alongside each other. But his chair appeared curiously higher than hers, making her look smaller, a bit like a child, while Walz appeared taller, a bit like a father.[117]

As Election Night neared, old narratives resurfaced. Suddenly, Harris was not Black enough. At the National Association of Black Journalists conference in Chicago, Trump questioned her identity, saying, "I didn't know she was Black until a number of years ago when she happened to turn Black and now, she wants to be known as Black. So, I don't know, is she Indian or is she Black?" Trump's perverse musings mobilized racist rhetoric typecasting mixed-race women as the tragic mulatta figure, a racially ambiguous woman belonging to neither the Black nor white community by virtue of her "warring" blood. In explicitly calling into question Harris' racial identity, Trump evaded the more glaring truths of his ascension to the White House. Namely, a seeming prerequisite for becoming president in America is that one must be male and white. In the 248 years since Americans declared their independence from Britain, only one president has identified otherwise. In such stark terms, the question following Harris' election loss should not have been how one, lone woman failed to save democracy, but why and how have Americans consistently placed power in the hands of white men for over 200 years?

Instead, pundits and top democrats, in the days after the 2024 election, rushed to cast blame on Biden for staying in the race for too long, or on Harris for having the audacity to run and believe she could win. Reports indicating ripples of Democratic dissent at Harris' perceived leapfrogging over other potential presidential nominees surfaced. Nancy Pelosi's eventual endorsement of Harris' campaign quelled some of the rumors, but even she seemed to point out that there was a desire for "an open process." Following up on her statement, Pelosi noted that Harris "had the endorsement of the president, and she, politically astutely, took advantage of it and shut down—not shut down, but won the nomination. But anybody else could have gotten in."[118] There is a hint among Pelosi, and other Democratic officials, that Harris had ruthlessly shaped her own political needs to her own ends. And yet, her battle for the White House—launching the shortest presidential election in history with only 107 days before Election Day—was yet another indication of the speed with which white American capitalism recruits Black women to perform the dirty work of democracy. In the final quarter, Americans heaved up a hail mary and hoped Harris would clinch victory. Still, had America elected its first female president we may have needed to develop a new set of rhetorical tools for understanding Black women's relationship to power in the 21st century. For now, we may understand Harris' loss as a symbolic call for Black women to harvest our energies, labors, and talents for a season where those most in need of saving are ourselves.

Notes

1 Needham.
2 Romano.
3 "The Origins of 'Reclaiming My Time.'"
4 "Arkansas Sen. Flowers Makes Passionate Speech against 'Stand Your Ground' Bill."
5 "Arkansas Sen. Flowers Makes Passionate Speech against 'Stand Your Ground' Bill."
6 Carter Jackson, 8.
7 Davies, 123.
8 Davis, 149.
9 Hughes.
10 Curwood, 244.
11 Curwood, 244.
12 Curwood, 244.
13 Curwood, 244.
14 A. Davis, 2.
15 Hurston, 8.
16 Chisholm, 20.
17 Leshar.
18 Benjamin, 23.
19 Landers.
20 Curwood, 221.
21 Curwood, 218.
22 Curwood, 219.
23 Morrison, 281.
24 Shange, 25.

25 Shange, 25.
26 Curwood, 253.
27 Curwood, 218.
28 Curwood, 222.
29 Curwood, 222.
30 Chisholm, 2.
31 Curwood, 223.
32 Curwood, 2.
33 Perlez.
34 Collective.
35 Collective.
36 Collective.
37 Rudin.
38 Perlez.
39 Perlez.
40 Curwood, 46.
41 Morrison and West.
42 Mabry, 40.
43 Mabry, 40.
44 Mabry, 157.
45 Mabry, 40.
46 Mabry, 52.
47 Morrison, *Sula*, 54.
48 Morrison, *Sula*, 54.
49 Evers-Williams, 39.
50 Evers-Williams, 40.
51 C. Davis, 149.
52 Morrison, *Sula*, 16.
53 Morrison, *Sula*, 14.
54 Morrison, *Sula*, 121.
55 Mabry, 53.
56 Mabry, 52.
57 "Rice Defends Bush's Katrina Response."
58 Rice, 200.
59 Rice, 200.
60 Benjamin, 23.
61 Morrison, *Sula*, 120.
62 Morrison, *Sula*, 92.
63 Ikard, 22.
64 Morrison, *Sula*, 92.
65 Morrison, *Sula*, 92.
66 Morrison, *Sula* 52.
67 Mabry, 132.
68 Mabry, 133.
69 Mabry, 133.
70 Mabry, 86.
71 Mabry, 136.
72 Mabry, 137.
73 Mabry, 140.
74 Mabry, 97.
75 Mabry, 97.
76 Lockhart.

77 Clayton.
78 Marlette.
79 Kai.
80 Kai.
81 Dovere.
82 Dovere.
83 "Go F*ck Yourself: Jill Biden Slammed Kamala for Attacking Joe on Race Record at 2019 Debate, Book Says."
84 Dovere.
85 Dovere.
86 Chisholm, "Shirley Chisholm on Why She Ran for President."
87 Bennett.
88 Jones.
89 Cadelago.
90 Korecki, Cadelago, and Caputo.
91 Korecki, Cadelago, and Caputo.
92 Budryk.
93 Korecki, Cadelago, and Caputo.
94 Beckett.
95 Hakim, Saul, and Richard.
96 Ryan, xiv.
97 Ryan, xiv.
98 Morrison, *Sula*, 118.
99 Morrison, *Sula*, 78.
100 hooks, 115.
101 Demby.
102 Demby.
103 Purnell.
104 Bazelon.
105 Higginbotham, 694.
106 Testa.
107 Betts.
108 Betts.
109 Betts.
110 Garafoli.
111 Mason.
112 Mason.
113 "Vice President Kamala Harris on Becoming 'Momala' to Her Husband's Kids."
114 Jones-Rogers, 346.
115 Han.
116 Marans and Robillard.
117 "Kamala Harris and Tim Walz CNN Interview (Part 1): Plan for First Day in Office."
118 B. Clayton.

Bibliography

Arkansas Sen. Flowers Makes Passionate Speech Against "Stand Your Ground" Bill. 2019. 2 March 2020. https://www.youtube.com/watch?v=FNtEiAu4mtE.

Bazelon, Lara. *Kamala Harris Was Not a 'Progressive Prosecutor'.* 17 January 2019. 1 January 2020. https://www.nytimes.com/2019/01/17/opinion/kamala-harris-criminal-justice.html.

Beckett, Lois. *Kamala Harris: Resurfaced Video on Truancy Prosecutions Sparks Backlash*. 30 January 2019. 1 May 2023. https://www.theguardian.com/us-news/2019/jan/30/kamala-harris-truant-children-parents-prosecutions-clip.

Benjamin, Ruha. *Imagination: A Manifesto*. New York: W.W. Norton & Company, 2024.

Bennett, Jessica. *Overlooked No More: Before Kamala Harris, There Was Charlotta Bass*. 4 September 2020. 1 May 2024. https://www.nytimes.com/2020/09/04/obituaries/charlotta-bass-vice-president-overlooked.html.

Betts, Reginald Dwayne. *Kamala Harris, Mass Incarceration and Me*. 20 October 2020. 31 October 2020. https://www.nytimes.com/2020/10/20/magazine/kamala-harris-crime-prison.html.

Budryk, Zack. *Biden aide Symone Sanders Jokes that She 'Broke a Nail' Tackling Protester.*" 3 March 2020. 1 May 2024. https://thehill.com/homenews/campaign/485864-biden-aide-jokes-that-she-broke-a-nail-after-seen-tackling-protester/.

Cadelago, Christopher. *How Kamala Harris Went From "Female Obama" to Fifth Place*. 5 November 2019. 1 June 2023. https://www.politico.com/magazine/story/2019/11/05/how-kamala-harris-went-from-female-obama-to-fifth-place-229901/.

Carter Jackson, Kellie. *We Refuse: A Forceful History of Black History*. New York: Seal Press, 2024.

Chisholm, Shirley. *Shirley Chisholm on Why She Ran for President*. 1 November 2022. 2 June 2024. https://lithub.com/shirley-chisholm-on-why-she-ran-for-president/.

Chisholm, Shirley. *Unbought and Unbossed: Expanded 40th Anniversary Edition*. North Carolina: Take Root Media, 2010.

Clayton, Bruce. *Pelosi Claims to Have Wanted Open Process to Replace Biden*. 21 August 2024. 21 August 2024. https://sjvsun.com/u-s/pelosi-claims-to-have-wanted-open-process-to-replace-biden/.

Clayton, Mel. *Black Women CAN Save The United States But It's Not Their Responsibility*. 18 August 2020. 1 May 2023. https://blackwithnochaser.com/black-women-can-save-the-united-states-but-its-not-their-responsibility/.

Collective, Combahee River. *The Combahee River Collective Statement*. 1978. 1 May 2023. https://www.blackpast.org/african-american-history/combahee-river-collective-statement-1977/.

Curwood, Anastasia. *Shirley Chisholm: Champion of Black Feminist Power Politics*. North Carolina: The University of North Carolina Press, 2023.

The Daily Beast, "Go F*ck Yourself: Jill Biden Slammed Kamala for Attacking Joe on Race Record at 2019 Debate, Book Says." May 19 2021. 2 March 2023. https://www.thedailybeast.com/go-fck-yourself-jill-biden-slammed-kamala-for-attacking-joe-on-race-record-at-2019-debate-book-says/.

Davies, Carol Boyce. "'SHE WANTS THE BLACK MAN POST': Constructions of Race, Sexuality and Political leadership in Popular Culture." *Agenda: Empowering Women for Gender Equity*, 2011, pp. 121–133. https://www.jstor.org/stable/23207211.

Davis, Angela. *Race, Women, and Class*. New York: Vintage, 1983.

Davis, Christina. "Interview with Toni Morrison." *Présence Africaine*, vol. 145, 1988, pp. 141–150.

Demby, Gene. *The Story Behind Kamala Harris' Truancy Program*. 17 October 2020. 2 May 2023. https://www.npr.org/sections/codeswitch/2020/10/17/924766186/the-story-behind-kamala-harriss-truancy-program.

Dovere, Edward-Isaac. *The Inside Story of the Biden-Harris Debate Blowup*. 19 May 2021. 1 June 2023. https://www.politico.com/news/magazine/2021/05/19

/edward-isaac-dovere-2020-campaign-book-excerpt-joe-biden-kamala-harris-489347?nname=playbook&nid=0000014f-1646-d88f-a1cf-5f46b7bd0000&nrid=0000016a-25a3-d780-abea-b7ff639f0000&nlid=630318.

Evers-Williams, Myrlie. *Watch Me Fly: What I Learned on the Way to Becoming the Woman I Was Meant to Be.* Boston: Little Brown and Company, 1999.

Garafoli, Joe. *Fact-checking the Democratic Debate Attacks against Kamala Harris.* 1 August 2019. 5 August 2019. https://www.sfchronicle.com/politics/article/Fact-checking-the-Democratic-debate-attacks-14275081.php.

Hakim, Danny, Stephanie Saul, and Oppel Richard. *"Top Cop" Kamala Harris's Record of Policing the Police.* 9 August 2020. 1 May 2021. https://www.nytimes.com/2020/08/09/us/politics/kamala-harris-policing.html.

Han, Jeongyoon. *Want to Know What Biden Said When He Dropped Out? The Full Letter is Here.* 21 July 2024. 1 August 2024.

Higginbotham, A. Leon, Jr. "Race, Sex, Education and Missouri Jurisprudence: Shelley v. Kraemer in a Historical Perspective." *Washington University Law Quarterly*, 1989, pp. 673–708.

hooks, bell. *Black Looks: Race and Representation.* Boston: South End P, 1992.

Hughes, Langston. *The Negro Artist and the Racial Mountain.* 13 October 2009. 1 August 2024. https://www.poetryfoundation.org/articles/69395/the-negro-artist-and-the-racial-mountain.

Hurston, Zora Neale. *Their Eyes Were Watching God.* New York: Harper Perennial, 1937.

Ikard, David. *Breaking the Silence: Toward a Black Male Feminist Criticism.* Baton Rouge: LSU P, 2007.

Jones, Martha S. *Vanguard: How Black Women Broke Barriers, Won the Vote, and Insisted on Equality for All.* New York: Basic Books, 2020.

Jones-Rogers, Stephanie E. *They Were Her Property: White Women as Slave Owners in the American South.* Cambridge: Yale U P, 2019.

Kai, Maiyshai. *"We Can't Be Afraid to Challenge Our Own People": The Root Presents: It's Lit! Gets Crunk With Brittney Cooper.* 2 October 2020. 2 May 2023. https://www.theroot.com/we-cant-be-afraid-to-challenge-our-own-people-the-root-1845253474.

Kamala Harris and Tim Walz CNN interview (Part 1): Plan for First Day in Office. 1 September 2024. https://www.youtube.com/watch?v=Dl9gPBasyv4&t=195s.

Korecki, Natasha, Christopher Cadelago, and Marc Caputo. *"She Had No Remorse": Why Kamala Harris isn't a Lock for VP.* 27 July 2020. 1 July 2023. https://www.politico.com/magazine/story/2019/11/05/how-kamala-harris-went-from-female-obama-to-fifth-place-229901/.

Landers, Jackson. *"Unbought and Unbossed": When a Black Woman Ran for the White House.* 25 April 2016. 1 June 2020. https://www.smithsonianmag.com/smithsonian-institution/unbought-and-unbossed-when-black-woman-ran-for-the-white-house-180958699/.

Leshar, Stephan. *The Short, Unhappy Life of Black Presidential Politics, 1972.* 25 June 1972. 1 June 2021. https://www.nytimes.com/1972/06/25/archives/the-short-unhappy-life-of-black-presidential-politics-1972-black.html.

Lockhart, P.R. *In 2018, Black Women Want More than Thanks. They Want Political Power.* 8 January 2018. 1 September 2018. https://www.vox.com/identities/2018/1/8/16849720/black-voters-women-midterm-2018.

Mabry, Marcus. *Twice as Good: Condoleezza Rice and Her Path to Power.* New York: Modern Times, 2007.

Marans, Daniel, and Kevin Robillard. *Democratic Convention Anoints Harris as a Commander in Chief Ready To Lead.* 23 August 2024. https://www.huffpost

.com/entry/kamala-harris-commander-in-chief-dnc_n_66c8106ee4b0b9c7b360c473.

Marlette, Andy. *Cartoons of the Week! January 22.* 22 January 2021. 1 May 2023. https://www.pnj.com/picture-gallery/opinion/2021/01/22/cartoons-week-january-22/6678364002/.

Mason, Charlotte. *Misleading Claim Says Harris Jailed 1,500 Black Men for Marijuana.* 20 October 2020. 1 June 2021. https://factcheck.afp.com/misleading-claim-says-harris-jailed-1500-black-men-marijuana.

Morrison, Toni. *Sula.* New York: Vintage, 2004.

Morrison, Toni. *Tar Baby.* New York: Vintage, 2004.

Morrison, Toni, and Cornell West. *"We Better Do Something": Toni Morrison and Cornel West in Conversation.* 6 May 2004. 2 May 2020. https://www.thenation.com/article/archive/toni-morrison-cornel-west-politics/.

Needham, Vicki. *Waters Gets Testy with Mnuchin at House Hearing.* 17 July 2017. 2 June 2019. https://thehill.com/policy/finance/344152-waters-gets-testy-with-mnuchin-at-house-hearing/.

Perlez, Jane. "Rep. Chisholm's Angry Farewell." *The New York Times.* 12 October 1982: 24. https://www.nytimes.com/1982/10/12/us/rep-chisholm-s-angry-farewell.html.

Purnell, Derecka. *Many Americans Are Ready for a Black Woman President. Just Not Kamala Harris.* September December 2019. 1 May 2021. https://www.theguardian.com/commentisfree/2019/dec/03/black-woman-president-kamala-harris.

Rice Defends Bush's Katrina Response. 4 September 2005. 1 June 2023. https://www.nbcnews.com/id/wbna9206731.

Rice, Condoleezza. *No Higher Honor: A Memoir of My Years in Washington.* New York: Crown, 2011.

Romano, Aja. *Reclaiming my Time: Maxine Waters's Beleaguered Congressional Hearing Led to a Mighty Meme.* 31 July 2017. https://www.vox.com/culture/2017/7/31/16070822/reclaiming-my-time-maxine-waters-mnuchin-meme.

Rudin, Ken. *Ed Koch, New York City And The Politics Of Resentment And Race.* 4 February 2013. 1 June 2023. https://www.npr.org/sections/politicaljunkie/2013/02/04/170842922/ed-koch-new-york-city-and-the-politics-of-resentment-and-race.

Ryan, April. *Black Women Will Save the World: An Anthem.* New York: Amistad, 2022.

Shange, Ntozake. *For Colored Girls Who Have Considered Suicide When the Rainbow Is Enuf.* New York: Scribner, 1997.

Testa, Jessica. *The 13 Women Who Accused a Cop of Sexual Assault, In Their Own Words.* 15 December 2015. 2 May 2016. https://www.buzzfeednews.com/article/jtes/daniel-holtzclaw-women-in-their-ow#.agbk8LqM5.

The Origins of "Reclaiming My Time." 2017. 3 March 2024. https://www.searchablemuseum.com/the-origins-of-reclaiming-my-time.

Vice President Kamala Harris on Becoming "Momala" to Her Husband's Kids | The Drew Barrymore Show. May 2024. 1 August 2024. https://www.youtube.com/watch?v=d_XCKpxsp5k.

Index

#BlackMothersStill Matter 2
#Blackwomen 144
#ReclaimingMyTime 126
#SayHerName 112
#YouOKSis 113
18th-century colonial America 57

abuse 45, 49, 58, 71, 114–116, 118, 152; Black men's 110; Black women's 116–117; child 34; domestic 90; guardians 43; medical 8; physical 105; sexual 50–51, 58–59, 152; shelter 1; systemic 118; verbal 24
access to health and education 8, 113
activism 15, 20, 22; communal 105; political 2, 7; violent 88; voting rights 13; working-class 90
adultification of Black girls 80
African American Male Resource Center 103–104
African Female Benevolent Society 56
afterlife of slavery 3, 8, 28
anti-Black(ness) 23; America 43; antagonisms 26; candidates 134; conditions 41; regimes 27; state apparatus 35, 46; state violence 23; terrain 36; views 134; woman world 74; world 10, 16

Bambara, T. C. 5, 109–110, 120
Barnes, D. 114, 116
Basquiat, J. M. 9, 28
Benjamin, R. 33, 130, 142
Betts, R. D. 152–153
Biden, J. 146–148, 151, 153–155; inauguration 145; patronizing tone toward Black voters 148; presidential statement 154; Super Tuesday speech 148
Birmingham bombing (1963) 19
birth(ing) 7, 15–16, 21, 24–25, 42, 101; child- 8, 20; difficult (dystocia) 10; experiences 13; -givers 2, 5, 8–9; home 11; injustices 11; new worlds 26; people 18, 25; -place 121; positions 11; process 11; stories 12; workers 2, 5, 11
bitter baby mamas 3, 9
Black: birth-givers 5; birth-workers 5; caregivers 2, 32–35; Civil Rights 15; feminist foundations 1; feminist mothering 1–3, 58–59, 68, 71, 94, 101, 128, 131; legacies of resistance 4; lesbians 63, 74; Liberation Army 15, 26–27, 103; Lives Matter 2, 13–14, 101, 103, 113, 126; matrilineal consciousness 2, 9–10, 22, 27; Panther Party 1, 14, 23, 90, 105, 121; patriarchal stealth 5, 101, 106–107, 109, 114–115, 121, 139; power 13–14, 101, 109–110, 112, 129, 131; resiliency 15; Revolution 13, 15; Women's Revolutionary Council 90
breeders 3, 32
Brown, E. 105–106, 121
Bynum, T. 58, 59, 65

campaign 128, 130, 132–133, 147, 156; aggressive 87; Civil Rights-inspired 96; fundraisers 128; national 128; organization 128; paraphernalia 134; presidential 24, 132–133, 144; slogan 147; smear 11; staffer 128, 131, 146–147; university ad 143

capitalism 7; American 128; slaveholding 39; white American 39, 156; white patriarchal 3–4; white supremacist 33, 36
captive maternal 2
caregivers 2, 27, 52, 108; Black 2, 32–35
Center for Disease Control 102
Chisholm, S. 5, 127–136, 146–148
Civil Rights: activist 87; era 82, 88; icons 3, 96; -inspired campaign 96; leader 15; movement 130, 137; widow 82, 86, 91, 97; years 88
Clinton Correctional Facility for Women 13, 16
Collins, P. H. 81; 'othermother' 22; Black feminist 2; motherwork 2, 22, 33
Combahee River Collective 134, 149
communities 5, 11, 43, 73, 101, 105, 113, 120, 129, 137, 149, 152; African American 22; beloved 2; Black 16, 24–25, 41, 82, 86–87, 95, 129, 137, 151; Black lesbian 89; collective solutions for 2; disadvantaged 112; marginalized 128, 149; rural Black 11; survival of Black 13; sustainability of 13, 102; vulnerable 7
consciousness 44; erotic 61; *see also* Black
Cooper, B. 20, 101, 145
COVID-19 96, 147

Daughters of the Confederacy 145
Davis, D. A. 8, 34
death-bound conditions 7
deathscapes 33–34, 40, 49–52
dehumanization 81
Democratic National Convention (1964) 21, 23, 145
De Veaux, A. 64, 90
discrimination 8, 40, 42; racist 88; sexist 61–62, 88; white supremacist 7
Douglass, F. 36–37, 44, 76

economic: challenges 64; depression 147; deprivation 7; exploitation 3, 109; healthcare crisis 147; insecurity 62; position 135; realities 64; subjugation 65

enslaved 1, 11, 38, 44, 49, 51; Africans 48; artist 67; Black children 44; Black girl 50, 59, 65; Black man 36, 45, 48, 67; Black mothers 3, 34; Black parents 35; Black people 4, 32, 40, 48–50, 66–67, 154; Black women 4, 12, 32, 42, 45, 48–49, 56, 58–59, 65, 71, 152; Negro girls 70; status 45
environmental: activist 41; aggression 41; crises 41; injustice 41; racism 40
Evers-Williams, M. 82, 84, 86, 95–96, 138–139

Faculty Senate Women's Caucus 143
feminist 76, 101; activist 64; circles 90; ethos 62; literary circles 69; literary foremother 68; literary icon 64; literary politics 72; literary traditions 74; literature 101; model 68; white 132; writers 64
Free Breakfast for Children program 14, 112
Freedom Farm Collective 23
Fugitive Slave Act (1850) 43, 49

Genocide Bill 21
Georgetown Law's Center on Poverty and Inequality 80
GirlTREK 96
Gonzalez, S. M. 45
Goodwin, M. 25
Gumbs, A. P. 2, 8, 27

Hagar, S. 110–111, 120
Hamer, F. L. 7, 13, 18, 20–24, 81
Harris, K. 5, 127, 144–156
Hartman, S. 3, 8, 70–71
hatred 68, 75, 80–81, 84; deep 86; fervor of 131; unyielding 49
high-risk rage 18–19, 21, 23, 26
Homeland Security 141, 154–155
homophobia 72, 74, 90
hooks, b. 22, 65, 150
Hurston, Z. N. 57, 62–63, 69, 100, 102, 115–118

impoverishment 8
incarceration 8, 13, 16, 25, 105, 151–152

Jemisin, N. K. 2, 33, 40–41, 48, 50
Jim Crow: America 11; fields of Mississippi 20, 139; rule 7, 142; violence 2
job instability 7
Johnson, L. B. 22
Jones, E. P. 2, 33, 36, 40
Jones, M. S. 147
Jordan, J. 5, 23, 66, 69

King, M. L. 22, 82–84, 87–88, 140
KKK 18

Lorde, A. 3–4, 13, 19, 57, 59–60, 64, 70, 72–74, 76, 80–82, 86, 89–94, 109, 119, 134

Malcolm X 4, 82, 84–88, 94–95, 119
maternal 5, 13, 15, 57; ancestors 16, 57; archetypes 8; captive 2; care 2, 23, 60, 69, 111–112; consciousness 27; decision-making 10; figure 20; genius 28; healthcare crisis 10; inheritance 28; knowledges 10–12; labor 2–4, 22, 25, 45, 57–58, 62, 65, 68, 71, 95, 112, 154; legacy 15; manifesto 15; monitoring 18; persona 148; positive outcomes 8; practices 11–12, 15; praxis 20; purity 23; strategies 33, 48; tenderness 69; visions 13, 23, 28; wisdoms 10, 17
M'baye, B. 58, 66
McQueen, B. 1, 4
Morrison, T. 2, 9–10, 17, 33, 44, 46, 88, 109–111, 120, 127, 131, –139, 141–142
mortality 82

National Association of Black Journalists 155
National Association of Colored Women 145
National Council of Negro Women 145
National Urban League 62
neonatal outcomes 8

Oakland Feminist Women's Health Center 90
obstetric: positions 11; racism 8, 12

oppression 35, 49–50, 56, 71, 81, 129, 135; -free lives 113; gendered 57, 106; race-based 105, 141; soul-crushing 18; structural 105; systems of 94, 135; targeted 56; unique 113; white supremacists 91
orogene 42–44, 48–49

Parker, P. 3, 57, 72–74, 82, 89–94
patriarchal: capitalism 3–4; codes 118; hetero- 143; male supremacist 60; power 38, 134, 136, 148; racist white men 66; stealth 5, 101, 106–107, 109, 114–115, 121, 139
perverse racial calculus 39
poverty 2, 7, 24, 59, 88, 128
Progressive Era of the 1900s 11

racial: ambiguity 155; calculus 13, 39, 132; context 83; dynamics 126; effects of environmental aggression 41; ethnic community 2, 22, 33; hierarchies 132; identities 137, 155; ideologies 148; implications 150–151; intra- 5; issues 148; lines 148; loyalty 134, 137; oppression 59; paradigms 129; politics 82; profiling 35; scripts 146; signifiers 41; solidarities 152; subjugation 127; tensions 144; violence 33, 80–82, 86, 137
racism 21, 50, 72, 129, 134, 140; clear 132; corporeal toll 28; environmental 40; indignities of 20; institutional 24; obstetric 8, 12; overt 132; relentless 4; structural 59; unbearable pressures of 134; victims of 116; white supremacist 129
Rector, J. 103–105
Rice, C. 5, 127, 136–138, 140–141, 143 144
Rikers Island Correctional Facility for Women 13
Roberts, W. R. 67–68

sexism 59, 116, 130, 134
Shakur, A. 13–17, 23–27, 112
Shange, N. 119, 131
Sharpe, C. 35, 101, 112
Sheppard-Towner Act (1921) 11

SisterSong Women of Color Reproductive Justice Collective 102
sisterwork 3, 56–57, 61–63, 65–66, 75, 81–82, 92–93, 95–96
Sixteenth Street Church 137–138
slaveholding 38–39, 43; American 36, 41; capitalism 39; colonies 45, 48; customary 36; power 40; records 70; society 70; whites 40
slavery 8, 22, 40, 42–43, 59, 120, 128–129, 132; afterlife of 3, 8, 28; anti- 58, 60; chattel 2, 35; decline 11, 20; pro- 43, 48, 59; strictures of 50; transatlantic 33
Smith, B. 64, 90, 134
Sojourner Truth 35
Stover, J. M. 3, 57
Student Nonviolent Coordinating Committee 7, 21
Suicide Day death march 140

Tanner-Collins, O. 3, 56–62, 65–73, 76
truancy law 149–150

victimhood 58, 101–103, 113, 115, 117
violence 2, 19, 34, 37–40, 48, 50–51, 67, 71, 101, 114–117, 141, 152; anti-Black state 23; crushing 19; exposure to 7; gender-based 113–114; intimate partner 102, 115; lingering 65; police 34–35, 116; racial 137; racialized 80–82, 86; racist police 113; reproductive 2, 9, 13, 18, 33–34, 40, 42, 45, 47, 90, 103; rhetorical 9; sexual 33; state 45; state-sanctioned 7; structural 3; unprovoked 42; unspeakable 47; white 18, 20; white supremacist 2, 38

Walker, A. 27–28, 56, 60, 69, 72, 76, 107–109
Wallace, M. 5, 109
welfare queens 3
West, D. 57, 62–64
Wheatley Peters, P. 3, 56–62, 64–73, 75–76
white supremacist 19, 23–24, 38, 94, 126, 134, 137; capitalism 33, 36; cowardly 18; discrimination 7; forces 91; incursions 24; oppression 91; patriarchal capitalism 4; patriarchal power 148; power 5, 65–66; racism 129; rendering 59; rhetoric 59; savagery 20; state 19; stereotypes 86–87; structures 82; violence 2, 38
Women's Press Collective 90

Printed in the United States
by Baker & Taylor Publisher Services